What LIES Beneath
from LIES to Love

FOREWORD BY:
COURTNEY COHEN
The Sacred Shadow

STEVEN COHEN

.

DISCLAIMER

Due to the content of *What Lies Beneath*, by proceeding, you agree to read and utilize the advice within at your own discretion. This book is neither intended for self-help, nor is it meant to replace any sort of counseling, therapy, or pastoral guidance. As used within this Disclaimer, "Author" refers to all Now Found Publishing products, Steven Cohen, any family members, agents, successors, Now Found Publishing, LLC, and assignees.

  This book is a tool designed to encourage a deeper, investigative relationship with God and His Son through the Holy Spirit and DOES NOT make any promises, judgments, or diagnoses of your mental health. It is intended for adults and, by reading this book, you state that you are at least 18 years of age or are reading this under the guidance and supervision of a parent or guardian. The Author cannot be held responsible for injuries, loss, or other consequences resulting from reading this book or any action taken as a result thereof. No information provided in this book shall be construed as legal, financial, psychological, and/or medical advice.

  If you have destructive thoughts or are exhibiting destructive behaviors, please contact a local counselor, the National Suicide Prevention Hotline at 1-800-273-8255, and in an emergency please dial 9-1-1 or your local emergency response number.

What Lies Beneath: From Lies to Love

Published by Now Found Publishing, LLC

Southlake, Texas

NowFoundPublishing.com

Copyright © 2019 by Steven Cohen

Edited by Courtney Cohen

Cover design by Steven Cohen

Trade Hardback ISBN: 978-1-942362-13-5

Trade Paperback ISBN: 978-1-942362-14-2

eBook ISBN: 978-1-942362-15-9

What Lies Beneath is also available on Amazon Kindle, Barnes & Noble Nook, Google Play Books and Apple iBook's.

All rights reserved. No part of this book may be reproduced or transmitted in any form or by any means, electronic or mechanical, including photocopying, and recording, or by and information storage and retrieval system, without permission in writing from the publisher.

All scripture quotations, unless otherwise indicated are taken from the Holy Bible, English Standard Version, copyright 2001, by Crossway Bibles, a division of Good News Publishers.

TABLE OF CONTENTS

Introduction – Your Foundation — i

Section 1 – The Truth About the Lies Beneath

1 – The Definition of a Lie — 3
2 – The Father of All Lies — 13
3 – The Birth of a Lie — 23
4 – The Anatomy of a Lie — 37
5 – The Nature of a Lie — 71
6 – The Role of a Lie — 95
7 – The Fruit of a Lie — 103
8 – The Addiction of a Lie — 113

Section 2 – The Lies Beneath

9 – Recognizing the Lie and the Liar — 125
10 – Discovering the Lies About the Truth Beneath — 135
11 – Lies Upon Lies — 181

Section 3 – Here Lie Your Lies

12 – The Lie of Your Disbelief — 223
13 – The Lie of Your Belief — 231
14 – The Lie of Your Justifications — 239
15 – The Lie of Your Actions — 247
16 – The Lie That They Are Your Lies — 257

Section 4 – What Lie's Beneath

17 – The Father of All Truth — 265
18 – Discovering the Truth Beneath — 277
19 – How to Believe and Live That Truth — 283
20 – The Nature of Truth — 293
21 – The Fruit of Truth — 299
22 – Feeding Authentic Identity — 303

Section 5 – Applying Truth

23 – Our Testimony Is Powerful — 313
24 – Confronting the Lies of Others — 319
25 – Loving Others Despite Their Lies — 325
26 – Guarding Against New Lies — 331

Wrapping Up — 337
Resources — 340
Endnotes — 342

ACKNOWLEDGEMENTS

First things first. Thank you for trusting me with your valuable time and walking with me on this journey of freedom. I hope you find that your time has been invested well and that God speaks to you through these words.

    I would also like to thank my precious family. God has blessed me with extraordinary favor in my wife, my bride, my sweetheart, and best friend, who are all one person, Courtney Cohen. I am honored to be the father of three remarkable children, whom I am so proud of and thankful for, simply for being who they were created to be. To my son, daughters, and my wife, thank you for loving, supporting, and inspiring me.

FOREWORD

Steven rarely lets me get away with anything. It's one of the primary reasons I married this man. After all, how could I grow personally if falsehoods and selfishness within me were never challenged? So, with any lie I've believed that's skewing me off course, leading me to live in a way contrary to God's call of freedom and identity on my life, Steven takes unapologetic issue. As my husband, his primary goal in our relationship is to help me become the person that God has designed and desires me to be.

Steven isn't afraid of a confrontation. And, while my former, non-confrontational self would have preferred an argument-free marriage, looking back, I see God at work through those uncomfortable conversations across the years. Steven's love for me isn't expressed through satisfying my every whim; it is expressed through helping each family member gradually and authentically become the people whom God created us to be.

Reading *What Lies Beneath* has caused me to question my perceptions and challenge what is comfortable. Steven and I come from drastically different places. While I grew up in the church, with church-language that became so familiar many of the often-repeated words lost their rich meaning, Steven grew up an atheist, immune to Christian-ese terminology. Perhaps that's one reason why he can approach matters of the soul with such clarity, like looking through an entirely new lens. He will share in profound detail his encounters with God that led him into a relationship with Jesus Christ, so I won't tell his story here. Simply prepare yourself to see reality from a new frame of mind.

What Lies Beneath is not always a comfortable read, but it's a vital one. This is no fluffy, arbitrary book. In these pages, truth is spoken, lies are uncovered, biases are revealed, and internal contradictions are challenged. Through down-to-earth language, Steven reaches into the depths of profound revelation to help every reader experience the freedom that God always designed and desired for us. Equipping readers with practical tools immediately applicable to daily life, Steven acts like the leader of an excavating crew. Boldly and diligently sifting beneath the surface of what we think we believe, he exposes the source of our struggles and confusion, knowing that we need to clear out the debris in order to build on a solid foundation.

So, reader, I encourage you to turn the pages here boldly, prepared to have your paradigms shifted, with a heart open to the revelation God has for you. He has a profound work to do in each of us, a work that uncovers lies and establishes a foundation that can never be fractured: one framed in love.

- Courtney Cohen
Co-Founder of Now Found Publishing
Author of *Refining Identity* & *The Sacred Shadow*

What LIES Beneath

I have to stand under what is over me before I can stand over what's under me.

- ED YOUNG SR.

INTRODUCTION

The *What Lies Beneath* journey began in the early 2000's at Gateway Church in Southlake, TX. My wife, Courtney (or Court, as I typically refer to her), enrolled us in a class on this weird topic of *freedom*. Bored, I sat in the classes watching Court take pages of notes, while I got nothing from them. Then, at a men's conference in 2012, this topic of freedom came up again. This time it felt like I had different ears. They shared about how we become bound by believing lies spoken over us by demons and how God's Truth and Love, His Essence, is the only thing that can truly set us free.[1] This time I was enthralled.

At the mention of freedom, you may have some of the same questions that came to my mind:

- What is freedom?
- How do I get free?
- If I'm in bondage why don't I know it?
- If freedom is so important why is this the first time I have heard about it (ironic, because I had heard it years before)?

That second time, however, I remember thinking that although I didn't fully understand it, I needed and wanted more.

While many people struggle with the question: "What is freedom?", there is no one set definition. It's a concept or a state of being, which is why I like to define freedom through a hybrid of a few definitions I've encountered. Simply put:

Freedom is living as the individuals that God designed and desires, Jesus redeemed, and the Holy Spirit leads us to be.

Court and I were married in 2005 after a two-year courtship. While I have one very full-time job, Court has about six. I don't know how she handles it all. Together, we have three beautiful blessings, our son Reece and daughters Shelby and Makayla. My wife and I, primarily my wife, have the responsibility and honor to homeschool our children. The wonderful experience of guiding the development and foundation of our children's education can be a challenge, but a special bond forms through the process.

One evening, my daughter and I practiced reading. She was five at the time, and we were reading something brief. What we were reading doesn't matter, neither do the words on the paper, but what is important is that I had my little girl on my lap, pouring into her the love, knowledge, and experiences that God has given me. As we progressed through the words, which she was doing well with, we came to a word that looked a little intimidating. I watched her countenance change. She became scared, unsure, and frustrated. She didn't want to continue reading, starting to cry as I pressed in to find out what was going on.

During the next ten minutes, I tried to encourage her to read this three-syllable word and asked her what was wrong, while at the same time trying to stay sensitive to God's Voice speaking. The Holy Spirit revealed to me a lie she was being told. The lie: that she wasn't a good reader, that she would never be as good of a reader as her big brother, and that the word was just too big for her.

As tempted as I was to get up, pace around the house praying, cuss satan out for attacking my little girl, demand that he leave her alone, that would have been giving in to his attack and failing to address the root issue that she believed the lies she was being fed. Instead, I took a break from the words on the paper, turned my daughter to me, and asked her to help me identify the lies she was hearing. At first, she acted defensive, insisting that she wasn't believing a lie, as if believing a lie is the problem. I encouraged her to press into God and ask Him how He saw her and if what she was hearing about her reading aligned with or was the same as what He said. She told me that she knew God created her to be smart and a good reader. So, I asked her if God had created her to be capable, smart, and a good reader, but satan was saying otherwise, who was she going to believe. Her response, beneath the heaving sobs, was, "I want to believe God." But she still seemed defeated. Although she verbally agreed with her daddy, as well as with her Father and Creator, she wasn't yet living in the *Truth*.

This is one of the hardest situations to witness as a parent, my little girl being attacked by the enemy. It's also one of the most challenging tasks to balance sensitivity toward my hurting daughter with righteous anger toward the enemy. So, we prayed for God's Truth to pour into her, for lies to break off of her, and for satan and the demons who thought they had control of her to be gone.

When we finished praying, I could see God's Essence and Love glowing, exuding from her. Knowing the truth, what both her daddy and her Father said *about* her and saw *in* her, and knowing and accepting who she was created to be changed something in her. I asked her if we could read the word and she looked at me with a smile and said yes. She looked down without hesitation, without even sounding out the letters, and simply said the word. A word that, in all honesty, I thought she was going to wrestle through a little, she simply blurted out. I was so proud of her, but not because she read the word. It was the excitement and joy that could only come from engaging together in a spiritual battle, exercising our dominion over satan and his demons. I was able to watch her lean into Jesus, rely on the Holy Spirit for counsel, seek her Father's Truth, and break off the lies that were beneath her fear and insecurity. Even now, she impresses me daily with her reading speed and capability.

Satan doesn't wait until we are older, wiser, and have developed our defenses to start attacking us. He is a lying, cheating thief who has no compassion for the young or weak. If he can take us out of the game before we get in it, he has one less thing to worry about. As parents, a large part of our responsibility is to recognize these lies and protect our children from them, but, even more, it's to help our children identify and work through them. As we receive Life being spoken over us, we can speak even more Life over those we love and encounter daily. We may have to dig down deep in order to find what lies beneath. What if something is binding you today which is based on a lie you believed 20, 30, or even 60 years ago? It's not too late to break free and experience God's Essence for the rest of your life.

Two foundational scriptures for this book have had such a tremendous impact:

> *...For they exchanged the truth about God for a lie and worshiped and served the creature rather than the Creator, who is blessed forever!*
>
> – Romans 1:25

Worshiping the created rather than the Creator has been a habit of God's people for a long time. Look at the Israelites and what they did as God and Moses met atop Mount Sinai. As God met Moses, interacting with him, the Israelites were down below, forming and worshiping a golden calf. Today we have traded our golden calves for fire-engine red sports cars, marble counter tops, double ovens, hand-scraped wood floors, and so-called reality shows. These things, in and of themselves, are not bad, but when we put them on the altar of our hearts, when we put these created things above the almighty Creator, we miss out on what truly matters.

Introduction

> *...seek first the kingdom of God and his righteousness, and all these things will be added to you.*
>
> – Matthew 6:33

This is not a get-rich-quick verse. Much like the previous scripture we considered, if we plug those material things into the place where God belongs, we miss the point. Thinking that this verse functions as a key to get what we want puts us right back in the situation of worshiping the created instead of the Creator. If there is nothing else you take away from this book, I want you to understand the gist of this passage. We should always ask our Father what He says about what we are going through, and how His power, strength, and righteousness will get us through it. We will spend a good amount of time in Genesis 1-3, recounting the Creation story where this all went awry.

Even while writing this book I have come under attack, told lies like, "The truth that God has for us isn't understandable; it's confusing and people just won't get it." So, before I go any further, I would like to lean into the Creator of all and the Author of Truth as we pray together.

> *Lord, thank You so much for Your wisdom and understanding, for Your freedom and redemption, for Your healing and restoration. Lord please reveal to us what lies beneath so that we can better understand who You are and who You have designed us to be. Please let the words here be revelation and create a deeper dialogue between You and Your children. And please, come and speak, pouring Your Life out on us as we read. Amen.*

One morning, my wife and I were discussing something (I don't remember what) while getting ready to go somewhere (I don't remember where). Really good story so far, right? Have you ever experienced one of those moments in time which, later, you don't remember much about except one main point? This is one of those moments, so please bear with me.

While my wife and I were talking, I felt the desire to tell her how wonderful and beautiful she was, so I gave her a compliment. As I spoke the compliment, it seemed as if God stepped in and slowed time, opening a window for me into His reality. It was like He gave me a glimpse into the Matrix.

For the deprived soul who has neither seen nor heard of the Matrix, it is a 1999 movie written and directed by the Wachowski brothers. A computer hacker, Neo, who is stuck inside of a computer-controlled reality learns the reality of the world he lives in, a world where humans are harvested for the electrochemical energy their bodies create. Rebels who have escaped the matrix contact Neo and give him an opportunity to have reality revealed or stay in the only reality he knew existed.

Several scenes in the movie slow down in order for the audience to see and comprehend intense action sequences clearly. For example, a bullet slicing through the air left compression ripples of sound waves in its wake. In that same way, when I spoke to my wife that day, I could see my speech. As the words came out of my mouth, I saw the words form, letter by letter, into tangible structures, projecting across the room like slow-moving, rapid-fire bullets toward my wife. They didn't create ripples as they flew towards her, but it was nevertheless impressive to see.

As the words approached and met her, instead of piercing or melting into her skin, penetrating deep into her heart, affirming her of her beauty, her righteousness, her importance to me (as I intended them to) they met an impenetrable obstacle as if she was made of Kevlar. The words struck a wall, each letter folded on top of the next, like a car crumpling as it collides with an immovable object. Because they did not make it to their intended destination, they fell to the floor in a mess of crumpled letters, failing to fulfill their created purpose.

God later showed me that the intent of my words – their meaning, their spoken purpose, and my desire for them – were distorted and deflected before they could reach their destination, my wife's heart. They did reach my wife's ears, but that wasn't where I needed them to be deposited. That would be like taking a check to the bank, giving it to the teller, but the teller never depositing it in your account, instead balling it up and throwing it on the floor to be swept up later. Even worse, it could be like the teller not only did not deposit the check, but then actually withdrew money from your account without notifying you.

That's what happened that morning. A lie my wife had believed, which satan told her many times over the years, created a lens (or filter) designed to alter her perception of incoming stimuli in order to match the heart of the lie. And, while she heard the words spoken, the lens shifted the meaning of my heartfelt, caring, encouraging words, to those of condescension, sarcasm, and cold-hearted indifference. The filter led to a withdrawal of love and warmth from her heart when I had intended to make a deposit.

At that moment, I had a revelation that God continued to unpack over the months to come. It wasn't that my wife doesn't listen to me or that she was a hard, uncaring wife. Because those suggestions are absolutely not the case. Those thoughts would be the lies satan wanted me to believe. The revelation was that even though someone else believes a lie, whether it's about me, themselves, or someone else, I don't have to believe the lie they believe. Crazy, right? I don't have to pick up a spirit of offense based on a lie that someone else chooses to believe. I don't have to bind myself and oppress myself with negative thoughts and emotions about myself or others just because they do.

In that moment with my wife, I don't know what lie she had

believed. Maybe it was doubt in my sincerity, that, although I was giving compliments, I really didn't mean them or I only gave them because she was my wife and I had to. No matter the lie believed, it changed my compliment into something else for her. That muddled, melted mess of words represented something deep within her, a bondage that satan and his demons had successfully created.

We've all got them, lenses that lie beneath the surface of our lives, tying us, binding us, preventing us from living the life God designed, desires, and redeemed for us. Not necessarily keeping us from *doing* something, but instead keeping us from *being* someone. Someone He fashioned: the person which He, and only He, knows us to be. Remember our definition of freedom is

Living as the individuals that God designed and desires, Jesus redeemed, and the Holy Spirit leads us to be.

I can't stress enough that freedom is a journey which will last the rest of your time on Earth. To get there, or at least get on your way, first know that it is a process to go through, not just a book to read or a class to attend. The freedom ministries mentioned in this book include various groups of people who walk beside others in the hope of helping them experience who God is and who He created those individuals to be. I hope that you find this book to be a valuable part of your process. My desire is that God uses the words here to produce revelation, love, and freedom in your heart.

The Baseline

Before we journey into the rest of the book, it is important that we create a baseline of understanding, a picture if you will. What's directly beneath you? It's not a trick question. Go ahead and look. What about below that? And below that? Depending on whether you are on the first floor or the hundred and tenth of an office building, or even sitting outside on the grass, you may have reached the foundation in just a few, small layers of carpet and padding, there could have been 150,000 tons of steel, concrete, duct work, electrical wiring, insulation, desks, people, and so forth; there could be just a few blades of grass, or you could have no idea what's between you and your foundation. No matter where you are, that foundation isn't merely floating. There is something that supports everything else in existence. Even the grass is being supported by something, right? Even though we cannot always see it, there is always something beneath the surface.

Have you ever seen a construction site as workers manipulate the soil to level out the surface in order to pour a foundation for a building? Do they just pour concrete on that soil? No. What do they do? They create forms, or guides and barriers, that will restrain the liquid concrete until it dries. They also add reinforcement, typically rebar or steel, to help provide strength and rigidity. Often for larger buildings, workers excavate and drill down into the earth to pour pillars, which are needed to support the pier and beams that will, later, be placed on top. Those piers have complex skeletons, like the image on the cover, designed to bear and distribute the weight of the large structure above.

While in New York on business, I had a chance to visit some of my family and go to lower Manhattan to revisit the site of the Twin Towers. The last time I had been there, thirty years before, I was a kid. Then, I'd enjoyed watching the towers sway in the wind from the sidewalk below. I went to the observation deck atop the south tower and looked out over all of Manhattan, even seeing across to parts of New Jersey where my family lived. But this time was a totally different experience. Instead of seeing the Twin Towers I was familiar with, I found myself at Ground Zero. The new Freedom Tower stretched into the clouds. I went below the original site of the Twin Towers into what is now a museum beneath the 9/11 memorial. While I will never forget 9/11, it was especially somber and emotionally difficult to remember what happened that day. It was also remarkable to see aspects of the original construction and foundation used to support those two iconic buildings.

      The twin towers extended one hundred and ten floors, in excess of 1360',[2] into the air and approximately sixty-five feet below the earth's surface down to bed-rock. The towers, as a pair, weighed approximately 1,500,000 tons, or some 3 billion pounds. They were constructed using the majority share of some 200,000 tons of steel. And over 860,000 tons of concrete were used in the entire World Trade Center complex[3]. Yet, as impressive and massive a construction the towers were, we humans, at an average height measuring five feet, four inches[4] and weight of one hundred and fifty-three pounds, created from primarily water and carbon, have an even more impressive foundation than that of those behemoth structures.

      1 Corinthians 3:11 says, *"For no one can lay a foundation other than that which is laid, which is Jesus Christ."* And, unlike our foundations here in Texas, He doesn't shift around or need repair from time to time. In Matthew 7, Jesus talks about building houses (which represent our lives) on shifty or unstable soil, and how those who build on that type of soil are considered foolish. The problem isn't limited to Texas, according to Geology.com. Expansive soils... also known as "expandable," "shrink-swell," "heavable" soils, and "expansive clays," ... "are present throughout the world and are known in every US state...causing billions of dollars in damage [per year]. The American Society of Civil Engineers estimates that ¼ of all homes in the United States have some damage caused by expansive soils... [causing] greater financial loss to property owners than earthquakes, floods, hurricanes, and tornadoes combined." This is important to point out because, as King points out, "even though [these] expansive soils cause enormous amounts of damage, most people have never heard of them... because their damage is done slowly and cannot be attributed to a specific event." The article goes on to explain that because there is a lack

of knowledge of these phenomena, that incorrect blame is often placed on poor construction or damage due to aging.5

A foundation of truth rests beneath all of existence; it was both spoken and present "In the Beginning."[i] I would argue that most people don't agree with that statement. Although the Bible is the best-selling book of all time and the average American household has, on average, three to four Bibles in it, most people have not heard or do not believe that non-relative truth exists. Statements like "truth is relative," "truth is scary," "truth is beauty," or "truth is stranger than fiction" tend to make me believe truth is under attack in the name of tolerance. This attack has taken place so gradually that, often, people never realize there is, in fact, an immovable, permanent, absolute Truth which doesn't conform to our wishes, desires, or personal bent. Nor does it originate from philosophy or our thought processes which easily change based on current trends.

Although Truth can be factual, it is not always the same as fact. The simple existence of data can create fact, but the truth behind the existence of data transforms the meaning of it. The existence of man is a fact. It is provable, but that rarely quenchable question, "Why?" forces us to dig a little deeper. The fact is that man exists; the truth as to why man exists is simple, but much deeper. Love. Love, while true, is much more difficult to prove because it is not fact. For those who do not believe in the Creator, the search for *why* becomes a never-ending quest for factual data to create an unfulfilling, artificial substitute for the why behind the fact through more facts.

As complex and wonderfully made as our minds are, being one part of this human body crafted in the image of God, we are limited in our capabilities here on Earth, which prevents us from being able to prove certain inalienable truths. That being said, just because we cannot prove something within the realm

---
[i] John 1:1

of our abilities does not mean that it is not God's Truth. Dr. John MacArthur accurately describes the origins of Truth when he states,

> The one most valuable lesson humanity ought to have learned from philosophy is that it is impossible to make sense of truth without acknowledging God as the necessary starting point.

I also like a quote I found on, author and speaker, Steve Cha's blog,

> Truth is Truth even if no one believes it. A lie is a lie even if everyone believes it.

And, Dallas Willard addresses truth and reality, stating that the,

> Acceptance of...[something's] right to exist in a pluralistic society does not make it any more correct, and will be of no help to those following it when they finally run into reality.

Willard continues to point out that those who believe there are different standards as to what reality is or isn't, and variances between fact and faith,

> are victims of the unfortunate delusion of current culture that "fact" is limited to what is sense-perceptible. The implication is that for faith things are, somehow, as you think them to be... [many assuming] there is no 'way things are' with God, or at least that we cannot know how they are. Hence all views of God are said to be equally true because all are equally in the dark-an astonishingly fallacious inference.[6]

As Matthew 7 states, Christ is the Rock we should be building on. He was there in the beginning. He is one part of the Triune foundation of our existence.

Going back to Romans 1:25, the issue comes when we try to

pour our own foundation over the one Christ has poured. Like the earthmovers at the Freedom Tower, many times we move around or arrange our thoughts and actions – create relationships with others who have like minds, choose our clothes, style our hair, buy houses and cars and jewelry – all in an attempt to support our own truths, our own realities if you will, instead of simply relying on God's Truth and the foundation Christ has already poured for us. Second Corinthians 4:16-18 gives us a good picture of not only life's challenges but also our truths, goals, and aspirations.

> *... We do not lose heart. Though our outer self is wasting away, our inner self is being renewed day by day. For this light momentary affliction is preparing for us an eternal weight of glory beyond all comparison, as we look not to the things that are seen but to the things that are unseen. For the things that are seen [our goals, our truths] are transient, but the things that are unseen [God's truth] are eternal.*

A challenge for you: Are "our truths" God's Truth? Or are they lies that we have believed? And how can we tell the difference?

This book is designed to help you hear God, the only One who can reveal what lies beneath and identify whether what we find is a lie. Do we want to stop there? Nope. When we find a lie, we want to dig the support structure out from beneath these false foundations, these lies, so that they will crumble and fall into the pit of hell where they belong.

Keep in mind that this is a process. You can have lies built on lies, built on lies. Much like when I asked you to look below you and to continue examining what was below what was below you, this can go on and on. You may have been sitting on the first floor with very little between you and the foundation or you could have been on the top floor of the Freedom Tower with a monstrous structure between you and the foundation below. As these lies are revealed, we need our Rock, Jesus, to be our foundation. We need to understand that even when it seems as though everything we've believed is crumbling around us, as it says in Psalm 91:4, *"He will cover you with his feathers. He will shelter you with his wings. His faithful promises are your armor and protection."* He's got us covered and, remember, He is our foundation, so He's also got us supported. He's got you.

Introduction

What LIES Beneath

Steven Cohen

SECTION 1
The Truth About the Lies Beneath

But the king will rejoice in God. All who swear by Him will boast, when the mouth speaking lies is shut.
- Psalms 63:12 TLV

1
The Definition of a Lie

What LIES Beneath

There are all sorts of lies: manipulative lies, noble lies, polite lies, barefaced lies, fraud, bluffs, fibs, exaggerations, contextual lies, cover-ups, "THE BIG LIE," little white lies, deflection, omission, minimization, perjury, and pathological lies. We each have our own reasons and uses for each one, using them at various rates and times. Like tools in a toolbox, we have organized lies into nice and neat drawers, ready to be utilized when the situation arises. And while each of these lies has its own definition and nuance, they also have things in common with one another. I believe the greatest commonality between them all is that they are all lies. Even factual lies which manipulate factual data to portray a certain viewpoint are lies. I know that seems elementary, even obvious, being that I just listed them as types of lies. But it seems that, because of how often we use them, we lose sight of the fact that we are lying. No matter our motive, how we express, or how someone receives a lie we tell, our justification does not change the fact that they are lies. Even if our intention is to protect, to avoid hurting, or to lessen the pain someone experiences in a situation, we are still lying.

In a society and time where relativism has made great strides, where we are to COEXIST, as the bumper sticker says, it's become difficult to know what truth really is. So let's create that baseline. Truth is an absolute, unwavering, unmovable reality, sometimes based on facts, but, more importantly, founded on and rooted in love. God's design and desire for His people is to do so much more than simply COEXIST; it's to love one another like He does. While the outward message of that bumper sticker message is simply to live or exist together peacefully, the deeper implication is that we must accept each and every religion and worldview as if they are unquestionable truth simply because they are true to the person who believes them. But if Jim's truth (just a fictitious person) says all versions of "truth" are truth and the truth that I believe says all other "truths" are based or built upon a lie, can they both be true? How can all thoughts or beliefs be true when they contradict each other?

When Supreme Court Justice Kennedy heard arguments in the Masterpieces Cakeshop vs. Colorado Civil Rights Commission, he commented that,

> *Tolerance is essential in a free society, and tolerance is most meaningful when it's mutual. It seems to me that the state in its position here has been neither tolerant nor respectful of Mr. Phillips's religious beliefs.*[1]

This is a landmark case where Mr. Phillips refused to bake a wedding cake for a gay couple, based on his Christian beliefs, not wanting to endorse or support gay marriage. There are two conflicting beliefs here: one says that gay marriage is acceptable and right, and another declares that gay marriage does not align with the way God created humans to live. What happens when we come across this situation? What did Jesus do? What does God say about *all* of His kids?

While I think that we as clients or consumers should have the ability to choose whom we do business with, I also believe that businesses should too. The challenge I pose here is this: why does this cake baker, and all who agree with him, stop at gay marriage and not all sinful living? Liars have the same punishment as the sexually immoral, the unbeliever, the fearful, idolaters, murderers, and the like. They all deserve the lake of fire.[i] I want to challenge your belief: if you agree with the cake baker, why stop there? Why not extend that rule to include liars? If it is true that God wants us to shun, boycott, condemn, belittle, or refuse to love on His children who are living in a sinful lifestyle, then we are to love no one. But that does not line up with the God whom Phillips, the cake baker, says he is trying to align his business with.

Former commissioner Diann Rice said at a 2014 hearing that

---
i   Revelation 21:8

"freedom of religion, and religion, has been used to justify all kinds of discrimination throughout history, whether it be slavery, whether it be the Holocaust."

How often do we do the same thing in the name of God, likely without even seeking His view of the situation? I am not making assumptions that Phillips didn't consult God. The challenge here is simply for us to make sure we are.

If something is said to be "true to you," or "my truth," is it truth, or is it a belief? There are beliefs which are inaccurate, but Truth is infallible. I used to believe there was no God. Regardless of how hard I believed, how close I pulled that lie to my chest, how tightly I held onto it, my belief was wrong. Truth is truth and lies are lies. Not every inaccurate belief is a lie, but it is based on a lie and a judgment. We'll tackle that twist a little later.

A common belief people struggle with is the consideration about how we get to heaven. How can you get to heaven through your works and deeds via one religion, get to heaven only by grace in another, heaven not even exist in another, and all still be true? C.S. Lewis in *Mere Christianity* points out that Christ was either a Liar, a Lunatic, or Lord. Yeshua (Jesus' name in the original Aramaic) claims to be the Son of Yahweh, Lord and Creator of all, and that "no one... [could] come to the Father except through Him," which is straightforward and contradicts what many other works-based religions say.

All thoughts and beliefs cannot be Truth. But if our beliefs and our truth, are based on and formed by Love, God's Love to be specific, then when we experience someone who is living, breathing, teaching, or preaching something that is opposite of the Truth, we will simply love them despite their belief. We don't have to believe what they want us to, but we can still love them, honoring them with encouragement, respect, and compassion. God does that with us when we make mistakes, when our beliefs don't align with His Truth. He doesn't change His mind to align with ours so that our feelings aren't hurt. God is the One who created love, the One who is Love, and is the one Truth. He doesn't want us staying stuck, soaking in falsehoods and misperceptions. He cherishes us too much for that, but He also loves us too much to withhold His Love from us just because we're stuck. We are His children and He wants to see us grow and mature in His design and desires for our lives. You will hear that a lot in this book, that He designed us and desires us. He wanted us to be here and wants to be an ongoing part of our lives. That was a belief I had wrong for the greater part of my journey. I believed a lie to the contrary; that God didn't hear us, or if He could, that He didn't care, or was incapable of helping.

So how do we know? How does a person believe they know the truth? That, in itself, is part of the problem. Many times, they don't *believe* they know, they *think* they know. For much of my life, as an atheist, I relied on my knowledge, the "facts," more truthfully defined as theories and opinions I had gathered to guide my understood "truth." Opinions of the scientific community shaped my thoughts at an early age. While facts were being presented to educate us, opinions and propaganda were infused to convince us that there was "in fact" no God. Based on so-called fact, we were told that the written Word of God wasn't reliable, that the Christian creation story didn't hold water, and that the people of that time were simply barbaric and couldn't have understood such complex "science."

In the foundation of this book, I stated that just because something is fact does not mean that it is true. And while a fact is sometimes defined as, "a thing that is indisputably the case,"[2] that is not the case. Facts are always disputable; facts are commonly massaged and manipulated in order to make the case of the person presenting them. On the first day of class, my statistics professor asked what we thought statistics were. Most of the students suggested they were analytics of data to present fact. I surprised him with my answer: "Statistics are a manipulation of data to present the end result you prefer to present and methods you used to do so." He asked that question to see if he could change his students' perception of a class that so many dreaded. Needless to say, on the last day of class when he asked the same question, my answer had not changed; it had been confirmed.

Facts are simply judgments placed on information that we have accumulated, compounded, compiled, and processed through the knowledge we have obtained. All of those components are movable, malleable, and fallible. As our knowledge increases, our ability to accumulate, compound, compile, and process information increases, possibly changing our judgment regarding the information. Definitions and thoughts change, therefore "facts" change. Facts are facts; facts are not, by definition, truth. Facts can be based on lies; truth cannot. Facts can be based on truth, but that doesn't make them truth. How much of a statement has to be false before the entire statement is false? We should all know from elementary school true or false test questions, the answer is *any portion*, no matter how small it is.

Our relativistic culture is much closer to the truth than they believe. I'm not saying that they are closer to being right, just closer to the Truth. If you think about where relativists' statements come from, in reality they are not far off. If a person bases all of their thoughts and beliefs on facts, something disputable and capable of being manipulated, then everything is relative. Until, that is, when you expose the facts to truth. Once a person has seen and accepted God's truth, all facts moving forward have an anchor, Truth, to keep them steady and to be compared to.

When I was young, I didn't have much knowledge of the Bible other than that it existed. We did not have one in our house and my parents' experiences with "the church," or "God's people," had been tainted by lies and deception as well. So, when I was told over and over that certain scientific theories, presented as law, were more reliable than the Bible, I had nothing to weigh it against, nothing to test their theories with. When I heard stories about how the Bible was simply an old Jewish tribal account of traditions and superstitions, similar to that of every other heritage in history, I thought those opinions to be accurate. They were coming from my parents after all. Aren't our parents always right?

People from Noah, Moses, or Joshua's times are, today, often viewed as unenlightened barbarians. I watched a debate between Bill Nye ("the science guy" for everyone who grew up in the 90s) and Ken Ham, CEO of Answers in Genesis, where Nye implied that the individuals recorded in the Bible, sages and prophets if you will, were incapable of thought, reason, or intellect worth comparing to modern-day "science."[3] Someone once pointed out that people tend to believe that their generation is the first and that all reality began with them. This concept basically states that, as a people, we cannot grasp what occurred before us in totality. Although we know that historical events took place and relate to how we came to be, on an individual level, all ideas and reality begin at the point when *we* become conscious of our existence. This may be the reason God says,

> *What has been is what will be, and what has been done is what will be done, and there is nothing new under the sun. Is there a thing of which it is said, 'See, this is new'? It has been already in the ages before us. There is no remembrance of former things, nor will there be any remembrance of later things yet to be among those who come after.*[ii]

There is a lie often believed that the knowledge attained in today's modern age is greater than the ancient wisdom attained by those who've followed God's Word across time. This isn't a new thought, so where does that lie come from? It sounds a lot like the

---

[ii] Ecclesiastes 1:9-11

story told in Genesis, right? Just moments before Eve took of the forbidden fruit, the serpent spoke to her,

> *God's lying to you. He's keeping something from you. Knowledge makes you like God; knowledge is God. God is holding out on you because He knows you will be like Him and you will no longer need Him.*[i]

That's the first lie we see in the Bible, the first in the existence of the world, and it is the lie beneath all other lies. Lies are not Love; even with the best motives, lies strip the essential foundation of love away, replacing it with an unmet desire and longing our Father created us to experience in fullness, True Love.

---

[i] A paraphrase of Genesis 3:1-5

The Definition of a Lie

I was born to be royal,
I was born to be free.
But I was torn from the garden,
When that devil lied to me.

- "Back to the Garden" David Crowder

2
The Father of All Lies

In an era when many of us either have no father, a dad who wasn't our father, an absent or misguided father, or even two fathers, it is easy for us to struggle knowing who our real Father is. There is a reason that God created us to desire parental relationships even once we are grown. It is a type, or model, of Him. He fulfills the characteristics of both a mother and a father. But we face a challenge in recognizing and accepting Him as our heavenly Father because our parents, our children, and we as parents and children are all imperfect. I think we all know that we are imperfect, but I am not sure we all truly believe and understand how our imperfections only accentuate our need for the Father. On the other hand, if we think we are perfect, or righteous, then we may not see our need for dependence because we're perfect just as we are, right? The enemy of our souls knows the importance of our dependence on our Father and how powerful that relationship is designed to be. So, his goal is to substitute himself as our parental figure. The Bible says that satan is *a* father, but he is not *our* father. He is the father of lies.

> *Jesus said to the Jews who had believed Him,*
> *If you abide in my word, you are truly my disciples, and*
> *you will know the truth, and the truth will set you free.*

And they answered him,

> *We are offspring of Abraham and have never been*
> *enslaved to anyone. How is it that you say, "You will*
> *become free"?*[iii]

While it may seem kind of comical, as Pastor Robert Morris once pointed out, their rebuttal to Jesus also seems tragic to me, saying that they, "have never been enslaved to anyone," while they were essentially enslaved by the Roman government. Not to mention the reality that the Israelites had been enslaved by the Egyptians, Babylonians, and Assyrians across their history. It's comical that

---

iii   John 8:31-33

they argued with God that they had never been slaves even as they were being ruled over, but it's tragic that they did not realize the lie that they had believed. The lie that they were free and in control of their own lives. And while that is one lie they believed, it wasn't THE lie Jesus came to set them free from. Jesus answered them,

> *Truly, truly, I say to you, everyone who practices sin is a slave to sin. The slave does not remain in the house forever; the son remains forever. So if the Son sets you free, you will be free indeed. I know that you are offspring of Abraham; yet you seek to kill me because my word finds no place in you. I speak of what I have seen with my Father, and you do what you have heard from your father." They [the Jews] answered him [Jesus], "Abraham is our father."*[iv]

Here Jesus first reveals a fatherless generation. He acknowledges that the Jewish people are the offspring of Abraham, but He also points out how He knows that Abraham is not their father. So, although they proclaim that Abraham is their father, God reveals the truth of their situation. Yes, the Jewish people can trace their lineage back to Abraham, but through their own righteousness, their own verity, or, as we discussed, the lies they have believed, they have made themselves their own gods, their own salvation. Even today, many Jews believe that simply because they are descendants of Israel they are automatically in relationship with Y-hw-h (the Great I Am). They believe that, although they are not performing sacrifices to atone for their failures and shortcomings as demanded in the Torah, they will still go to heaven simply because they are Jewish by lineage. Jesus asserts that bloodline doesn't establish a relationship with Him. Family means so much more to Him:

> *...but it is not as though the word of God has failed. For*

---
iv   John 8:34-39a

> *not all those who are descended from Israel are Israel, nor are they all children because they are Abraham's seed; rather, "Your seed shall be called through Isaac." That is, it is not the children of the flesh who are children of God; rather, the children of the promise are counted as seed.*[v]

Although these Jews were descendants of Abraham, they were no longer sons and daughters of Abraham. These men were devout followers of the Law. They dedicated their lives to living by the Law. They believed they were righteous on their own, and the primary reason they even looked to God to deliver a messiah was to restore a Jewish state, to bring a king or ruler over them, and to set them free from relying on other governments. You see, when we are not looking to our Father to be our father, we are willing to substitute Him with someone or something lesser, something not at all fitting to fill such an important role in our lives. Jesus exposes this lie and goes on to reveal not only how the fruit of their actions and beliefs reveals who their father is not, but also who is now filling the void of that role.

> *If you were Abraham's children, you would be doing the works Abraham did, but now you seek to kill me, a man who has told you the truth that I heard from God. This is not what Abraham did. You are doing the works your father did." They said to him, "We were not born of sexual immorality. We have one Father--even God." Jesus said to them, "If God were your Father, you would love me, for I came from God and I am here. I came not of my own accord, but he sent me. Why do you not understand what I say? It is because you cannot bear to hear my word. You are of your father the devil, and your will is to do your father's desires. He was a murderer from the beginning, and **has nothing***

---
[v] Romans 9:6-8 TLV

> ***to do with the truth**, because there is **no truth in him**. When he lies, **he speaks out of his own character, for he is a liar and the father of lies**. But because I tell the truth, you do not believe me. Which one of you convicts me of sin? If I tell the truth, why do you not believe me? Whoever is of God hears the words of God. The reason why you do not hear them is that you are not of God.*[vi]

During a time of enslavement, the Jews ironically stated that they had never been enslaved. Ironic, but sad. The lies Jesus speaks of sometimes reach so deep that we cannot see the very thing being revealed. Because we have believed the lie so deeply for so long, we become blind to God's reality. Look at the last few verses of that passage. Although He knows the answer, Jesus still asks, "...why do you not believe me?" It's one of those rhetorical questions which He really didn't want them to answer, but instead used to make a point: if they were not listening to Him, then they were listening to someone else. And, although these followers of the Law thought they were listening to laws and precepts of their Father and Creator, Yahweh, they were not listening to the Word of God standing directly in front of them. If they were not willing to listen or follow Him, then they were following someone else. Jesus did not shy away from telling these religious leaders who they were listening to. He wasn't telling them that their father was satan like kids talk about other kids' parents on the playground. He also wasn't intending to be rude, hurtful, or demeaning. It seems to me that He just didn't want to pull any punches or be vague and chance them missing the truth behind the matter. They were indeed listening to and following satan, the one entity all of the laws, precepts, and traditions were trying to point them away from. Ironically, the 613 laws they were trying to uphold emanated from the knowledge of good and evil. Now, you may be saying, *but they*

[vi] John 8:39b-47 ESV (emphasis mine)

were laws given by God; how can they be from the knowledge of good and evil?

Prior to the Fall in Genesis 3, there was only one warning, rule, law, or command. Whatever you want to call it, aside from that one command, nothing kept Adam and Eve from their relationship with God. The single, original commandment was to not eat from the Tree of the Knowledge of Good and Evil. That warning did not say,

> *...neither shall you touch it, lest you die,*

as Eve stated in Genesis 3:3. Instead God, just after He placed Adam in the Garden,

> *to work it and keep it... commanded the man, saying, "You may surely eat of every tree of the garden, but of the tree of the knowledge of good and evil you shall not eat, for in the day that you eat of it you shall surely die."*

Notice, it mentions nothing about touching it and also notice the definitiveness of the consequence as well. "Lest you die," in the Hebrew is less emphatic than, "you shall surely die." It is interesting that Eve, even before Satan challenged her, apparently had God's word twisted in her mind.[4] Now, we don't know for sure that God did not say those exact words to her during one of their morning walks, whether this was her interpretation of what He said or if this reflects Adam trying to emphatically stress the importance of the command, attempting to remove any temptation Eve may have had to eat of the fruit. No matter the situation, the information we have been given shows that they indeed could have and almost would have been required to touch the fruit. After all, it was Adam's job to work and keep the Garden.

When thinking of the Garden of Eden, I like to imagine what it was like to live there, to have such unhindered intimacy with God, to know Him, and to grow in relationship with Him more each day. Questions rise up, like: What if fruit fell from the tree? That begs the question, *did fruit even fall from the tree?* Did the fruit ever get so full, so ripe with life that it could take no more, dropping to the ground, spilling life into the soil below? What happened when mischievous and curious squirrels chased each other through the trees of Eden, or a deer strolled through the Garden with its eighty-four-point antler rack and bumped a pleasantly plump and ripe knowledge of good and evil fruit? Then, that leads to the question, *did the animals eat from the forbidden tree?* I can only assume that it was the serpent's favorite fruit in the Garden. I enjoy letting my mind go on rabbit trails like this so that I can never forget what we were promised and what we lost when that single commandment was broken.

    The six hundred and thirteen laws culminated in a world that had lost its connection to God, its connection to Truth. For centuries, many theologians have pointed out that the law is a way in which God points out how desperately we need Him. It points to the Cross and how there is no way to reconnect to God without Him having created the way. These are all results, consequences rather, of Adam and Eve listening to satan in the first place. The laws that the Pharisees and Sadducees so diligently followed and tried to fulfill all emanated from the knowledge of good and evil. Had Adam and Eve not chosen to walk away from God's design for them, eating of the fruit, gaining the knowledge only designed for Himself, good and evil, there would not have been a need for those laws. The relationship would have never been broken and we would not have needed the Law to show our inability to keep a perfect standard. Instead, we simply would have received all we needed to know from our Father.

    Hearing that satan was their father had to be a hard pill to swallow, like in *The Matrix*, where Neo had a choice to take one of two pills. The first so-called pill was this newly-revealed reality which changed everything; it revealed the underlying foundation of lies and beliefs they had built their lives upon. The second pill would allow them to keep living their lives as they always had. It was easier, more comfortable, and more familiar. We face the same choice. What happens when you realize everything you have thought and believed is a lie? Satan would have you believe that life is over, but in actuality, only life as you have known it is over.

Who are YOU listening to?

You have an opportunity to know the Truth and be born again, this time not born from flesh and knowledge, but from the Spirit. To live LIFE to the fullest, the way God, from the beginning, intended, designed, and forever desires for you to live. Ephesians 1:13-14 says it this way,

> *...when you heard the word of Truth, the gospel of your salvation, and believed [or put your trust] in Him, [you] were sealed with the promised Holy Spirit, who is the guarantee of our inheritance until we acquire possession of it, [all] to the praise of His glory.*

To initiate that journey, you must make a choice. You don't have to take a pill, but you do have those same options before you: continue reading, asking God to reveal what lies beneath, or put the book down and continue to rely on the lies you have believed. (I've included a prayer here simply to be a guide, to help you begin a conversation with God. Keep in mind, your prayer doesn't have to follow my wording exactly. Let it be conversational, let it come authentically from your heart. He does understand, even if you don't speak eloquently or have perfect words.) If you are ready, let's pray:

> *God, Father, Daddy, I am unsure of where to start. I need Your help to begin this journey of truth, love, identity, and freedom. I want to see me as You see me. I want to know who You created me to be, who You*

desire me to be, and who I am in Your eyes. Please reveal to me the lies I have believed and how I let myself believe them. Please let this book minister to my heart and help me understand, reveal, and protect against future battles for my heart. Lord, I love You and want to experience Your Love like never before.

Are you ready? Let's begin at the beginning.

Even the most beautiful lie is both born from and conceives deception and death.
— Courtney Cohen

3
The Birth of a Lie

Anything born or created must not only come from something, but it also must reside, live, or exist somewhere. A lie is no different. Like a baby, if a lie has no host to carry it, no one to feed and nurture it, it will fail to live.

Have you ever tried to trace back to the root of a lie? Looking at the motivation behind why we lie – our reactions to things people say or do, the feelings which make us feel that we must lie, and when we typically feel the need to lie – we can see that all these are based on deception and death. It might seem that pride should be included as a root of a lie, but pride still falls back to deception, creating a false persona to convince ourselves or others that we are "better" than we really are.

Some people, perhaps even you, would say that they have lied in order to make someone feel better or to prevent confrontation or pain. But even if a lie has prevented confrontation, or if it makes someone feel better by avoiding pain, the lie is still rooted in death and deception. Digging even further, what lie exists beneath our belief that lies have the power to prevent pain and create peace? Just because we alleviate pain doesn't mean we prevent death; lies only numb the soul to the reality of life and possibly death.

Consider this: One of the most common lies told, believed, and perceived manifests in the question, "Do I look fat in this?" Profound, right? Were you expecting something deeper, more religious, more spiritual? When we dive into it, we can see how deep this really goes. It doesn't have to come in these exact words. Some people may simply say, "How do I look?" Or, they may not say a word, but simply will look in a mirror, full of self-doubt. In our image-obsessed world, I doubt many people have failed to come across some form of this question. You may even immediately think that the response given to the question is the lie I will address here, and I will, but first, I must address the lie whispered in the ears of many of God's children today.

The Birth of a Lie

It is no longer merely a woman's issue, and I am not sure it ever truly was. Men are, and have been, just as affected by this lie. They have typically internalized it and "toughed" it out because they are, well, "men." The lie is that our beauty is dependent upon the amount of cellulite we do or do not have on our bodies, whether we have 0, 2, 4, 6, or 8 abdominal muscles showing, or how well a designer pair of jeans fits us. I bought into this lie for quite some time. I still struggle with it every once in a while when I find myself looking in the mirror and, instead of seeing a very healthy forty-something-year-old man, satan whispers to me that I have gained ten to fifteen pounds since I was in my prime physical condition. Some of you may be saying now, "Really, ten pounds? You're getting bent out of shape over ten pounds?" But it is the same lie, whether it's two or two hundred pounds. There are people who are extremely underweight, anorexic, and bulimic because of this same lie.

Jesus was not a super model, *"...he had no form or majesty that we should look at him, and no beauty that we should desire him."*[i] Some even argue that He didn't have long, flowing hair. (I should also tell you that He wasn't a blue-eyed Caucasian either, despite what various artists' depictions may show.) But what is the easiest way to keep us from knowing who someone is? It's to lie to us about what they look like, about their personality, and about who they are so that, when we do encounter that person, our perception of them is so distorted we don't recognize them. This might be why Jesus said that His sheep know His voice, so that we are not deceived by the physical, but rather, we rely solely on our relationship with Him. The same goes for us. We have been lied to so often regarding our identity: that who we are is defined by what we do, what we look like, what sins we have committed, what we wear, what we will never achieve, what status we have, and who our friends are or aren't. And when we look in the mirror we don't even recognize the beauty in front of us.

---
i   Isaiah 53:13b

What LIES Beneath

A lie was presented at some point that our body is a true representation of who we are and who we were created to be. We believed that lie, became ashamed, and decided to cover it up with either clothing, exercise, or food.

It's no different than what happened in the Garden. The simplest lie implies so much. Deception and death spread through our entire beings. They don't stay put in the one lie. The original lie was that we are not good enough as God created, intended, designed, and desires us to be. That one lie, when believed, set off a chain reaction of death. It makes us feel that we need more, to be more, to do more. Being with God isn't quite enough; we need to be doing something "for" Him. And if we need to be doing stuff for Him, then that means we need to earn our way into heaven, which leads to the belief that if we are not perfect we cannot get into heaven. That then leads to self-doubt and the destruction of our identity, of who we were created to be in the first place: His children.

This can be like the chicken and the egg, or like a bowl of spaghetti. Similar to the chicken and the egg, sometimes when we start to look at the lies we have believed and passed on to others, it becomes extremely difficult to see which belief led to which thought, and ultimately which action. This results in a belief that either confirms or conflicts with another belief. It's also like a bowl of spaghetti because, when we unearth a lie, or a noodle, and try to pull it out, it is impossible to do so cleanly without disturbing or shifting other noodles. When we uncover lies that cause conflict or self-doubt, they will reveal other possible mistakes or lies believed. It's like the Prego "Bad Decisions" commercial where a lady tastes Prego Spaghetti Sauce for the first time. Realizing she has been buying Ragu for the wrong reasons, she poses the question, "What other bad decisions have I been making?" and then proceeds to reflect on her 80s' attire and choices of music. We will start to discover other incorrect decisions we have made which have been based on what we believed to be true.

If it's like the chicken and the egg, how do we ever find the root or beginning? You keep looking back until you find Jesus. I am *not* saying Jesus was the root of the lie. We need to continue digging down until we reveal His Truth about whatever lie is affecting us. If we must, we can go all the way back to the beginning. For the chicken, that would have been the fifth day of Creation when God created the birds. I am not sure which form He created them in and I am not sure it really matters. But you find out by asking the One who created them. In the same way, you ask the One who was there at the beginning about where the lie you believed came from.

> *In the beginning was the Word, and the Word was with God, and the Word was God. He was in the beginning with God. All things were made through him, and without him was not any thing made that was made. In him was life, and the life was the light of men. The light shines in the darkness, and the darkness has not overcome it.*
> *- John 1:1*

Matthew Henry's Concise Commentary elaborates on this section of scripture, providing a simple way to understand what the Word of God means. It scratches the surface of who the Son of God is, but this commentary also says, "The plainest reason why the Son of God is called the Word, seems to be, that as our words explain our minds to others, and so was the Son of God sent in order to reveal his Father's mind to the world.[5]" If I could convince *Matthew Henry* to make a change, it would be to change the word "mind" to "heart." Although millions of people do dissect, discuss, and debate the Bible, it isn't something created to logically debate with our own wisdom, intelligence, or knowledge. It simply wasn't created for that purpose. Rather, it describes and annotates what God's heart was from our creation to the end of time. When we look at the Bible as merely a list of rules, or as evidence for a debate, we lose the simple truth behind it. God gave us a window to look into His heart and a door to walk into it.

One of the most profound truths revealed concerning quite possibly the largest lie ever believed, was that God existed. For the longest time, I was an atheist in search of explanations. Yet, no matter how eager I was to find purpose or reason for our existence, I resisted every conversation with Christians who talked about a God whom I had been convinced didn't exist. After my ex-fiancé and I split, the lie I had believed was pointed out. I believed that God didn't exist which was supported by my die-hard belief in evolution, natural selection, and the Big Bang **Theory**. You may wonder what my ex-fiancé has to do with this. Remember, I was not a Christian at that point. So, when she moved out, I gave her all the furniture except the couch, entertainment center, and electronics. (A typical bachelor thing to do, right?) In one of the cabinets of the entertainment center, she had left a series of pirated videos behind. For whatever reason, I chose to pop one in. A scientist, dedicated to showing how the universe was *created*, not manifested from nothingness, instantly intrigued me.

This scientist revealed the possibility of a lie I had been believing, and I chose to investigate further. I ended up watching the entire series, which left me reeling in unsurety. My foundation had been shaken out from under me. A lie revealed, but not resolved, will leave you insecure and unsure. I was seeking purpose and the explanation of our existence even more than before. And, while those videos spoke of this God who created everything, mere knowledge of His existence wasn't enough. I reached out to a coworker and asked to borrow a Bible. (This is before Bible.com, YouVersion, or access to a thousand online bibles existed.) What he did showed me the love of this God he believed in. He didn't bring a Bible to let me borrow; instead, he purchased a brand-new study Bible for me. This Bible contained explanations and commentaries that helped me better understand what I was reading, but it somehow wasn't enough. That insecurity and volatility was still present. People told, videos portrayed, and this Book informed me of a God I had never believed in. And, although much had changed as a result of my research, revealing patterns, explanations, and logical proof of His existence, nothing *real* had changed.

It wasn't until one evening, while sitting on my bed, totally lost in what I was reading, that I turned my attention from the words in the Book towards the Author of the Book. I did something I hadn't tried to do since childhood—I prayed. Something to the effect of, "God, if this is real, if You are real, show me." And immediately a hardness in my soul, my heart, my emotions, and my thoughts broke off. I knew immediately the lie I had believed. The foundational lie I had based my life on, logic, shattered like glass below my feet, but below was not a black hole or abyss I would fall into, leaving me desperate and alone. There He was, waiting to catch me. For over twenty-six years, God was ready and waiting to show me who He was, is, and will be. He replaced the foundation of lies I had created with Himself, His Truth, His Love, His Life, His Spirit. The insecurity, the unsurety and the questions were not all answered, but they became different questions. I had to hear from Him in order to have His Essence revealed to me. In John 14-16, Jesus talks about how and why the Holy Spirit was to come, how He was sending Him as our Helper and Counselor. Without even knowing of John 16:8-11, I benefitted from it:

> *...when he comes, he will convict the world concerning sin and righteousness and judgment: concerning sin, because they do not believe in me; concerning righteousness, because I go to the Father, and you will see me no longer; concerning judgment, because the ruler of this world is judged.*

Immediately after the hardness broke away, weeping like I never had before, I confessed my belief not only in His existence, but also in His Son as my Savior and Deliverer from my sin and my separation from my Creator, my Father, the God of the Universe. The ceiling of my apartment didn't lift off to reveal the heavenly host applauding, although I know now that they were cheering. I didn't hear satan bawling over losing his grip on me. Truthfully, I didn't hear anything at all.

Because I did not hear an audible reply or see an immediate response to my prayer, I want to address a core lie I believed at a young age: God doesn't listen or care. While seeking God about that lie, He brought me back to the moment I believed it.

I lay on the ground next to my dresser where our almost twenty-year-old cat lethargically hid from me, something she never did. She always cuddled in our arms, purring, kneading, and kissing us. That's where she got her name "Kissy." She had been with me since I was born, literally staying with me in my crib. So, when I noticed her hiding, I knew something was wrong, and I did something I had never really done before. I'm not sure where it came from since I had very little exposure to church as a child, but I started to pray. However, I didn't hear anything.

I don't know where I got the idea that I should hear something audibly, except an assumption that if I am talking with God that He should talk with me. But recently God showed me how I felt as a child after I talked to Him, petitioning Him for help for the healing of my cat. While lying there on the ground, peace came over me. My body lay prostrate on the floor and my right cheek rested on my crossed hands as I looked under the dresser. I simply felt peace. I was crying and sad, but I felt peace. Although I didn't know it then, that peace was God speaking to my soul. I heard Him, just not in the way I thought I was supposed to. Through the Freedom Ministry at Gateway Church, I have learned that, while God speaks in many different ways, He primarily uses three vehicles: auditory, visual, and kinesthetic. We will cover more on this later, but I can see now how He spoke to me that day, how He knew I needed to hear Him.

God knew that, as a child in my personal situation, I could not have handled hearing the audible voice of God. What would have happened had I faced an unbelieving family with a story that I had heard the voice of God? No doubt, there would have been years of endless ridicule, putting another barrier between Him and me. On my bed that evening, like years before as a child lying on that floor, I heard God speak directly to my soul. You may be asking, "Well, what did He 'say' to your soul?" While I can't express the "words" He spoke, I know what happened in my soul. My heart softened for Him. He impressed the essence of peace on me and I felt something come alive that never had been before.

Robert Morris explains that we are born with a dead spirit as a result of the fall and when we are saved, or born again, God breathes His breath of Life into us as He did to Adam at creation. My spirit came alive for the first time ever and a comforting warmth replaced a cold hatred for God. He simply welcomed me into His arms like a long-lost son coming home. The kindling for a fire that I could not yet imagine had been sparked. I felt as if a huge weight, or yoke, had been lifted from me.

This experience with Him had broken off another lie, that in order to hear God you have to *audibly* hear Him. But that is not the person He created me to be. When I was young, satan attacked me with this lie. He may have attacked you with it as well. It is one of the common lies he tells. While my childhood cat, whom I spent almost every day with, was struggling to stay alive, I prayed for God to heal her. And I heard nothing. The next day, my parents came home with her in a box, not much larger than a shoebox, and we buried her in the garden behind our house. So, not only did I not hear a response, but the request in my prayer went unfulfilled. Satan took that opportunity to pour his spiritual death into a moment which was simply the physical death of our pet. As much as I didn't want her to go, Kissy was nineteen years old and had lived a full life of love, happiness, and great fun. Satan and his demons wanted to capitalize on my hurt by trying to kill me, trying to finish me off before I had even started. The lie that God couldn't hear me and, if He did, that He didn't care enough to respond to or grant my request, deceived me. I took satan's lie and believed it, making it a foundation for my life, and built a wicked, jealous, hurt, and hate-filled life on top of it.

    I look back now, and while I am sure God would have preferred that I walk with Him all those years, my experience is exactly what I needed to have the testimony that I have, for my story to help share with you how great He is. That's why God let evil to influence and attack me like that. From what I saw, my parents were not spiritual in any way, agnostic at best. Had nothing happened to break me apart from their ambiguity, I, too, could have easily lived in spiritual obscurity.

    God knew when He designed me with an intensely passionate heart, that I would push Him away for years. Yet, instead of letting me live lacking the passion He created me with, He allowed it to remain, and a rage and passionate hatred developed. Because of the lie I believed – that God didn't hear or didn't care – the passion God created me to have towards Him was still there, it just manifested hate rather than His original intention of love and worship. How is that in any way a good thing? Well, when we look at it from our lens of the knowledge of good and evil, we tend to put hatred under the category of evil. But, strangely, because my heart and mind constantly turned that passion against this God I claimed not to believe in, I stayed close to Him. I found myself reading the Bible, searching for "ammunition" to use against His followers in debates. Satan quoted Scripture, right? And while I thought I was finding ammunition, my Father, my Savior, my Counselor knew that He was depositing His Word in my heart. His Word gave me tidbits of His Love, time after time after time, until it built a new desire to know Him, which would one day help not only in my salvation, but, more importantly, in bringing me into a deep, loving relationship with Him. What satan intended to be a death blow was full of Life, full of my Father's Love for me.

I look back and see how easy it would have been for me to have spent my childhood like my parents had, not sharing their lives with the One who created them, not even glancing at the Bible. What satan intended for harm was possibly the best thing for me. Looking at my hatred now, I believe I was simply hurt by my disbelief in God, who I knew in my heart not only existed, but loved me and created me to be in communication and relationship with Him. That hate was simply conflict between the truth in my heart and the perception in my head. I, like you, am made to live with and worship Him. And, when we are separated from Him and cannot express our adoration for Him, it muddles up our original design, causing undesired results. In my case, hatred grew towards Him instead of the direction He intended it. Psalm 97:10 in the Tree of Life Version says, "*You who love Adonai, hate evil...*" Unlike what many of us are told as children, we are actually built to hate; and if we love the Lord, Adonai, and seek Him first in all we do, then our hate should and will be directed toward evil. Not *evil* as a synonym to *bad* (antonym of good), but as in the opposition to God. We should hate the things He hates.

> **There are six things the Lord hates; seven that are an abomination to Him: haughty eyes (or the attitude of self-righteousness or placing yourself over anyone else), a lying tongue, and hands that shed innocent blood, a heart that devises wicked plans, feet that make hast to run to evil, a false witness who breathes out lies, and one who sows discord (or spreads rumors) among brothers.**[ii]

It doesn't say which is the one He doesn't hate and is

---
ii Proverbs 6:16-19

simply an abomination, but, either way, those things are evil. They stand against God. Did you notice that three of them, verbatim, referenced lying? Look further and you will see that they are all based on a deception. Remember from the chapter title here, a lie is both born from and conceives deception and death. When we believe a lie that we are greater than others, greater than the One who created us, it's an abomination. Hands that shed innocent blood are attached to someone who has incorrectly placed judgment on another based on their knowledge of good and evil, thus exacting their own punishment. God is the Judge, not us. The heart that devises wicked plans surely must be evil, plotting against what God would have for us. And the feet that quickly run to evil, instead of toward the Love and Life He has for us, must be attached to someone like I was for so long, believing God to be who He is not. Deception and lies are full of evil, and we, who love the Lord, should hate evil.

    There is no way to never believe lies. At some point, we will also tell, re-tell, or fabricate a lie. We are all imperfect. But God is bigger than all of the lies. His Truth and His Life will be revealed and overcome as we start to realize where and when the lies were born and the effects those lies have had. As lies are broken off, you are broken free from what lies beneath.

The Birth of a Lie

Sin, taking an opportunity through the commandment, deceived me and through it killed me.
- Romans 7:11 TLV

Steven Cohen

4
The Anatomy of a Lie

What LIES Beneath

Anything that is born must have an anatomy to live, to thrive, even to exist. A developed skeletal support system makes up part of your anatomy. Beyond your skeleton exist millions of complex organs, cells, muscles, tendons, nerves, and microorganisms, all various elements of your anatomy which work together, allowing you to live. Like these living organisms, a lie too has an anatomy. A complex, intertwined existence of possibly millions of contributing factors allow for the lie to exist, perhaps even to thrive.

We are not going to go through the millions of intertwining complexities of a lie. But, much like anatomy class (without the disgusting worm, frog, or cat guts lying everywhere), we will open up a lie to see the larger organs, or foundational components of that lie, and delve into how those affect and help support a lie's existence. Much like our bodies, when one or more of our organs fail to work properly, the other organs often compensate and can prematurely wear out, fail, or begin to break down. My goal with this chapter is not to help you tear down all of the lies at one time, in one big chunk. But if we can break down one or more aspects that a lie depends on to thrive in our lives, the lie will start to fail too. Also, like our bodies, a lie will not go down without a fight; even with a few failing parts it will strive to thrive. If you are trying to overcome the bondage of lies on your own, it is very difficult. But with Christ, our Lord and Creator, as our support system and Counselor, it becomes much easier, freeing even. He does all of the heavy lifting, but it is still a challenge we need to engage in. When we experience the spiritual, emotional, and mental health benefits we gain from disconnecting life-support from our lies, we will realize the value of the effort we made. There will likely be tenderness or pain involved, but only for a little while as we get familiar with using parts of our emotions, our spirit, and our will that have atrophied.

Death

We discussed in the previous chapter that a lie is born out of death and deception, so, fittingly, the first anatomical part of the lie we will discuss here is Death. But what is *death*? For that matter, what is *life?* A lie has been prolifically spread that *life* is simply a state of humanity, a culmination of vital statistics and symptoms found only in organic objects. What if that is only a limited understanding of what life really is? If you have a heartbeat, you breathe, grow, or metabolize food, then you are alive, but there are plenty of people, including myself for much of my existence, who, although we are alive, we actually are or were dead. I was full of hate, anger, rage, separated from my Creator, perceiving myself as god. Although I felt the emotion of love, more like comfort and infatuation, my heart was full of hate. It wasn't the righteous Hate that is spoken of in Psalm 97, hating evil, but it was full of jealousy, judgment, and a yearning for control of this thing called *life*. In reality, I was yearning for Life, but I didn't even know how to identify what I was looking for in order to start looking for it. Just as bad, I was suffering from death, but couldn't diagnose it.

To diagnose a condition, a doctor must know more than simply the existence of a condition; they must also understand its symptoms, its cause, and its cure (if available). I believe the cure to death is life. But this brings us back to the question, *what is life?* I like to define life as the absence of death and the presence of Life. You may think, "That's crazy. You can't use a word in its own definition," or "This is circular logic." But the Word is not just any word and the Life is not just any life. They are the reference point, the power, the origination of all existence. They redefine our definitions simply by being present. That's how life is better defined by the presence of Life, because in the Creator of life's presence we experience Life, and death disappears. On the flip side, death is simply the absence of Life. This is how God's warning in the Garden of Eden was true, even though Adam and Eve's hearts did not stop beating and their lungs did not stop breathing after eating of the fruit. From that moment, they were dead, full of death, separated from their Creator, separated from Life. God was not talking about the state of living – breathing, eating, or metabolizing – when He warned that they would "surely die."[i] Just as there is a difference between Love and loving, there is a difference between Life and living, Death and dying. Take a moment and seek God to show you the difference. Let Him speak to your heart. A prayer could look like this:

> *Lord, thank You for the breath in my lungs,*
> *the blood my heart pumps.*
> *Your concept, known as me, is such a complex and beautiful creation, I can only imagine how delightful it would have been to see Adam formed from the dirt. And, while the formation of his body is extraordinary, it was nothing until*
> *You Breathed Your Life into it.*
> *Lord, please show me Your Life, breathe into me as You did into Adam Your Life, Your Love. Break the chains of my knowledge and reveal to me Your Wisdom, Your Love, Your Life.*

God is Love. He is Life. He is Truth. We, on the other hand, are adored, and we need to believe it. We can feel and express love, are living and have the ability to accept and tell the truth. There is a difference between a state of action and the essence of something. For instance, before coming into a relationship with Christ, whether I believed it or not, God was still God. He created me, He knew me, He desired me to be with Him. His Essence of being God could not be removed from existence even if I didn't believe it. Even more than that, I had a heartbeat, but until I let Him breathe His Life into me, I was spiritually dead.

---
[i] Genesis 2:17

With a lie, there is almost no difference. The death found in a lie doesn't take our breath away or stop our hearts. It simply takes the Life out of us. Its goal and intent is to take God out of the equation, to lessen our dependence and connection with the "Truth and the Life." If you are no longer eating from the fruit of Life, you lose the connection to it. Eating from the fruit of the knowledge of good and evil connects you to the curse of the knowledge of good and evil. We'll visit this curse more in chapter ten.

Although I am not a doctor, I do have a good knowledge and understanding of the body God created for us. While God did create our bodies to continue to exhibit the symptoms of living regardless of our relationship with Him, they still need food, water, and oxygen to continue to work correctly. If we do not consume enough nutrients and sustenance, the symptoms of life begin to disappear and symptoms of an impending death appear. Think about it. If we breathe cancerous smoke from a cigarette, some of the symptoms of the death we are breathing include coughing, upper respiratory infections, black and less elastic lungs, emphysema, and possibly cancer. What about when we drink alcohol or energy drinks full of caffeine, sugar, and artificial stimulants?

Let me ask. Are there other ways to get the same benefits as drinking a glass of wine or an energy drink? Grapes for instance, where wine comes from, have almost all of the same chemical components that are believed to be beneficial to your heart, without the negative effects to your kidneys and other parts of your body. What about energy drinks? God created the seventh day for that. When we live a healthy lifestyle, one that consists of healthy activity and rest, we have more energy. But death tells us we can just rely on supplements and stimulants to give us what we need.

One symptom of that death-rooted belief is an ongoing, deeper dependence on these substances to continue to have more energy. Drinking not merely one, but now two or three or four coffees or so-called "energy drinks" per day to stay awake, to stay stimulated. Even the ones which claim to be all-natural need to be questioned. Arsenic and feces are natural, but that doesn't mean I want to consume them. The Mayo Clinic even advises doctors not to recommend the use of wine or other alcoholic beverages for their believed health benefits because of the increased chance of addiction, abuse, and other health risks.[6] For those who just use a little wine to take the edge off and relax, I ask, why is there the need to take the edge off? And, above that, is there another way that could allow you to relax without the adverse effects of alcohol? This is not just about intoxication. In a *Sleep Medicine* journal published by sleep specialist Michael Grandner, it is noted that a glass of wine at night, although calming or soothing for some people because of the melatonin provided by the grapes, actually prevents you from sleeping in a REM state because of the alcohol. The suggestion from the article was to eat red grapes with the skin on to get the melatonin if needed, but most food and drink habits before bed were found to be placebo. Meaning, we have deceived ourselves into thinking these things somehow give us rest.[7]

When we live close to God, we are continually being freed, and the world's burdens, anxiety, and stress dissipate. Psalms tells us to, *"Cast your burden on the LORD, and he will sustain you; he will never permit the righteous to be moved."*[iii] So, although wine is consumed in the Bible, it is not used in God-glorifying contexts to take the edge off. It is typically part of a celebration or gathering. Take your burdens to the Lord and leave them there. Don't go back to visit them; just let them go.

I am not anti-alcohol; I know that Jesus drank wine, but just because He drank it doesn't mean we should abuse or worship it. I spent many years doing that and I know where it got me. While I was having fun with my friends then, feeling uninhibited and free,

---

iii   Psalm 55:22

I can do that now without alcohol. I don't need the excuse to be stupid silly. We don't need alcohol to lower our inhibitions so that we can simply be the people God created us to be. Just as I hope for you, I am no longer dependent on the lie, the excuse, or the need for alcohol to reveal the fun that God created us to have. The difference is that, without alcohol or whatever substance is being used to numb the pain or lower inhibitions, all of our other faculties, processes, and functions are not inhibited.

Consider drunk driving as an example. I don't know of a single person who drinks for the purpose of going out to drive drunk. Now, I don't know everyone in the world and there may be some, but in my experience substances were used simply to have a good time, to give an excuse to get crazy, to dance freely, to laugh like they can't while at work, to do less serious things. So many of us are hiding or aren't even aware of who we are, how much fun we can have, how pleasurable this world really is supposed to be until something brings those inhibitions down.

But, let's look at what lies beneath. Why can't I dance freely? Why can't I laugh out loud? Why can't I sing (however out of tune it may or may not be)? Fear. Fear of judgment, fear of embarrassment, fear of looking silly or stupid or imperfect. Fear. We have let the opinions and judgments of others reduce us to stiff, protected, professional people who aren't willing to reveal ourselves because of the lies of our accuser that say we are weird.

My drinking story, like so many others', begins in childhood while I watched my dad and his friends drink on Sundays, watch "The Game," yell and scream at a TV, high-five each other, laugh, joke, cut up, and sing crazy songs. Many times, they did stupid things those days, but it seemed to be excused because they were drunk. Around that same age, I found myself singing in the shower one morning. Of all songs, I was singing Aretha Franklin's "Respect." Shouting, "R.E.S.P.E.C.T, find out what it means to me," over and over. I was having a blast. Until my family razzed me about it when I got out of the shower. I don't remember their exact words, but they don't matter because I remember the pain and hurt they caused. I didn't have a good enough singing voice to express the joy in my heart. So, I shut that down.

      Years later, at my homecoming dance, I found myself having fun, dancing, like only a thirteen-year-old boy who had never been to a dance before could. I am sure my moves looked hideous, but man, it was fun. Fun, until a close friend came up and started laughing at me. I am sure they did not mean to hurt me with their laughter, but it still cut deep because I took it as a judgment of my identity. I couldn't simply let loose and have fun because it was fun. I wasn't a good enough dancer to express the joy in my heart. So, I shut that part of me down in public. I didn't want to experience that betrayal again. It hurts to have someone laugh at you, at your pure expression of inner joy, especially a good friend.

      Embarrassments and wounds like this continued throughout my younger years. I kept shutting down every authentic expression of my personality until confusion and uncertainty clouded who I was. I became capable of only expressing pain, hurt, and anger. No one laughed at me when I was yelling, no one laughed at me when I was punching. No one laughed. I thought I had control of my emotions and that I could even control others' emotions through my actions. I could keep that embarrassing joy hidden away. I still had fun, but I couldn't really express myself. In the darkness and quiet of my own room, away from other people who could judge me, deep, dark music met me where I was at. They say misery loves company, but I felt absolutely isolated. Various substances and behaviors gave me a false sense of freedom from the hurt, from the loneliness. I started sniffing glue, cutting and carving, smoking, and drinking. These forms of self-medication are rampant today. You may have even taken part in some of these as well.

      But, when we lower our inhibitions artificially through substances or destructive behaviors, we expose ourselves to real threats, disabling our ability to protect ourselves. *Inhibition* is defined as, "a voluntary or involuntary restraint on the direct expression of an instinct."[8] In the example of driving under the influence, while driving drunk was not the intent (the reason for using whatever substance was used), once all protective restraints are gone, so is that instinct, that protective barrier that allows for good judgment. We've all heard of the Christian teen guarding their sexual purity, saving themselves for their spouse, ending up pregnant or getting someone else pregnant after a party where they were introduced to some sort of substance that lowered their inhibitions. They just wanted to have fun, but ended up pregnant.

(By the way, being pregnant, although it is a consequence, is not a problem. The life created there, while unplanned and possibly unwanted by the surprised parents, is still desired by someone, and did not take God by surprise. The lie that the deceiver whispers in that moment is that there is no way to live with that consequence. But he doesn't tell you about the horrible guilt, pain, and remorse associated with aborting the child after you've believed and acted on the enemy's lies. I was not planning on discussing abortion here, but it does show how there is a consequence for every action we take. Some are life-producing, some are full of death. Don't get death confused with pain or life confused with joy. Placing an unexpected child up for adoption is full of Life, both for the child and for the family it creates with the adoptive parents. I am not oblivious to the hurt and pain associated with adoption, because there are intense emotions involved. As an adoptive and foster parent, I know these all too well. But they pale in comparison to the death of the child and the wracking guilt and sorrow of the mother and father following an abortion.)

Some of you may be thinking that I am harping a bit too much on drugs and alcohol, or, on the flip side, that we should tighten down regulations, but I do not think these are the case at all. The problem is not the substances, the problem is that we have believed the lie that we need them at all. Where did these inhibitions come from? They act as a lens, or a mental protective layer, whether innate or created through various psychological processes. Many times, our inhibitions are created as a result of words from our parents, teachers, complete strangers, pastors, leaders, friends, and every person who has corrected or warned us of the repercussions of our actions. These inhibitions are protective layers created by the pain associated with failure, betrayal, correction, discipline, and struggle. Many times, they are healthy and protective layers that God created us with, as part of a complex and in-depth psyche designed to help preserve our mind, body, and soul. But when we rely on that psyche instead of the One who created it, the situation becomes unhealthy.

> ***They exchanged the truth about God for a lie and worshiped the creature rather than the Creator.***[iv]

Earlier, when I shared my past and the rejection I felt, was the problem the way I took their laughter, or was it that they were the ones who laughed at me? Was the problem that they believed it was acceptable to laugh at someone, or was it that I believed my worth was based on someone else's reaction to my behavior? While I am only responsible for my own actions and responses, the answer to both of those questions is still "yes." Both were problematic because the people in both situations, in both questions, were not seeking or relying on the Truth. If just one of them is not willing to continue the lie and, instead, seeks out the Truth, the cycle stops. If the cycle never stops, then the cycle never stops, and the questions and situations causing pain and rejection can seem endless, turning into a web of confusion and overwhelm. Is that what we are called to by our Creator? To live in a state of overwhelm, confusion, and addiction, reliant on substances, behaviors, or other people for our comfort?

Again, many doctors are hesitant to suggest drinking as

---

iv Romans 1:25

a way to relax because of the risk of opening that gateway to addiction. How many stories bear witness to one glass of wine turning into two, then half a bottle, and so on?

Lies poison us slowly, building in us a tolerance and dependence on them which grow greater and greater. Before we know it, practically the only thing that comes out of our mouth is a lie. What if the only breaths we breathed were through the end of a cigarette, the only liquid we provided for our bodies was alcohol or energy drinks, and the only food we consumed was Twinkies or super-sized French fries? Would you agree that the symptoms of death would appear much more quickly?

We have all seen the person, and this may be you, who predictably embellishes almost everything they say. The person who thinks they need to lie about everything in order to gain acceptance, and for others to listen to or value their contribution to the conversation. It's ironic that, typically, the reason people don't want to accept, listen to, or believe that type of person is because all they do is lie and embellish. Even if others see through the lies and accept that person for who God created them to be, the person stuck in the cycle of embellishing is likely not going to feel that acceptance until they, themselves, can accept who they truly are, who they were created to be.

As I sit here at the local coffee house, sipping on my tea, I see person after person approach the counter, dragging in, tired and groggy, talking about how exhausted they are. I have even heard, on occasion, the barista behind the counter reply, "Let me fix that." Are they actually fixing that or are they simply covering up symptoms? When we eat or drink poison, our bodies start to fail, they no longer recover as quickly as they were designed to, their capabilities diminish, the requirement for sleep seems to increase, although many times activity is actually needed.

Newton's first law of motion states that a body at rest will stay at rest unless an outside force acts upon it, and a body in motion at a constant velocity will remain in motion in a straight line unless acted upon by an outside force.[9] Sometimes we need an outside force to barge in and knock us off our current course or get us in motion.

Deception

The next organ we will explore in the anatomy of a lie is Deception. We hear this word and understand its concept, but what does it mean practically for our lives? Multiple resources simply define *deception* as "the act of deceiving." But can we use a word, or a form of a word, to define itself? "NO," my classmates and I would yell to our fifth grade English teacher. This was one of the rules drilled into my brain over and over that just stuck.

So, what does *deception* mean? I asked God this question one morning while noticing a connection between deception, perception, inception, conception, and about twenty other words. You have probably caught on to what I saw. They all have different prefixes for the same base, "ception." But, as my spell-checker points out, "ception" is not a word. Breaking it down a little further, "*ion*" indicates action or a state of doing something.[10] That leaves "cept." What are we doing when we are "cept-ing" something? This segment is derived from the Latin word *capere*[11]*,* meaning "to take." It has the same root as the word *capture*. (I guess those high school Latin classes are paying off.) So, when we *accept* something, we capture it towards our self. *Perception* is taking in or capturing our surroundings in our minds. A *precept* is something we have taken in as understood, prior to all other understanding. When we *intercept*, we take something away from its original destination. (As a football fan, I find this to be one of the most emotional words in this group.) *Susceptible* would be something or someone that things are easily taken away from.[12]

What about *deception*? The implied subject here is truth. So, deception is the act of taking away truth. Not just hiding it, not just fibbing, but the intentional removal of truth from a statement or action. Jesus said He *is* the Truth. If God is Truth, there is no wonder why, in Psalms 101:7, God says that, "No one who practices deceit [or deception] will dwell in [His] house." He is saying that those who practice taking Him out of what they say and do will not stay with Him. Deception is so destructive and divisive, but it can also be quite discrete.

Remember what a lie is born from: death and deception. So, not only is a lie born *from* deception, but deception is key to its survival or existence. In addition, one of the core components to deception is that it must be believed or accepted not only by the receiver, but also by the deceiver. Satan created a lie long ago which he then believed himself. Isaiah 14:12-15 shows how satan believed he could replace YHWH, or Yahweh, as God. But think about it. Satan not only tries to deceive others, he himself is deceived. The word *satan* in Hebrew means enemy or adversary. He is our enemy, exactly as his name describes him. You may have noticed all non-grammatically required references to satan are not capitalized in this book. It's because satan is a title, or descriptor, undeserving of worship. God is a title that deserves worship and honor; satan not so much, even though he believes it should be the case. It almost makes you feel sorry for him, that he himself has bought into his own lie, but remember that is simply an invitation into another lie. Feeling sorry for or emotionally burdened by someone else's decisions is an easy way to enter into judgment or acceptance of their burdens as if you are responsible for their decisions and actions.

You may be asking, how does sympathy for others open us up to lies? Let's first clarify what I mean by sympathy and how it differs from empathy. They both share the same Greek root word *Pathos*, meaning suffering, emotion, depraved passion or lust.[13] However sympathy, broken down as, *sym – pathos,* means "the same *pathos*" or *sharing in one's suffering.* In an attempt to relate, we become emotionally deceived, taking on a state not our own, associated with someone else's hardship. This limits our perspective to a similar experience and vantage point, making it difficult to help, possibly even trapping us with them.

Empathy on the other hand, breaks down to *"em – pathos"* or "in *pathos*," which sounds similar, but what is missing is the sharing component. Instead there is an understanding of the pain and suffering. We are *in* it with them, cognizant of how or why they feel the way they do, possibly having been in a similar situation at some point, but without assuming the burden as our own. While empathy creates an "emotional connectedness,"[14] to better understand what others are experiencing, there is not a transfer of feelings or emotions. This allows for a deeper understanding and alternate vantage point, all while keeping ourselves alert.

But aren't we supposed to, "**bear one another's burdens, and fulfill the law of Christ**," like Galatians 6:2 instructs us? Well, what is the law of Christ? Isn't it love?[15] In context, from the end of Galatians 5 through the beginning of Galatians 6, Paul talks about producing the fruit of the Spirit, becoming more like Christ. In Galatians 6:1 he says,

> *...if anyone is caught in any transgression, you who are spiritual [or having a relationship with the Holy Spirit] should restore him in a spirit of gentleness. Keep watch on yourself, lest you too be tempted. (emphasis mine)*

It is very easy to witness someone choose to walk away from God and feel sorry for them, allowing their situation to affect your emotional state. And, then, to justify or condemn their choices based on our own feelings or experiences regarding their situation. But just two verses earlier in Galatians 5:22, we who have the Holy Spirit are told to reveal the fruit of the Spirit:

> *...love, joy, peace, patience, kindness, goodness, faithfulness, **gentleness**, self-control. [emphasis mine]*

Notice, there is no mention of being sympathetic or emotionally burdened. A few verses later, Galatians 6:3-9 continues to warn against taking on judgment or emotional burden, stating,

> *For if anyone thinks he is something, when he is nothing, he deceives himself. But let each one test his own work, and then his reason to boast will be in himself alone and not in his neighbor. For each will have to bear his own load."*

These verses do not contradict themselves. They complement each other. When we become emotionally burdened over someone else's choices, we make a judgment about them, as though we could have done it better, or that we know the choice they should have made. But these verses tell us that if we think we know better, in reality, we don't. We have deceived ourselves. Being responsible for our own choices and decisions, we too are responsible for our own relationship with Christ, our own journey with the Holy Spirit. If we see someone who may have stumbled, we are to fulfill the law of Christ over them. To love them, not judge them. To restore them, as emphasized above, gently, not to sympathize with them by bringing ourselves into their world. We are to empathize and lift them up with Love into His world. This way we continue to exude the love of Christ while we also "bear" the burdens of others. In reality, He bears all of our burdens anyway, right? It is utter deception that we have to take on the emotions of others in order to bear their burden or to help them walk through hardships and challenges.

If we look at Genesis 3:4-5a, "But the serpent said to the woman, 'You will not surely die. For God knows that when you eat of it your eyes will be opened, and you will be like God…,'" you can reasonably infer that, because I am bringing attention to this verse, there is some sort of lie being presented. But what about it is a lie? Where is the deception here? If you break it down literally, you can justify how this entire statement is true. Did God know that Adam and Eve, once having the knowledge of good and evil, would feel as if they no longer needed their Father, nor would they be accepted by Him? Did God know that their hearts wouldn't stop beating and their lungs wouldn't stop breathing? Of course. But, let me also ask, can a true statement be deceptive? We just considered how deception is the removal of truth from a statement or action. Where this gets sticky is that simply because some truth is removed does not mean that all truth is. This is where so many of us allow ourselves not only to believe, but also to spread lies. We are not seeking the *whole* truth. The truth that was taken from Genesis 3:4-5 was that God loves us so much that He advised Adam of the consequences of eating from the Tree so that he would not ever have to experience separation from Life, separation from Him, simply put, death. I don't believe Adam and Eve would have taken and eaten the fruit had they known that this attractive and delicious fruit would have resulted in their separation from God.

    I am convinced that satan played this deception card to the angels who followed him in heaven and were eventually cast out with him. He is not the creator, he is neither capable of creating nor bringing life to anything. He is skilled at killing, stealing, and destroying. He is a liar and, of course, he has bought his own lies. He thinks that he has a chance at "winning." But, in order to win, there must first be a competition. Here, there is no competition for 1st Place. It is God, and God alone, who can sit on that throne. But there is a battle. A battle for you and your friends and family. A battle, not to win the universe, but a battle over whether or not you fulfill God's design and desire for who you are.

    Deception is deception both of self and others. If a lie were intended to deceive only one person it would not spread as fast as lies spread. Imagine deception as a vineyard. Intertwining vines spread from support to support, making it difficult to tell which root they originate from. The deception that one person believes may not be the deception someone else receives. Let's use the example from chapter three: if a woman has been continually fed the lie that her appearance determines her worth, she may ask her husband that age-old question, "Does this make me look fat?" But her husband probably won't hear, "Sweetheart, I have believed a lie that my self-worth is determined by what you or others think about my appearance." The lie he may believe is, "I'm trapped; no matter what I say I cannot win here, so I won't even try." We will explore and expand on this later, but these are the moments when we have choices to embrace the lies presented to us, therefore reinforcing the lies spoken to others, or we can identify the lies, confront them, and, with God's help, restore His truth, tossing the lies to the pit of hell with the liar where they belong.

Now, once a deception becomes revealed, you might think that the lie is broken off and freedom is instantaneous. While in many situations that can be the case, more often a battle rages in an attempt to prevent you from becoming who the Great I *AM* created you to *BE*. Have you ever known something to be wrong, but you were unwilling to believe it? In those times when deception is revealed, but we refuse to accept it, deception continues to brew and pour over our lives. This, again, is how lies intertwine like a vine to sustain and support each other. They become so interdependent and entwined that the unraveling process seems daunting and sometimes insurmountable (yet another lie trying to keep you from the freedom God desires for you).

If I were a liar trying to prevent you from realizing that I lied to you, I would work to confuse and confound you by pouring on more lies, possibly even factual lies that could make it hard to identify what was real and what was fake. In reality, they would all be lies.

In Shelley Taylor and Jonathon Brown's article, "Positive Illusions and Well-Being Revisited: Separating Fact from Fiction,"[16] Taylor and Brown make convincing arguments that Positive Illusions truly create healthy minds. Part of the argument centers on what they called "Accuracy as Essential for Well-Being," where they form a baseline for what they believe is healthy. The issue I see with this often-cited and research-inspiring study is that the base foundation is, I believe, founded on a lie. The lie is that healthy "life" is defined as "contentment, positive attitudes toward the self, the ability to care for and about others, openness to new ideas and people, creativity, the ability to perform creative and productive work, and the ability to grow, develop, and self-actualize, especially in response to stressful events." And while I agree that those all make our time in this world more pleasant, they do not constitute life or health.

Let's go back to God on this and simply ask Him what life is. If we look at *life* as created by God, then the study falls apart. Life is an essence of God, it was found as a fruit of the Garden of Eden, it is a tangible connection, relationship, and dependence upon our Creator. The concept of *life* or *well-being* within the article referenced above may intertwine with symptoms of a blessed life, but it is not the foundation or definition of life itself. When you only focus on symptoms you open yourself up to an endless line of lies being supported by other lies which help support themselves, all in an effort to feel, look, and be good, especially during stressful events.

During one of my recent conversations with God, the Holy Spirit gave me comfort and confirmation in the face of adversity. A result of that time was the following:

Give Up and Stay Weak

People tell us to "stay strong" in the rough times. "Just hold on" is another phrase proclaimed to be words of encouragement. But Paul says something totally different. In a time of hardship, having a "thorn" in his side, he prayed three times for the thorn to be removed, each time being refused by his Father:

But he said to me, "My grace is sufficient for you, for

> my power is made perfect in weakness." Therefore I will boast all the more gladly of my weaknesses, so that the power of Christ may rest upon me. For the sake of Christ, then, I am content with weaknesses, insults, hardships, persecutions, and calamities. For when I am weak, then I am strong.
> – 2 Corinthians 12:9-10, ESV

Like so many things the world has backward, I encourage you in the hard times, the days when you don't have anything left, the times when you feel like giving up, to do it. Give it up to Christ and let His Spirit come and rest on you, delivering you from whatever pains your heart. Be content in your weakness, knowing that it is not up to you to save the world. It's not even up to you to save yourself. He has already done that too.

While Paul was considered by most to be a righteous and holy man, in this passage he admits the only reason he is such is because of the power and grace of Christ. That means we too should give up and stay weak.

Paul says to stay content with our weakness, to acknowledge it and embrace it in order to embrace our reliance and dependence upon Christ who makes us strong. The study by Taylor and Brown seems to suggest something totally different; they believe that embracing lies makes us strong and capable of dealing with hard times. The lies that they have believed encourage others to believe in more lies. That is why it is so important to be sensitive and to seek the kingdom of God for His view of everything. When we break up the foundation of their premise and lies are removed, we are still broken people dependent on a Creator to make us, support us, love us, and redeem us. Remember, we have the choice to be restored to Life as God created it or to hold tight to our knowledge of good and evil.

Paul Ekman, who many would refer to as the world's expert on lying, pioneered the study of micro-expressions which reveal, very reliably, lies of commission and omission in the story of the person exhibiting these expressions. He wrote an interesting article considering whether we would want our President to never lie, presenting many convincing stories as to why we want our President to be a liar, primarily in the name of national security. But where does that line get drawn? I believe that is why presidents today are often thought of as talking heads or puppets for the "machine." In most cases, our men and women in public service begin with good intentions, but then are compelled to lie in the name of protecting the people they serve. Lines get blurred and reality and lie become confused.

When we lie to ourselves, we not only live in a bound and deceived state, which is opposite from how God created us to live, but we also end up deceiving others. When we deceive others, we also destroy the foundation of trust, honor, love, and respect that friendships and relationships are based on. It is hard to develop deep, honest relationships, and it takes both or all parties to invest in that depth. If one holds back when all parties have committed to open, honest communication, they still deceive themselves and their so-called friends. That's not to say that all information needs to become public knowledge. However, we must be honest about feeling uncomfortable. Letting all parties know that as we become comfortable or ready to talk about a topic we will reveal it, but telling everyone we are being totally forthcoming and transparent while still hiding secrets in the deep, dark corners of our lives is damaging and deceptive.

Have you ever had a dream where you stood naked in

front of a class or large group of people? What is the deal with feeling exposed or naked with a group of people? Is it actually our skin that we do not want others to see, or is it something deeper, something more intimate than our most intimate parts? Could it be a fear of rejection, a fear that others won't see the beauty hidden underneath? God knows what's going on,

> *For the word of God is living and active, sharper than any two-edged sword, piercing to the division of soul and of spirit, of joints and of marrow, and discerning the thoughts and intentions of the heart. And no creature is hidden from his sight, but all are naked and exposed to the eyes of him to whom we must give account.*[i]

And, more important than Him seeing and knowing, we must remember that He loves what He sees. He created us, after all.

In order to have relationships with others that glorify His design for community, we must seek Him and His Truth and let others see who we are, what we are feeling. Transparency is not easy; exposing our true feelings is difficult and makes us vulnerable. Vulnerable to attack, judgment, hurt, and pain. These are the parts of vulnerability that others see as weak. But, if you look at the Latin root, *vulnerable* actually means *susceptible to being wounded*. We can consider that as weakness or we can think of it as a willingness to lay our lives down for the benefit of others. This willingness to die or experience pain should not only be for ourselves, but as Jesus showed us, it is important to die even for those who may want to persecute us, who may hate us, who may want to take advantage of our vulnerability. Jesus tells us that if the world hated Him, they will hate us as well.[ii] We need to understand that following Him is not easy. We will get hurt, we will feel pain, we will face spiritual attack, but that is all part of it. If we are not experiencing challenges

---

i   Hebrews 4:12-13
ii John 15:18-21

or forces against us, then there is a very good likelihood that we are not being vulnerable.

If we are not vulnerable, then we are deceived. We are fooling ourselves to think that others can't see our pain, that others themselves are not experiencing the same pain and fear we are, and that hiding from God what He already knows benefits us somehow. It really only keeps us trapped behind a fig leaf hoping it will keep us from being seen.

Confusion

Another anatomical component of a lie is confusion, which can also contribute to hurt and fear.

Confusion (not Confucius) says, "You know the things you can't conceive, and can't discern the things you have intimate knowledge of." The lie or deception behind confusion is that it removes your confidence in your knowledge of something. With a goal of diminishing your faith, confusion creates an insurmountable mound of doubt. But doubt is not the problem. Without doubt, there is no such thing as faith. Without doubt, there is no reason for exploration, experimentation, growth, or the pursuit of someone or something. Sometimes our doubt is confirmation for others that they are not alone.

Have you ever had to stop doing something you enjoyed – serving someone, going somewhere – for some reason or another? A few years ago, I felt led to start a small group for men. This wasn't just any fly-by-the-seat-of-your-pants notion. I had years of experience attending, assisting, leading, facilitating, training, and even serving on a team responsible for successfully rejuvenating a small group ministry at our church home in Colorado. So, when I started this new group, it was destined to succeed, right?

Let me give you a glimpse into one of our meetings.

I sit here today during what is supposed to be group time, with my laptop, writing about the group we are supposed to be having. No one showed up today. While my passion and reality are in conflict right now, I am okay with them not aligning. My passion is not wrong, my desire is not wrong, both are godly. Reality today is that no one was available, not that this group is a failure.

I wrote that entry not as a journal entry, but as a section of this book you are reading today. Instead of sulking or writing a steaming email to the guys who didn't show, I just continued to write in this book that God had placed on my heart. Satan attempted to confuse the issue by whispering (though his whispers often feel like shouts) that the group would never succeed, that men won't come, and that men won't or can't learn from me.

I had the choice to fold, or I could call satan's bluff. The easy part about playing poker with satan is that no matter what disguise he wears, no matter what move he makes, we can be sure that he's lying about something; he is trying to rob the truth that God has spoken into our lives. He is a liar, the father of all lies, after all, right?

Fast forward a few years. Although I contemplated the idea of cancelling the group, I didn't. I simply submitted my desires for the group to God, for Him to do what He desired. With that, He has brought the guys He's wanted every week, one of which surrendered his life to Christ shortly after starting to attend. While we have more guys now than the zero who showed on that one day, our numbers vary. And while the increase in attendance is not the purpose, it is an outward sign of the Life being generated within. The size of our group can't be the measuring stick. The purpose of the group is to help men break off lies, not break attendance records. We are restoring the Life God intended, with the intent for each of us to then go out and help others do the same. As that great statement goes, "Free people free people."

Satan tried to tell me that I couldn't pour into and be refilled by interaction with other men. He took my knowledge that sometimes men's schedules are hard to align, and that some men struggle to open up and be vulnerable and tried to twist those facts to tell me the group was a waste of time. Liar! I know this group works and works well. Our Guild of Guys is going strong; God continues to allow us to be a part of bringing more men closer to Him every time we meet. By submitting my desire and hope for the group to God, He showed me and let me be a part of His hope and desire.

When God speaks His will, hope, and desires to His children and we listen, that is simply hearing God. Sometimes, for various reasons, we don't or can't hear Him when He speaks, so God, in His Love for us, will speak to someone close to us to relay the message for Him. When He does this it is called *prophecy*.

Has anyone ever spoken a prophetic word over you that didn't manifest in the way or time you thought it would? How do you deal with the internal struggle between your desire or understanding of how and when to do something and a message that you couldn't or shouldn't follow through with it right now? God is not limited to time or space. His words are reality. In the movie *Bruce Almighty*, Jim Carrey's character, Bruce Nolan, has been given the task of filling God's role. When he speaks, the content of what he tries to say simply forms in his mouth. He ends up spitting out a toy car, for example, simply by trying to say the word. It's a hilarious picture, but still an amazingly accurate portrayal of how God's words function.

God speaks reality, but we have to understand that our limited view of reality may not align (yet) with what He says. Has God ever given you a word or a desire for something that you jumped into quickly, just to have it fail miserably? Were you confused or left hurting that it didn't work out? It's not that His words are not true. It's that time has not caught up with reality. In Ray Cummings' *The Girl in the Golden Atom*, he explains that, "time is what keeps everything from happening at once," but our minds living in this realm ruled by time, struggle to make sense of this dichotomy. These struggles are examples of cognitive dissonance.

To better understand how satan works, you must understand cognitive dissonance. Don't let the formal, psychological terminology intimidate you. *Cognitive*, simply defined, refers to the processes in which our mind acquires or processes knowledge. *Dissonance* is a lack of alignment or harmony, or, more easily defined in today's vernacular, it is the presence of tension. So, *cognitive dissonance* could simply be defined as tension we experience when what we know and what we are experiencing or learning do not align. In studies on cognitive dissonance, people typically conform their thoughts about something to the amount of friction, consequences, or repercussions that come as a result of the experience.[17]

    I found one study performed on children particularly interesting. The moderators showed one group of children a set of toys, asking which one they wanted to play with the most. Once the most desirable toy was selected, they advised half of the kids that there would be severe consequences for playing with it, while the others were warned of only a moderate consequence. After some time passed, the moderators came back in to give the kids an opportunity to play with that same toy and what happened was very interesting. The kiddos who were advised of a moderate consequence were less likely to play with the toy than those who knew there would be severe consequences. Sometimes, when the consequence is greater, it feels like the risk is worth it.

    In a world where we think everything must be fair and eastern mysticism says everything balances out, yin and yang, if the consequence is unfathomable, then the forbidden must be astonishing. If the consequence isn't that big of a deal, then neither is the object of law against it. I believe this is, in part, how satan tricked Adam and Eve. Yes, he downplayed death, but even more he built up the reward to offset the extreme consequence of eating the *forbidden fruit*. This is how satan works in our lives too, playing tricks on our minds to manipulate and conform our thoughts to be out of alignment with what God has said. He infiltrates with even more dangerous thinking: the enticing things of this world are worth damaging our relationship with our Creator, Savior, and Lord.

This shift in focus is dangerous and harmful because when the time comes to use our passions and desires, if we have changed our minds that they just weren't that interesting or important, we will not act on them. We will neither fulfill our purpose nor understand the reason why God gifted us with that passion. Additionally, our passions and desires may have dire consequences if used at the wrong time. But if used at the right time, in the right place, that same passion or desire can have life-changing results. It's a spiritual war, which, in its essence, is conflict. It will cause discomfort, especially if you choose to go at it on your own.

When we are passionate about something, but God says no for a while or a reason we may not understand, it creates dissonance or internal conflict. Instead of allowing conflict to exist, or for His timing to manifest His reality, we try to relieve the tension by ourselves. Instead of bringing it to God, and discussing the tension with Him, too often we listen to satan's whispers that say we didn't really want it anyway. We become confused about what our desires really mean. We become willing to conform our thoughts about our passions to say that we were wrong for desiring what we desired, or that it just wasn't that desirable, when, in fact, we desire our passions for a reason. We were created in a fashion and for a purpose that only the Creator knows. Unless you talk with Him about it, how can He reveal it to you? Keep in mind, it will come in time, His time, not limited to now or a couple of weeks from now. His reality spoken in this moment may be manifested years from now. Remember, if it wasn't for time, we would have instantaneous satisfaction, but at the same time, our lives would also be over by now. Let that reality simmer on your heart. Let His words and desires marinate and create desire in you to learn and prepare for whatever He has next.

I find this cartoon helpful in illustrating how satan tries to manipulate things.

The Anatomy of a Lie

(Who knew that satan was a little dog whispering behind our backs while at work?) I, like many people, had a huge battle with addiction, addiction to cigarettes, alcohol, attention, and pornography. I knew they were wrong, but I lied to myself, saying there was no problem. Even when I did realize they were real issues, I lied to myself by saying something like, "I am going to quit, starting Monday." Why do we lie to ourselves when we know that both the lie and the thing we are lying about are wrong? Did I truly believe I was going to quit at the beginning of the next week? No, but it was my way of logically justifying the continuation of my habit. It was my way of trying to ease the guilt I felt for the things I was involved with.

I have had the awesome opportunity of teaching a class entitled *Hearing God*, part of Gateway Church's *Freedom Basics* classes. In this class, we discuss how hearing God is crucial to our being set free from bondage. Often, we find ourselves wishing or hoping that something would simply happen instead of seeking God's will and listening for His response to the matter at hand. Like it says in Romans 10:17, *"Faith comes by hearing and hearing by the word of Christ."* When we hear God, it starts to grow faith, or complete confidence, within us. Faith, Hope, Love, and Life all come back to this critical component of hearing from the One who created us.

Before entering into a relationship with Jesus, I had no power over my addictions and I had faith in nothing. So, to make myself feel better, I would lie to myself and justify my actions. Dr. James Richards speaks to this point in his book *How to Stop the Pain*. "There are times when we want to violate wisdom...we feel the need to justify our actions, so we pass good judgments," or find good reasons, and "when we create enough good judgments to justify our actions, what usually results is a bad decision." In my case, and in many others', the pain of the lie was much less than the pain the addiction caused. When we justify our actions, we make ourselves "like God" and judge our actions as righteous or sinless. In my experience, the quasi-hope the lie created was an attempt to cover up or mask the pain experienced by continuing in my addictions.

Manipulating the thoughts and emotions of others is much like fighting those addictions. It's a form of protection of and from our self. We are trying to establish control in an environment that we feel is out of our control. We confuse ourselves into thinking that we are like God. Isn't that the same lie satan wanted us to believe, that the knowledge of good and evil would provide? But because we are not God, nor were we created to be in control, it takes substantial effort to maintain these lies. An article on the science of deception points out that,

> Although several brain areas appear to play a role in deception, the most consistent finding across multiple fMRI studies is that activity in the prefrontal cortex increases when people lie. The prefrontal cortex, situated just behind the forehead, is a collection of regions responsible for executive control (the ability to regulate thoughts or actions to achieve goals). Executive control includes cognitive processes such as planning, problem solving, and attention, all important components of deception, so it's no surprise the prefrontal cortex is active when we lie. Dishonesty requires the brain to work harder than honesty, and

> *this effort is reflected by increased brain activity. Studies even show people take longer to respond when lying.*[19]

Think about this. When we lie, we have to think about what we are saying in order to make sure the lie we are about to tell checks out with all of the other lies we have already told. We dig an even deeper hole for ourselves. When we try to manipulate others, we bury ourselves, tightening the shackles of bondage even more. Richards states,

> *We think we are discerning and that our judgments will protect us from future pain, but...instead we create a world of conflict and suffering through the very judgments we think will protect us.*

Additionally, other studies have identified common physical ticks that people exhibit when they are lying. Because the mind and body were not created for dishonesty, we, through our nervous system, manifest symptoms as a result of accepting falsehood. A few years ago, a show on TV called *Lie to Me* aired, based on the work of Ekman, Friesen, Haggard, and Isaacs, who discovered micro expressions. Dr. Paul Ekman was the scientific consultant for the show, whose main character, Dr. Cal Lightman, played by Tim Roth, assisted in criminal investigations by interviewing and analyzing suspects' responses for these micro expressions. Dr. Ekman's studies scientifically confirm that there are negative personal, physical, and psychological ramifications to lying. We were not made to lie, nor to be lied to. I believe this is why Jesus told His disciples that when they knew Him and followed His teachings they would know the truth, and that truth would set them free.[iii]

Confusion has no place in truth and, although sometimes Truth can be confusing, Truth will reveal itself in increments that

---

[iii] John 8:31-32

God knows we are ready for. Paul in 1 Corinthians poses the question,

> *For who knows a person's thoughts except the spirit of that person, which is in him?*

He then goes on to explain how we can know what's on God's mind,

> *...no one comprehends the thoughts of God except the Spirit of God...we have received not the spirit of the world, but the Spirit who is from God, that we might understand the things freely given us by God... not taught by human wisdom but taught by the Spirit, interpreting spiritual truths to those who are spiritual (or those in relationship with His Spirit).*[iv]

If I could put a voice to Truth, I think it would say, "I know the things you can't conceive, the things you can't comprehend. I know the dreams you have and hope for. I know you, I love you; you are my child. And, if you come to Me, trust Me, and listen to My Spirit, I will reveal Myself to you."

[iv] 1 Corinthians 2:11-13 Commentary Added

The Anatomy of a Lie

No one who practices deceit will dwell in my house. No one who utters lies will endure before my eyes.
- Psalms 101:7 TLV

Steven Cohen

5
The Nature of a Lie

Our perception of our identity is often blurred, creating doubt in our minds that we are worthy or capable of receiving God's love. Many times, we even attempt to fool others into believing our misperception. Remember from our previous look at deception, perception is how we take in or capture our surroundings in our minds. Often, we survey our surrounding environment and its situations for what we can apply to ourselves, speaking to who we are instead of simply to what has happened. It's as if, somehow, the things people say, the events which happen, the feelings we encounter, and the desires we have all determine who we were created to be. Worldly advice says to be who you want to be; go with your feelings. But we see throughout the Bible what happens when people do that. Their feelings tell them to do things that don't make sense. The Israelites felt scared of God at Mount Sinai with Moses. They had just witnessed their salvation from, and the wrath of God on, the entire Egyptian army. Yet, when presented with an intense storm sitting on top of a mountain, their feelings told them to be afraid and stay away. Rather than approach, they sent Moses and, while he was gone, made a golden statue of a cow to worship. In Egypt, idol worship was the norm. So, it had become familiar to the Israelites. When fear stepped in, they returned to the familiar.

  Many times, our feelings and emotions tell us to do the same thing. We start to idolize things and take our attention off of what really matters. On that mountain sat what really mattered, but it was uncomfortable and intimidating and it was easier to look for something else. Our golden calves are typically much less intimidating, they may even seem more fun or exciting. But they are powerless and have no capability to love, save, redeem, or help transform you into the person you were designed to be.

  In Sodom and Gomorrah, the people gave into their emotions and desires, ending up worshiping sex and sensual fulfillment rather than spiritual fulfillment. They chose to eject God from their lives and eventually the evil, or lack of God, in their villages overcame and reigned intensely in their lives. Their hatred towards anything of God was so fierce that God sent two angels to survey and confirm, as well as remove, anyone who loved Him. The town was then struck with burning sulfur to remove such a great threat from His people. Feelings can be deceiving; they have the ability to strip reality out of the situation if God is not sought after when those feelings emerge. If we let our perceptions rule over our emotions and our emotions determine the direction of our lives, we can simply get lost and forget who we are.

   Thankfully some people don't fall for our perception of ourselves. Granted, that is *their* perception of *our* self, but many times their point of view, free from our emotional responses, about the exact same situations can either frustrate or challenge our beliefs. You may be wondering how frustration benefits us. Frustration is an agitation. And agitation can help clean up our perception. In a day and age of front-loader washers, this may seem a little old school, but there is a reason top-loader washing machines have an agitator. The agitator is the cylinder in the middle of the drum of a top-loader washing machine, which typically includes downward spiraling fins to pull clothes down into the water. It helps stir up the clothes to remove the dirt, oil, sweat, and dead skin that transfers from our bodies to our clothing every time we wear them. Much like our perception, our clothes, although designed to protect us from the elements, were not designed to continue to contain those elements. We were created with a way to see danger, to see other peoples' reactions to our actions, to see the beauty around us. But when we place judgment on those things and take them on for ourselves, we have soiled and stained who we really are, who our Designer fashioned us to be.

   That is not saying that just because someone else does not agree with us they are right, but it may be a trigger, an agitation, which reminds us to check with God to make sure we are believing, living, and exhibiting who He says we are. The subtitle of *Refining*

What LIES Beneath

Identity, my wife, Courtney Cohen's, book reads, *I Am Who I Am Says I Am.* That's all we are designed to be, nothing more than who God says we are. But, unfortunately, many times we are far less, even when we try our hardest and we surpass our man-made goals of what we think we were made for. Many times, that just means we are nowhere close to what He designed us to be.

      Could one of the most successful business men in the world be less than what he was created to be? Could the president or ruler of a country fall short of the mark? How does that happen? Not long ago, our pastor who leads one of the largest churches in America, which is also influential around the world, shared about his own goals. He shared the goals he felt he had achieved, which then caused him unrest and a desire to figure out what was next. He was getting bored leading a church of over 30,000 people, no longer felt challenged, and had met all of his goals for the church. It was in seeking God that our pastor heard that, although he had met some goals which were made in discussion with God, the goals themselves did not define who he was, nor were they the fulfillment of his design. Had he stopped there, he would have fallen so short of what God's desire was. He said his life's purpose was, "to help people develop an intimate relationship with God." While fulfilling that purpose, being the son of God he is designed to be, doing the things that come from that calling, God gave him goals to achieve. These goals were simply that, goals to strive for while continuing to be who God called him to be. Once those goals were achieved, he continued to seek God and was given a set of new goals: "to preach and teach God's Word, inspire pastors and leaders, and mentor the next generation."[20]

      Notice, it was not another list of check marks he could do and cross off. Now imagine if he had not gone to God to find this list how easy it would it be for someone who has achieved their goals and aspirations, financially as well as aspirationally to simply retire. Not that retirement is bad, but think about all the people he could have missed out on loving, how many people he would have missed out on leading to Christ, or counseled through struggles, or consoled through times of grieving, just because he had checked a few boxes. The lie here that he thankfully didn't buy is that we *are* what we do, achieve, or have left to accomplish. The truth God spoke is that what we do comes from who we are, who He created us to be, and then our desires are derived from that secure identity.

Let's consider the parable of the prodigal son. This story is concentrated on a son who sinned against his father by prematurely requesting his inheritance and leaving the family behind for what, according to the culture at the time, would have been considered "The Life." It then illustrates his fall or failure, how he was humbled, and his eventual return to his father, when he requested to be a slave to earn his keep. Instead, his father forgave and restored him. The most common way to look at this parable, which is not wrong, is that it illustrates how no matter how far we travel or run from our Father, that He too will forgive us.

Another perspective, taught by Pastor Josh Morris, brings a deeper perspective of the kingdom and how it related to those Jesus was talking to. When we look at the story from the viewpoint of life and death, keeping the perspective of Jesus teaching first-century Jews, we see a different story. The Jews at this point, ruled by the Romans, may as well have been "in a foreign country, exiled, eating pig slop." Subjected to horrible treatment, oppression, and slavery, they had accepted much less than what their true inheritance would have been. Seeing them spiritually away from their promised land, away from the freedom available only through their Father's kingdom, taking the scraps the Romans allowed them, we can see how the prodigal son could be a representation of those Jews who eventually repented and came to know Jesus as their Savior.

Jesus was illustrating how they had been living by their own understanding of what God's kingdom would look like and be like.

Jesus was hoping through this story that they would see how living spiritually away, although not geographically, from their Father's kingdom was not all that was promised. Jesus' desire was not to rag on or beat down the Pharisees and Sadducees, but to reveal to them that they had been deceived by their misguided belief about who the Savior, Messiah, would be and what He would do.

At the end of the story, we meet another brother who resents his younger brother's careless choices. He also appears to resent his father for allowing his brother to run off and live so wastefully. The older brother proclaims his innocence in having never done anything wrong or in opposition to his dad. His disdain and disappointment for not getting his portion of the inheritance is all-too clear.

So, who did the judgmental, resentful brother in the story represent? In context, Jesus is addressing two crowds simultaneously: the tax collectors and sinners as well as the Pharisees and Sadducees who were grumbling because Jesus was hanging around such people. The brother in the story very well could be those who devoutly, legalistically stood by God's side, the Pharisees and Sadducees. Never living in a wayward manner, but also never able to see how remarkable their God and King really is, the correlation can be drawn. When Christ said, "Repent for the kingdom of heaven is at hand," He was not saying that we need to clean up our acts and be better people, they were already as good as the Law allowed; He wanted change. The original word there for *repent* means to change the way you think about things. His desire was to show them that the Messiah was standing right in front of them, that all their efforts to experience God were in vain as they were experiencing Him right then.[21] So often we pass on *experiencing* God in the now, for the things that we have to *do* now.

In this parable about the prodigal, Jesus was showing the Jews who were stuck in a legalistic mindset, that they, in fact, could also be seen as this lost son. The lost son was not necessarily a bad role to be compared to. They were in desperate need of coming back, humbly returning to their Father and King. He gave them a different way to look at and for Messiah. Jesus was within reach, expressing how phenomenal it would be to establish or rejuvenate a relationship with them. He wanted dearly for those He addressed to realize who the King was in the parable. At the same time, He illustrated that He understood that many of them, like the prodigal's brother, would never see what was standing in front of them. Jesus knew that many would not see the death in their laws and rituals, as a result of the heart of entitlement that had developed. Had they only opened their hearts to the Truth, their resentment of the Father would have fizzled, and He would have opened the treasure troves of who He is and all He has given them.

The often-quoted adage, *"Pride comes before the fall,"* is not scriptural. Although the words are found in the same verse of a scripture, they are not in the same order, which creates a totally different meaning. This is a great example of deception. Satan takes a few words here and a few words there, rearranging, removing, or questioning them, and twists God's Truth to say and mean something totally different. The idea behind the phrase, *"Pride comes before the fall"* comes from Proverbs 16:18:

> **Pride comes before destruction, and a haughty spirit before a fall. (emphasis mine)**

What is a haughty spirit? The definition of *haughty* is "arrogantly superior and disdainful."[22] The Pharisees and Sadducees thought they knew everything about God and His Word. They knew exactly what to look for in their Messiah, believing He would be constrained to their understanding of Scripture. Isaiah 40 not only tells of how incredible our Lord is but also warns us about limiting ourselves to our own knowledge and wisdom, pointing out that God, although He listens to us, is not limited to us,

> *Who has measured [or directed] the Spirit of the Lord or what man shows Him his counsel?*[i]

The lie that many of the elite Jews believed was that they were, in fact, elite, that they were so knowledgeable about the Messiah that there was NO way they could miss Him. Yet there He was standing in front of them, telling them a story about them missing out on Him. Sometimes our perception of our situation distorts our vision of reality so seriously that we cannot even recognize Truth for what it is. This prevents us from experiencing the love others have for us because we believe we are unlovable. Much like the story I began with, describing my wife's and my conversation, compliments and genuine encouragement can simply bounce right off of us.

    I would argue that the primary deception Jesus reveals through the parable of the prodigal son is that our Triune God, in all of His love, wisdom, and power, is fixated on and cares primarily about what we *do* as His children. I believe Jesus sought to restore the truth: that God cares about us more than we could ever conceive. He cares about who we are and our perception of Him, that we recognize God as more than just a white-bearded image in a painting. He yearns for us to know "God" as Father, His Son, Jesus, as our Lord and Savior, and the Holy Spirit as our Counselor. Just as important as recognizing Him for who He is, He longs for us to be comfortable coming to Him for who we are. That's why He sent us the Holy Spirit as our Counselor, so that all of the walls could be broken, and we can now live freely with Him.

    What we do is simply a symptom of who we believe we are. If we think we are unworthy, we will always strive to do better, to be more, to be perfect. Our lives will be law and rules-based instead of confidently humble, knowing we are exactly who God made us to be. When we are willing to humble ourselves, be teachable, and listen to what the Lord has to say, we can experience the kingdom of heaven here on earth. Remember, "the kingdom of heaven is

---

i   Isaiah 40:13

at hand."[ii] His Peace, His Love, His Life are all available here and now, not just when we die and go to heaven, and definitely not because we have earned it. You see, in telling this story, Jesus was addressing a group of Pharisees and Scribes who had begun to grumble about Jesus spending time with tax collectors and sinners, something that a "righteous" person would not do. This parable is the third story Christ uses, "to illustrate the point further."[iii] Along with the two other parables about the lost sheep and the lost coin, Jesus was illustrating to the Pharisees that the prodigal son was all about a righteous God who mourns the loss of His children to anything other than what He created them to be.[23]

    That same God, that same Shepherd, that same Father, that same King who mourns His losses, never gives up, never ceases to look, never loses vision of how valuable, how precious the lost are. And, because He never loses sight of that, He never buys the lies of the enemy that their "lost-ness," for lack of a better word, diminishes their importance or somehow should lessen His fondness for them. As Papa (a character representing God the Father) says in *The Shack* about even some of the most heinous people we could ever think of, "*I am quite fond of them.*"[24] Note, He is not fond of their actions or emotional reactions, but is a fan of *them*, their personhood, their being His child, no matter how broken they are or how many lies they have believed.

    Our Father, our King, celebrates in spectacular fashion when His children come back to Him. A party doesn't adequately describe how grand of a celebration takes place every time one of His kiddos comes to realize who God is. Don't let your time-limited thought processes say there is not enough time in the world to throw a celebration every time someone comes to know God as God. He is the God of all and time is nothing to Him. He is reality and the most massive party we could conceive can happen in a mere microsecond in our world. In C.S. Lewis's *The Lion the Witch*

---
ii   Matthew 4:17
iii Luke 15:11a

and the Wardrobe, Lucy, playing hide-n-seek, enters a wardrobe and stumbles upon another world, Narnia. After spending hours exploring, she becomes concerned about her brothers and sisters back home who must be worried about her being undiscoverable for such a long period of time. She exits the wardrobe to find that mere seconds have passed. While this is a fictional story, it is a helpful illustration of time's dependency on the dimension it is measured in.

    Think about how Scripture says we are knit in our mother's womb. Many, if not most, of us think about God knitting us over a forty-week period as we gestate and incubate in our mother's belly. And, while He is there with us for that period of time, and the rest of our eternity for that matter, I think this knitting refers to the instantaneous creation, the "knitting," of our DNA strand. In a moment, He "knits" our soul to our DNA, making us unique people, unique children whom He is fond of. More unique than just our finger print, we each have completely unique identities. There is no one and never will be anyone who is the exact same as you. There may be similarities, as God has patterns in His creation, but you are unique. As Max Lucado writes, "You are special, because I [God] made you. And I [God] don't make mistakes."[25] God is fond of us, and relishes in seeing us not only look to Him and rely on Him for Life, but also flourish in it. Flourishing in His design and fulfilling His original predestination for our lives.

    I truly, deeply enjoy and resonate with the prodigal's story, and I believe there is a question we may not ask often enough: *Why did the son leave in the first place?* Jesus tells us almost nothing about that. We can only deduce certain reasons by his demands and actions, or the fruit of his belief. So, what was it that he believed? Did it align with his identity, who he was born to be? We can see that, although he believed whatever it was wholeheartedly enough to squander his entire inheritance on it, this belief did not align with the reality of who he was. With that, we know it was a lie, but what lie did the prodigal believe? It had to have occurred before Jesus' starting point in the parable? And, although Jesus doesn't tell us, I'd like to imagine for a moment.

Normally, when I imagine these situations, I pull from my own experiences. Maybe he believed that he didn't belong, or that his father didn't listen to him, or want to be involved with him. Maybe he just wasn't having enough fun. My son has mentioned many times lately that he is sad that he just isn't having fun when we ask him to do chores. I think every child, and some adults, at some point, have believed the lie that they should only experience fun throughout the entirety of their existence on Earth.

As for the prodigal son, the second child of a successful, powerful man, it could have been that he felt he wasn't getting what he was entitled to, that no one understood him, or gave him credit for being himself. All of these attacks on who he was, all of these lies believed, changed his vision of who he was. Although the deception never changed who he was designed to be, it changed who he believed himself to be. So, by believing the lies about his identity, the son, the man he was created to be, was dead. And there would be no way to bring him back to Life aside from having an experience with the King, his Father; spiritually, being born again. No matter how we look at the depth of the lesson of the parable of the prodigal, I think it is safe to assume that the reason he left was the result of a lie he believed, overwhelming him to a point that he was willing to give up his true self, his true inheritance, his true family, for an empty promise of something better, he gave it all up for deception.

You can put your own story here, your own experience of believing a lie, allowing death to destroy you, your family, your ministry. Deception cannot destroy your story, your testimony, or who you truly are. That's one of the ways we bring glory to God, through everything in our lives. There is power in our testimony. To put things into perspective, I don't know that satan can destroy anything without human participation. Let that sink in for a moment. That's part of satan's lie, that he is so powerful that there is nothing we can do about it. But we have the choice to choose. Do we believe his lies, or God's truth? Do we choose to pass on his lies to those around us or kill and bury them?

The deception of others can be purposeful or, often like our self-deception, it can be unbeknownst. When we are telling our story, there is truth and then there are lies we have believed about ourselves. There are also lies that we tell simply to make our stories seem more dramatic. This isn't to say we lie about what happened. Many times, we simply add more facts to increase the drama or credibility of our story. A short time ago, I was dealing with a broken toe. My orthopedic surgeon placed me in a knee-high boot to protect not only my toe, but also to prevent me flexing my *flexor hallucis longus,* also known as the shin muscle.[26] He was afraid that, because of the way my toe broke, if I flexed that muscle, the end of the tendon that attached that muscle to my toe would break one of the bones off, requiring surgery. These are the simple facts of the matter. God revealed to me in the midst of this reality that I felt inadequate. I felt that I had to justify and explain the knee-high boot for something as simple as a broken toe. I felt the judgment of others, that I was a hypochondriac, something I was often told both my Grandmother and I were. After responding to the question, "How'd that happen?" hundreds, if not thousands of times over that six-week period, I asked God why I felt so compelled to justify the boot, telling all of the facts, expressing my frustrations with my limitations, instead of just having the freedom to say, "I broke my toe and this is what the doctor suggested as my treatment."

Because we don't always know the lie deceiving us, we don't know any better and think we're speaking the truth. But even if it is factual, we still could be passing along a lie for others to ingest. The lie I passed on was that I am inadequate and that I have to justify my actions and state of being because of others' judgment of me

The Nature of a Lie

or my state of being. That sounds hopeless and almost as if it would be best, out of our desire not to lie to others, that we should keep silent and not speak at all. But that is another lie that satan would like to spin.

The Bible, from Genesis to Revelation, speaks of God's desire for us to have relationship with Him and with our brothers and sisters. In Genesis, as God spent time walking with Adam and Eve in the cool of the morning, having conversations without shame, He demonstrates how He designed relationships to work. He shows us how important it is to be in relationship when, in Genesis 2:18, the Father, being in relationship Himself, says to Jesus and the Holy Spirit that, "It is not good that the man should be alone." Because relationships are so important and because He is such an amazing Father, He goes on to tell us how He is going to solve the problem at hand, "I will make him a helper fit for him." And then, putting Adam to sleep, He created a perfect companion or "help meet" for him.

While here, let's discuss the lie many believe about those two mysterious words, *help meet*. This help meet was not intended to be a slave or helper in the sense that Adam was to rule over her, manipulate her, control her, own her, or use her.

Author Heather Ferrell provides insight into where those two words *help meet* come from.

In Hebrew, the two words that "help meet" are derived from are the words "*ezer*" and the word "*k'enegdo.*" *Ezer* which is commonly translated as "help" is really a rich word with a much deeper meaning. In her book *Eve and the Choice Made in Eden*, Beverly Campbell explains,

"According to biblical scholar David Freedman, the Hebrew word translated into English as "help" is ezer. This word is a combination of two roots, one meaning

"to rescue," "to save," and the other meaning, "to be strong." Just as the roots merged into one word, so did their meanings. At first ezer meant either "to save" or "to be strong," but in time, said Freedman, ezer "was always interpreted as "to help" a mixture of both nuances."

Diana Webb in her book *Forgotten Women of God* also clarifies this word by explaining,

"The noun ezer occurs 21 times in the Hebrew Bible. In eight of these instances the word means "savior". These examples are easy to identify because they are associated with other expressions of deliverance or saving. Elsewhere in the Bible, the root ezer means "strength.... the word is most frequently used to describe how God is an ezer to man."

She continues, "It is hard to know exactly what the word *k'enegdo* means because it only appears once in the entire Bible. Yet Diana Webb explained that,

"Neged, a related word which means "against", was one of the first words I learned in Hebrew. I thought it was very strange that God would create a companion for Adam that was "against" him! Later, I learned that k'enegdo could also mean "in front of" or "opposite." This still didn't help much. Finally, I heard it explained as being "exactly corresponding to," like when you look at yourself in a mirror."

Eve was not designed to be exactly like Adam. She was designed to be his mirror opposite, possessing the other half of the qualities, responsibilities, and

> *attributes which he lacked. Just like Adam and Eve's sexual organs were physically mirror opposites (one being internal and the other external) so were their divine stewardship designed to be opposite but fit together perfectly to create life. Eve was Adam's complete spiritual equal, endowed with an essential saving power that was opposite from his.[27]*

I find it interesting that a large segment of those within the Christian faith believe that, while Christ is their Savior, salvation in great part comes through Mary. And while I do not believe the same tenants and requirements of the religion, God showed me a different way to look at it. Without the eyes or lens of judgment against that religion, I now see how the truth of this mirrored savior may be where the veneration, or perceived worship, of Mary came from. I can also see where the lie and deception came from that has allowed so many people who are a part of that religion to truly worship Mary and the saints instead, the created, rather than the Creator.

Looking at the oppression of women over time, regardless of whether we believe it is perceived or real, it has generated an immense amount of pain and yearning for the restoration of women as daughters of the Most High. Women have heard for millennia that Eve was the reason sin came into this world, as if Adam was not responsible for not stepping up to the plate and intervening when satan was trying to and ultimately did succeed in deceiving Eve. This concept of opposites or opposing forces in the article is not a yin and yang theology where God has to balance things out. The belief that everything needs to be balanced and fair is rooted in our knowledge of good and evil, as if we are God and we know the proportions of the universe. It is not balancing out our world, but instead restoring women to their rightful place; neither a place of servitude, nor a place of sub-male stature.

Here is how this plays out. Eve came from Adam, a male

body, through a miracle of only God's doing. Eve seems to be the first who believes satan's lie, then is the first to act on that deception, taking and eating the fruit from the Tree of the Knowledge of Good and Evil. Again, I am not absolving Adam of his responsibility, because he too was there and failed to stand up as who he was created to be, strong in that moment of Eve's weakness, as she was meant to be strong in his weaknesses. It was, at this moment, maybe for the first time, that she was not fulfilling her original design of being that opposing savior, help meet. Imagine Adam's reaction when this woman who complemented him in every way, fulfilled his desires and need for companionship, who had walked through the Garden in the cool of the morning with God, all of a sudden did something that didn't fit with who he knew her to be. And now, with different eyes, he saw her actions through the lens of good and evil. She had, in an instant, introduced death into the human race. Imagine the guilt and shame she felt, finding herself no longer attached to Life as she had been just a moment before. This knowledge of good and evil polluted her mind, tainting every thought with an infectious, foul sense of abandonment, separation, aloneness. The burden she surely shouldered was then passed on to all of her daughters, for the rest of time. She was in Eden and yet, by her actions, through her initiation of the process that we call the Fall of Man, Eden was hidden from man for the rest of existence.

    Then, Jesus, coming from Eve's womb, through yet another miracle of only God's doing again, provides a really fantastic illustration of His commitment to restoration. There is no exact quote that tells us who the parents of Mary are. There are a few theories, but the genealogic history debate is for another book.[28] While it is important to understand history, especially His history, I feel God impressing that the real importance here is the act of Jesus being born from a woman. Why didn't God just create Jesus, the second Adam, like He created the first? There was plenty of dirt for God to just pile up and breathe into again. I believe it is because that method, while impressive, would not have shown the Love of God to those who had been broken for so long. You may point out that it also would not have fulfilled so many prophecies, but remember, God was the One who spoke the prophecies to the prophets.

A very possible reason Paul wanted us to "especially" desire the gift of prophecy, was because it required hearing from God.[i] He could have simply told Isaiah that there would be an amassing of dirt at the Temple, and that He would breathe into it just as He did Adam and our Messiah would be "born." Creating Jesus, fully man like Adam, in this same manner would have gained a lot of attention, probably convincing so many of those at the temple who had seen it. But I think God, like a carpenter, likes to restore the old, dead and worn out. Selecting Mary may have been because of her lineage or Joseph's or possibly both. But the importance of Mary isn't who she was before He chose her, but instead *that* He chose her. He could have chosen from so many people, but in His timing and His understanding Mary was the one. The one to whom He would present the honor and burden of carrying the Savior of the world within her womb. To do that, however, she had to make a choice. Much like the serpent came to Eve with a story, the angel came to Mary with a story. This time the story that was presented, in perfect opposition to the serpent's lies and death, came bearing Truth, Life, and Love. Much like Eve, Mary had a choice to believe or reject this information, and, again, in perfect opposition to Genesis 3, Mary chose truth, and within her the Holy Spirit planted the fertilized egg we know as Jesus. Life was now tethered within Mary to humanity much like humanity was once tethered to Life in the Garden, perfect opposition restoring the perfect help meet. And while He restored the broken state of women, God bringing His Son into this world did so much more. He restored all of humanity and

---

i   1 Corinthians 14:1

continues restoring each of us, man, woman, boy, and girl; all of His children.

If we limit ourselves to half-truths, we leave ourselves open to deception. The worship of women, the created woman, instead of the Creator Himself is what satan wants. You see, the deception we have about women, creation, the Creator, and the intention and reason for relationship all affects how we look at and interact with others.

Acts 2:42-47 speaks on how the number of believers continued to grow and how they were purposeful to gather and break bread. That being said, in Genesis 3 we are shown how those critical relationships were perverted and what happens to them when death is introduced. Mistrust, hiding our true selves, hurt, fear, and shame all come from the death chosen in Genesis 3.

What if Adam and Eve had simply come clean instead of running and hiding and covering themselves? What might have happened when they ate the fruit of knowledge of good and evil, feeling death and disconnect occur if, instead of running and hiding, they had run to their Father, their Creator, their Savior? I believe He would have pulled them in close and forgiven them, restored them. We will never know, because the deception that clouded their vision and beliefs in that moment made their shame, embarrassment, and fear feel greater than the affection He had for them. That is sin, that is the death that God spoke of when He warned Adam of the consequences of eating the fruit of the knowledge of good and evil. Their intimate relationship with and attachment to Life had ended; death had set in. The death and deception of Adam and Eve then passed to all of humanity when they spoke death and blame back to the Father who had caringly, lovingly approached them about stepping outside the boundary that He had clearly set and explained.

Additionally, there is a belief that, if a lie benefits us, then

The Nature of a Lie

it is okay, as if the lie is a means to an end. Many celebrate this in just one example: gambling. Almost all year long, here in Texas, we are bombarded by advertising from the casinos in Oklahoma. Huge banners, television and radio ads about poker tournaments and loose slots are littered throughout the cities here, promising the opportunity to "win" a lion's share of cash.

And, while deception is utilized to convince people that, somehow, their chances of winning their share of the hundreds of millions of dollars paid out annually are greater than the house's chances of taking their money, I want to address the more personal deception of others. If you have witnessed one of these tournaments, you know how people go to great lengths to hide their tells. Beards are grown, hats and hoodies and sunglasses are worn to cover and disguise players' "micro expressions[29]" that give away lies about the cards they hold, or don't hold, for that matter. A recent billboard for one of the casinos read, "In Dallas it's lying; here it's bluffing." The game of poker is not just a card game of chance and statistics; it's a competition over who is the better liar. Who can "bluff" the other person into forfeiting their possessions?

Think about that. Where have we seen that type of lie? A lie that says, "I know you may think that you have something great, but I have something better. But you can't see what I have or know what its costs are unless you risk losing all that you have gambled." That lie is a perversion of the Gospel. The difference is that Jesus doesn't promise greener grass and He says that you can't just put in a little here or a little there. It's an all-in thing. But it's not that we have to give away everything we have, like many believe. This belief is often a result of a limited view of the parable of the Rich Young Ruler during which Jesus tells his disciples,

> ***Truly***, I say to you, only with difficulty will a rich person enter the kingdom of heaven. Again, I tell you, it is easier

for a camel to go through the eye of a needle than for a rich person to enter the kingdom of God.[ii]

Instead of giving up everything we have, it is giving up everything we have become, our pride, our self-reliance, our control. When we go all in, it's not about abandoning our family or our bank accounts, it's about abandoning our slavery and reliance upon sin and death and replacing it with His Life. There isn't Life in lies and deception. But when lies are exposed to the light of Jesus, blown away by the Holy Spirit, and are obliterated by the Heart of our Father, their hold on us is utterly destroyed. Once this happens, He replaces the hold they have on us with the true freedom He intended for us in the beginning.

Some of you may read this from righteous eyes, perhaps you have never gambled, nor ever plan to, but what other area could you benefit from these purposeful deceptions. Could it be exaggerations on a résumé, a story told at the water cooler, or a small group meeting? It could be withholding information on a job application, performance review, or counseling session. We were shown throughout the New Testament men who dedicated their lives to making sure the Torah (the Laws of Moses) were followed. Those same men, however, are also the ones who manipulated the testimonies and told falsehoods not just about Jesus the Messiah, but repeatedly about Paul and the disciples as well. Their traditions, behaviors, and lifestyle were being threatened and it seems that they were okay breaking laws and deceiving others in order to keep their way of life. If those around them knew that they were lying, they might not have been able to keep their positions of authority. In the second letter Peter wrote, he addresses this,

For by mouthing grandiosities that amount to nothing, they entice in sensual fleshly passions those who are barely escaping from those who live in error. They promise them freedom while they themselves

---
[ii] Matthew 19:23-24

The Nature of a Lie

are slaves of corruption—for a person is a slave to whatever has overcome him.[iii]

We see this today in many politicians, telling us what they think we want to hear, so we will continue to keep them employed. And while it's easy to spot those stories because we are bombarded with them in the news media and on social media, what about ourselves? What about the "speck in our own eyes?" How are we not living as our Father desires us to? Who do we believe we have become? What perceptions have been made, accepted as reality instead of responses to stimuli? We may want to look at our own lives to see what lies and deceptions prop up our own lifestyles.

We will leave this topic of *The Nature of a Lie* with a story. Imagine an elephant born and, much like the childhood story many of us grew up reading, he wants to fly. Except, in this situation, he doesn't have enormous ears, nor does he live in a fictitious story. He may feel like a bird, desire to be a bird, prefer the benefits of being a bird, and others may think it would be such a huge step for all those like him, to just pronounce himself to be a bird and start flying. But he is still an elephant. Now an outside force could come in and modify or change that design by adding feathers and perhaps a beak, creating a super-efficient diet to reduce his weight, shaving down the enormous nails to reduce his drag coefficient, maybe even adding a giant flying squirrel suit to the mix, but he is still an elephant. Even if he gets to fly, he is still an elephant. Even if others start to call him a bird, he is still an elephant. And the day that he is able to realize his desires originally were pure in motive, but were defiled by deception, he will take his first step toward becoming free. Asking God who He created him to be and where the desire to fly came from will help allow for God's Essence to overcome the death and deception fermenting within. Truth, in this instance, was that this elephant's desire to fly was created in him as a way to explore this phenomenal creation in a new way. A

[iii] 2 Peter 2:18-19 TLV

longing to see the earth from God's eyes was created in him so that he, a limited being, an elephant, would go to his Creator and ask for a vision of how He, God, sees the world. A pure desire was created, but misunderstood. The problem was not the misunderstanding, but it was instead where the elephant went to get clarification. God knew the elephant may get confused, but His yearning was always to meet in the Garden, spending time walking, talking about all of his questions and showing the elephant the staggering beauty that would address his concerns and cravings. It is only in God's kingdom, in His presence, with His wisdom, understanding, and love, that the elephant could understand who he was designed to be.

The Nature of a Lie

You've put yourself between a bullet and a target.
- "Bullet and a Target" Citizen Cope

Steven Cohen

6
The Role of a Lie

Sitting in a bakery one morning, I heard that resounding lyric by Citizen Cope, "You've put yourself between a bullet and a target." Although I do not condone Citizen Cope's music, this one lyric kept repeating and resounding in my heart and mind. When I asked God why I resonated with those words, He pointed out how we often set ourselves up for death. We place ourselves right in the crosshairs, between a bullet and the target. These lies that we believe, create, re-tell, and rely on aren't reducing our pain. They are making it easier for our enemy to place us in his cross-hairs. Once we have believed a lie, unless we have replaced that lie with truth, it is much easier to hit us with it again. And, as we have discussed, if there is one lie, there are usually others around supporting it.

The liar would have you believe the role of a lie would be to lessen pain, to reduce stress. But, in reality, a lie never reduces pain, it simply defers the pain to another time or place. The role of a lie is to further increase your reliance on lies. Think about that word *reliance*. (No, I am not going to tell you that this word came from the same root as *lie*; that in itself would be a lie.) Reliance is, however, two parts brought together: *rely*, or to be dependent on something, and *ance* which means the state of. So, *reliance* means to depend on a state of being. The point or role of a lie is to create further dependence on lies. What else in our world today continually deepens its hold on you, promising the reduction of stress or pain; promising the increase of enjoyment and fun? It sounds like every recreational drug, including alcohol, known to man. And while drugs, both recreational and medicinal, can supply a temporary escape from stress and pain, they typically bring you back down to reality in a worse place than you started, with some sort of side effect or the creation of a dependence looming. That, in turn, increases the desire to get back under the influence, in an attempt to get back to normal, which only deepens the hole being dug.

Some of us think that this only applies to "hard" substances like cocaine, heroin, meth, hydrocodone, or morphine, but that is part of the lie satan would have us believe. Now, I am not saying we should eat a "John the Baptist diet" of locusts and honey and move out to the desert to remove ourselves from all impurities and such. But we need to understand that many of our everyday routines, if not examined, may fall into this trap. The Bible says that satan is "more crafty than any other beast of the field."[i] His lies are subtle and are designed to make us further dependent on them.

There is a lie many of us believe, with plenty of propaganda to support it, that caffeine is our friend and we "need" it to get through the day. I know what seems to be an attack on coffee may turn many of you off as you sit and sip your *cup of joe* while reading, but think about this: How many of us say we can't function without caffeine? Is that statement true? What is the truth beneath that? What does God say about it? He may say that caffeine is a substance found in many of the plants He created. I believe He would say that He made caffeine for various reasons, including to help perk people up sometimes. But He also made the element of gold and an animal of the field, the calf. Nevertheless, He never intended for people to make a golden calf and worship or rely on it. There are plenty of His scriptures that specifically say there should be no other god before Him. If you cannot function before coffee, if you cannot read your Bible before drinking your latte, or you must have your afternoon spot of pick-me-up tea to get through the day, what are you relying on? What are you worshiping, something created or the Creator? The truth is that we can function and function well without caffeine or any artificial stimulant. The "need" for stimulants is based on the lack of true rest and rejuvenation. This is where the Sabbath comes in.

While I am sure Navy Seals, firefighters, and paramedics drink coffee sometimes, if they had to have their cup of joe before they could get up and go, we would be in a lot of trouble in an emergency. Picture the middle of the night, the firehouse is dark

---

i Gen 3:1

and quiet, full of sleeping firefighters, when the alarm sounds. Dispatch advises of the location and status of the emergency and the men start to brew their coffee, walking sluggishly grumpy throughout the house, stubbing their toes on coffee tables, forgetting their boots and helmets as they rush out the fire station. Even if they have a brewer that prepares a single cup in mere seconds, this would create a delay that could mean life or death for those involved in the emergency. Or imagine a Navy Seal, in the midst of battle, being incapacitated by a caffeine headache. Or a police officer, so tired while pursuing a violent offender, falling asleep at the wheel. We can't imagine these situations, right? Is it because these people are impervious to the side effects of caffeine? Likely not. Is it because they are perfect superhero-like humans with mutations that make them superior to all other humans? No.

These mind-blowing men and women who make it possible for us live in the freedom, safety, and comfort that we do, train their bodies to rest when they can get it. God created our bodies in a magnificent way, in that they recharge themselves and that rest gives us the energy we need. Some caveats to that, though, are that we must supply our body with proper nutrition to allow proper rejuvenation through the rest we get. One day, a coworker asked what supplements I would suggest to help him get up in the morning. I explained how his body was created in a magnificent way and advised him to quit dipping, replace eating garbage food with fresh, non-processed food, and go to bed early. He looked at me first as if I were crazy, but as he thought about it his expression changed. He seemed to realize that these simple ideas were revelational, that they could, or would, change his life.

He had bought a lie that supplements, energy drinks, and stimulants would fuel his body to operate at its best potential. But he realized that the more garbage he put in his body the more garbage he needed to keep operating at a normal level, and eventually he was just tired everyday no matter how many awareness-boosting energy products he consumed.

The lie about the truth in our lifestyle is that man-made substances make our lives better somehow, as if God needed help with His design. I am not sure if there was coffee in the Garden, but I can pretty much guarantee that there were no fast food chains nor were there canned, processed foods. There were fresh vegetables, fresh water, and although there was work to be done, there was also rest to be taken. Even more importantly, there was time with God, hiking through the wonders, chatting about the day, hearing Him share His thoughts.

That's where Life comes from. The energy available from the One who created everything is limitless, and our dependence should be on God and His Life, not on ours. Lies are designed to slowly chip away at our dependence on Him, replacing our relationship with God with a dependence on the lies themselves.

> ***Better is open rebuke than hidden love. Faithful are the wounds of a friend; profuse as the kisses of an enemy.***
> *– Proverbs 27:5-6*

Before meeting Christ, many so-called friends condoned and even supported the horrible evil going on in my life, which continued to feed lies and breed death. But my journey towards Truth, Life, and Love began with one person who was willing to shine God's light on the death and lies beneath my surface.

As we start to dig down and reveal light to the dark places below, our dependence on lies will be broken. The digging will likely be difficult at times and will rarely be comfortable. The light shining from friends who share the Truth may cause uneasiness and distress. But as those strongholds are broken and we gain freedom, who we were created to be is revealed. Christ supplants the foundation of lies we have built beneath us, replacing it with His strong and everlasting love. We then have the opportunity to share that with our family, friends, and neighbors.

The Role of a Lie

For there is no good tree that produces rotten fruit, nor again does a rotten tree produce good fruit. Each tree comes to be known by its own fruit. For figs are not gleaned out of briars; neither are bunches of grapes gathered from thorn bushes. 'Out of the good treasure of his heart the good man brings forth good, and out of the evil man brings forth evil. For from the overflow of the heart his mouth speaks.

- Luke 6:43-45

Steven Cohen

7
The Fruit of a Lie

What is your favorite fruit? In our family, we joyfully anticipate early summer when fresh watermelon starts coming in from the local Texas farms. Our children bury their faces in the fibrous, soft, yet crisp, sweet melon, with juice dripping down their chin as they attempt to slurp as much as they can. However, if you have ever had watermelon, there is one thing that gets in the way of pure enjoyment, the seeds. When it comes to watermelon, I have discovered that there are three kinds of people: the seed spitters, the seed chewers, and the seed avoiders who either pick them out or buy so-called "seedless" versions of the fruit.

      Like all non-genetically modified or non-mutated fruit, the fruit of a lie has seeds in it. Most of the time, the seeds are found in their own small, protective shell nestled deep within a sweet, moist, intensely refreshing, delicious fruit. I believe God created them this way so that animals and humans alike would eat the fruit, spitting or picking the seeds out or passing them along through their digestive system. The seeds would then be continually replanted, spreading that plant species throughout His creation. In this same manner, God designed His Truth to be spread as well. By word of mouth and through the testimony of those who have had encounters with Him, people share seeds of Life, allowing for His Essence to grow within someone else so they too can have encounters with Him. I am sure, or at least I hope, as you read this you will realize how satan simply copied God's design, again perverting it for his own use, to spread lies and death. Satan is lame in that fashion; he is not creative. If you look at it, every angle he can take is simply a perversion or contrast of God's love.

      Many people, believers and non-believers, grew up in church reading about, listening to, and studying the fruit of the Spirit: love, joy, peace, patience, kindness, goodness, faithfulness, gentleness, and self-control. Just as the fruit you eat comes from the presence or existence of the matching tree, bush, or vine, the fruit of the

Spirit can only come from the Holy Spirit. I believe that is what Matthew 12:32-35 speaks to:

> *Either make the tree good and its fruit good, or make the tree bad and its fruit bad, for the tree is known by its fruit. You brood of vipers! How can you speak good, when you are evil? For out of the abundance of the heart the mouth speaks. The good person out of his good treasure brings forth good, and the evil person out of his evil treasure brings forth evil.*

Remember that when we read Scripture we must read it in context. Right before these verses, Jesus talks about the blasphemy of the Holy Spirit and says:

> *...whoever speaks a word against the Son of Man will be forgiven, but whoever speaks against the Holy Spirit will not be forgiven, either in this age or in the age to come.*

Where does the fruit of the Spirit come from? From the Spirit, right? The discussion about blasphemy of the Holy Spirit resulted from the Sadducees and Pharisees saying that Jesus' power came from demons. Are you catching what Jesus says here? The fruit is a representation of the tree it comes from, words are a result of the heart that they stem from. The fruit of the Spirit can only come from one place, the Holy Spirit. Similarly, in Luke 6, you cannot get oranges from banana trees, nor pomegranates from a fig tree. But much like Monsanto, the giant agricultural company that continues to artificially modify and chemically mutate much of the food consumed today, satan tries to genetically modify the plant (that's *us*) so that we produce a contrasting version of fruit. Whether it be seedless (to prevent us from spreading the gospel), a new taste or various textures (that spin the Gospel of Me instead of Christ), easy-to-peel versions of that fruit (that make us feel unprotected or susceptible to losing our salvation), or a different fruit all together (losing our faith and belief in the One who created us), the plan is to pervert what God originally designed and desires for our lives.

Some of the modifications often accepted in our current society which contradict what God created are: gentleness meaning weakness (emerging from a state of fear), self-control becoming self-condemnation (as a result of shame), peace redefined as passivity (in an attempt to avoid communication and conflict), patience slowly becoming sloth-like (in an attempt for us to stop working while we wait and wait and wait on the Lord), joy being reduced to the emotion of happiness (so it is as fleeting as the minutes in a day), kindness moving toward simply acting kind (even when the heart behind harbors bitterness and hatred), goodness redefined as being perfect (in an attempt to convince us that our works can earn us a relationship with God or a ticket into heaven, even though God loves us as we are), passion succumbing to lust (redefining our identity through the lens of our sexual urges, feelings, and temptations), faithfulness not being truly rewarding (replacing it with drama, pornography, heartache, and sexual addiction)...and, while we gain freedom from releasing some bad definitions there, those are *lies about fruit*, not the *fruit of a lie*. What's the difference? Those definitions are an attack on identity, they are lies about our identity and who God created us to be. The fruit of a lie is what we let grow and manifest inside us when we believe those lies. The enemy spewed the lies themselves over us many days, weeks, and even years prior to us accepting, believing, and then cultivating them in our own lives.

So, what is inside and what comes from lies? To use pictures here, imagine your favorite fruit. It doesn't matter what kind it is, because like fruits, lies come in all kinds, shapes, and sizes. So, with almost any fruit you pick, this illustration works. Our family enjoys watermelon, but I really enjoy blackberries, especially vine-fresh blackberries from my parents' land in north Georgia. While they have no real shell, they have a skin covering each bulb of the fruit.

Those of you who may have picked a pomegranate, kiwi, coconut, or durian know that there is a protective barrier covering the fruit. These protective barriers vary from a gel-like cap, to a shell, to a fibrous husk, and even to a soft, furry skin. While one barrier may take a little more effort to get through, there is still something not only hiding, but holding and containing the fruit. When we eat the meat of the fruit, we intake the benefits, the nutrients contained within. Many of us thought as a child that if we ate a fruit's seeds then a tree or vine would start growing in our stomachs, so we avoided eating seeds. But most seeds are nutrient-saturated and packed with protein.

When we believe a lie, we consume or eat its fruit and its seeds along with it. Remember the seed chewers from the beginning of the chapter? Satan has perverted this process in us. Without truth, we cannot process the lie correctly and it gets stuck. Like the fears of a child, seeds nestle deep inside us, germinating, growing, if you will, into little lie trees. Picture this with me. Little trees take root, pulling resources from our minds, bodies, and spirits that it needs in order to continue its growth. Once the lie tree is mature, which for some may only take a matter of seconds, it starts to create fruit. And when the time is right, the harvest is ready, we start plucking the fruit from the trees growing within and vomit these lies on those around us. This perverted version of God's original design for spreading His truth continues to plant more trees, founded by the roots of death, in the belly of those who consume them. When we believe a lie, we are in essence consuming others' vomit. As unsavory as this picture is, I hope it helps us all to understand how vile and disgusting lies are.

In the parable of the sower, Jesus talks about four contrasting types of people who have prepared their hearts in various ways and how those ways accept or repel God's Word differently.[i] Similarly, people have prepared and tilled their hearts

---

i   Matthew 13:1-23

to either receive or repel lies. Some of us are willing to believe anything we hear. We are all-too-willing to listen and let seeds be planted by gossip. We stay up late watching or reading whatever media outlets throw our way about almost anyone in the public eye, presenting their opinions as fact. Remember, facts are not truth. Although they may be true, what lies beneath the facts?

When my daughter was six years old, we had a conversation about how gossiping about someone means that we are speaking death, condemnation, and judgment over them. I loved hearing her response, saying that she doesn't want to speak death over people. She wants to love them and speak Life over them.

How do we do that? How do we choose Life over people? If we can go back to our watermelon analogy from the beginning of the chapter, I think it can provide great insight. Remember, there was a seed avoider. This illustrates those of us who very excitedly, and sometimes dramatically, rebuke or refuse to hear gossip. This person stays away from gossips, avoiding them all together, picking and choosing either their friends or the conversations they partake in. Avoiding those people is like choosing seedless watermelons. While this can be a wise decision in some cases, a warning: if our avoidance of a gossip comes from a spirit of judgment, we are inviting death into our lives through a different avenue. A suggestion: ask God what He desires for you, the individual who is gossiping, and your relationship.

There was a second way seed avoiders get around seeds, by picking them out. This secondary method may be an opportunity to stay in relationship with a gossiper, but not get caught up in gossip. Simply avoid the conversations that allow for or create an environment for it. Much like picking out each individual seed, it takes effort to change the topic. It can be challenging, sometimes boring, not as fun, and may even seem forced at times. But many times, when we are willing to invest in relationship, watering the relationship with Life, giving each other grace and room to grow,

The Fruit of a Lie

gently weeding the fields to prevent the weeds from choking out the good fruit, working together, purposefully pursuing Life, those relationships are richer, deeper, sweeter, juicier, and more meaningful than gossip could ever be.

Just because we are purposeful and our intentions are to resist being a part of these lies and judgments doesn't mean that they will never happen. If you have ever eaten a watermelon slice as a seed avoider, you know it is impossible to get every single one. Sometimes they are just so small we don't notice them. Sometimes we're so eager to eat, we are willing to put up with a few. Then there are times when the seeds are simply soft and easy to digest. I hope you see the analogy for what it is. Like the almost impossible task of avoiding all watermelon seeds, the same occurs with avoiding lies; we may take a bite into life and realize we missed one. But instead of despair, there is hope.

As you hear God more clearly about His Truth, you are going to start identifying lies more often, which allows you to spit them out. You don't have to believe them. You don't have to defend why they exist. You can simply spit them out. This ability to hear God more clearly doesn't mean that more lies exist; that would be what satan wants you to think. It means that you can identify them more easily. Even the little white ones. The soft ones which have barely started to develop and really don't seem like a big deal. Those are the ones we need to be especially aware of as they seem innocuous, but are truly cancerous as lies, if not as watermelon seeds. As we identify and reject these lies we become freer and less bound. But what about the ones that we still miss or the lies we ate years ago?

We need to develop and cultivate an environment in which those seeds don't germinate. When we cultivate an environment of awareness instead of fear it allows us to better digest the seeds (lies) we have ingested, preventing their gestation or growth in our belly. To create this environment, we first need to know that even though we eat a seed, unlike the common joke parents play on their kids, a tree does not form in our bellies. Just because we hear a lie doesn't mean we have to believe it. It is important that we look for what lies beneath our struggles, however, because, many times, the root to our existing issues comes from something that happened in our past. Something as small and seemingly innocuous as a little, white lie can stick in the cracks and folds of our memory. And, if not addressed, it can turn from a thought to a belief, creating doubt and judgment over both our self and others, which is the perfect field for a heart of gossip to grow in.

    We also must know that when we resist something on a physical level (i.e. not hearing something or staying away from someone) we can forget that there may be the spiritual level we still haven't addressed. When the evil one (referred to in John 10 as the thief and a robber) enters, it is not by the gate or front door. John 10:1 says, *"he comes some other way."* This is not necessarily because he cannot use the front, but coming in that way is less likely because more attention is given to the front entry. If we simply try to avoid satan or evil in our physical selves (the front door or gate) then we are concentrating on only one aspect of the battleground, leaving the rest of ourselves open, exposed, allowing access to those **other ways**. Because we rely on our self to refuse evil, we may be exposing our spirit to an unguarded attack.

    In Dr. James Richards' book *Grace: The Power to Change*, he shows how *grace* is not merely that common definition we have heard in the Christian community for so long, "Getting something we don't deserve," in opposition to mercy being, "Not getting what we do deserve." Richards illustrates and describes a power given to us from God, the ability that grace is what gives us power to conform to His image and likeness. Grace, as Richards' subtitle implies, is not just a Christianese catchphrase or a one-time experience at the time of our salvation. It is God's power in us which allows us to change on all levels. It allows us to break strongholds, allows us to resist gossip and the death associated with it, and it also allows us to become the people, His children, whom He designed and desires us to be.

There are others of us who seek the kingdom, God's Word, His viewpoint, His truth on the matters at hand and let Him break the lies off. I hesitate to call this a method because there is no prescription to God. This third and final way of preparing the soil of our hearts is the easiest to perform, although sometimes the hardest to stick to, yet it produces the most fruit. As we till the soil, prepping the garden of our heart, we seek God's knowledge, will, and heart to discern what are the weeds that we should rip out, as well as which are the good seeds that we must allow to enter our soil. If we simply ask for Him to water what we put in the ground, then who knows whether it will produce life or death? Because God doesn't water just anything we put down, we may become disappointed, but it is for His reasons that He does or doesn't water any given thing. It could be that what we have asked Him to water is a toxic seed or simply that the seeds we placed in our garden were not designed for our garden. There is a season for everything, and even if that seed may be perfect for you, sometimes crops need to be rotated.

The disappointment we have when God doesn't do what we want is the fruit of the lie that so many people have believed, "God is here to make what we want become reality." While He may grace us with our desires out of His goodness and generosity as our Father, that is not His function. He is our Father, our Dad, our Creator. That's why it is critical to additionally ask Him what seeds He wants in our garden, what experiences, wisdom, and emotions He wants in our lives. Then He can fertilize, water, and grow those into fruit-bearing plants that glorify Him and what He has created us to do.

Truth and reality do not adapt to us. It is up to us to adapt to them. A four-thousand-year-old tradition does not become truer as the years go by. If it is false or wrong, it simply continues to be a long-standing error.

– Dallas Willard[1]

Steven Cohen

8
The Addiction to Lies

While growing up, I moved around so often it was hard for me to keep friends. I found that the older I got when we moved, the harder it was to make friends. By the time I started high school, I had reached a point of rejection I didn't think I could bear. I started cutting and carving as coping methods for the pain I felt. Cutting and carving are similar in that physical harm is inflicted and pain is created using sharp objects to cut through layers of skin. However, cutting is normally done in straight lines whereas carving creates shapes, letters, or images. I typically chose carving, masking my carving as a creative outlet instead of what it really was, an attempt to escape the numbness of my internal emotional pain. Either no one noticed, my deception worked, or everyone around me was oblivious to cutting and carving as a cry for help. Years later, after my urge to cut had mostly subsided, I heard a Nine Inch Nails remake of a Johnny Cash song called "Hurt" that I identified with; it nailed my pain on the head:

> *I hurt myself today*
> *To see if I still feel pain*
> *I focus on the pain*
> *The only thing that's real*
> *The needle tears a hole*
> *The old familiar sting*
> *Try to kill it all away*
> *But I remember everything*

Have you ever been there, feeling completely hopelessness and bound? I hope you can see now how those are filled with death and deception. A point came when I started to believe that I wasn't capable of making friends, *true* friends. Abandonment and loneliness ruled my world. I felt like no one would stick around and that people I met would leave at a moment's notice. I never let anyone too far into my world, leaving me with only superficial relationships. The song "Hurt" released on the album titled *Downward Spiral*; how highly applicable that was. I was stuck in a downward spiral. A stronghold grabbed a hold of me like it has so many others, and I couldn't break the cycle.

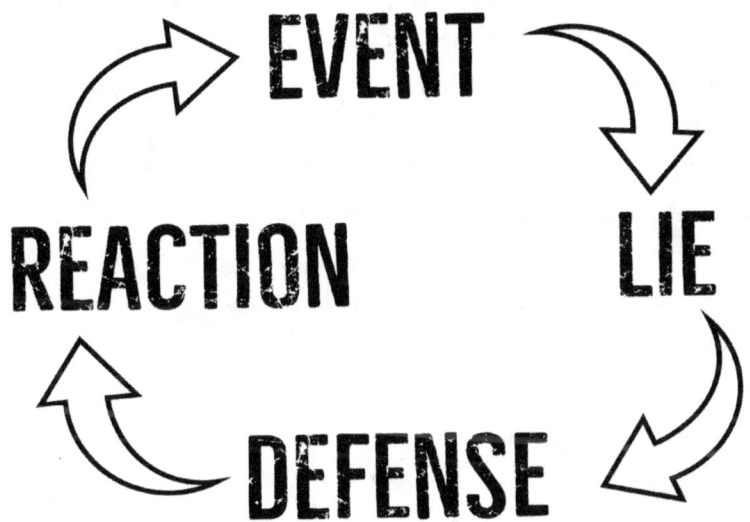

In this diagram, you'll see what was happening to me. This diagram of a stronghold is commonly used within freedom ministries and counseling sessions. It illustrates the proverbial "downward spiral" as causes and effects and shows its cyclical nature. The cycle begins with an event which creates negative emotions or consequences. This could be *any* event. There is not a qualifier for this other than it has had negative, hurtful, or harming effects.

One of the lies many of us struggle with is false humility, a belief that our hurts aren't big enough to concern others with. That is a lie from the deceiver who is trying to prevent us from bringing that hurt and pain to our Father to be healed. Through this event, and in our pain, the deceiver again attacks while we are vulnerable, telling us a lie about what happened. Instead of rejecting the lie, we accept it, placing a judgment on whomever or whatever was involved in the hurtful event.

With that judgment, we develop a defense mechanism to prevent further hurt from taking place. In my case, I had created a wall which prevented people from getting too close; I didn't trust that they wouldn't leave me. I was afraid they would abandon me like so many had before. But by building the wall, I was actually keeping those deep relationships I needed so desperately out as well. This created even more anguish. Maybe you know someone who has done the same. Maybe that someone was you. By creating these defenses, we may prevent a small amount of pain, but what we are truly doing is preventing healing, which in turn causes more pain.

Additionally, in response to our raised defense, others will possibly or probably (or as we say in our household, "prossibly") not understand and take offense. Therefore, the cycle continues as people react negatively to our defensive positioning. With that negative reaction to the defense mechanism – which was based on a judgment formed by a lie about a previous event – comes another event that only further reinforces the lie. Therefore, the need for the defense put in place strengthens. When this continues, we end up blockading ourselves behind a wall of defenses, preventing us from sharing or exposing our hurt. We become bound or shackled in this stronghold, this impenetrable fortress of hurt and pain. This is why it is so important that we not react to what people present as themselves, but ask God what He says, so that we can see behind the walls, behind the defensive posture, and speak to the heart of the matter, not merely to the symptom.

During my time of loneliness and pain, one of the "bad" kids, we'll call him Jonathan, was walking through the halls during class. I saw him look in at me from across the hall, positioned where the teacher could not see him from her desk. He motioned for me to come out and join him. I didn't know him all too well, but, in an effort to be accepted, I approached the teacher and lied to her, saying that I needed to use the bathroom. I was an otherwise trustworthy student, making A's & B's, and always attentive in class, so when I asked to go, there was no hesitation. The lie worked. She gave me a hall pass and I went into the hall to meet up with him. It felt exciting to break the rules, to be wanted and accepted. I felt free, although I was far from it. I had just added to my bondage and was about to further shackle myself with years of addiction and self-medicating my pain with drugs and various chemicals, in addition to the cutting and carving I already used.

Jonathan and I ended up going into the bathroom where he pulled out a pack of Camel brand full-strength, filter-less cigarettes and offered me one. I had been offered cigarettes before and rejected them plenty of times, but this time was different. I was on a rebellious high, my emotions were excited, and at that moment I chose to smoke my first cigarette. I didn't know what to do, but I was going to give it a shot. What he handed me was strange, it was filter-less, which was different from the cigarettes I had seen my dad smoke for so many years. I wasn't sure which end to put to my mouth, so I picked the end without the Camel branding, and, as I put it to my lips, he lit his lighter. I puffed a few puffs to get it lit but didn't inhale. It took a second for me to build the courage to take a puff and breathe it in. Only moments later I felt its intoxicating effects on the rest of my body and almost fell over. I don't know if the feeling was the cigarette, my body taking this rebellious high to another level, or a combination of the two. Regardless of the actual reason, I liked it.

That feeling of freedom soared as my body reacted to the nicotine in the toxic concoction of smoke. Moments later we heard the click-clack, click-clack of our principal's shoes coming down the hall. The cigarettes got flushed and we rushed out of the bathroom in different directions back to our classrooms. The adrenaline rush of trying to get away without being caught added to the high I felt from the cigarette. I felt invincible. Additionally, when I returned to class, a few kids noticed the smell of smoke that I was unaware of, apparently emanating from my existence like Pig-Pen in Charlie Brown. And although their comments said, "That is so bad," "I can't believe you smoke," their actions and interactions said, "You are so cool," "I wish I could be like you." These were kids who wouldn't give me the time of day not ten minutes prior. Their reactions added acceptance as a benefit to my rebellion and, in less than ten minutes, I had gone from no one to someone.

What I thought was one of my best days bound me in a fashion similar to when I prayed for God to heal my "Kissy-cat." The day I heard the deceiver tell me that my Father and God either didn't listen or didn't care effectively ruined my life. And while an addiction to cigarettes developed into a real physical bondage and dependence, something else occurred which was much worse. An addiction to that attention was forged and I believed a lie that relationships and friendships were based on my actions, instead of on unconditional acceptance and love. I liked the way cigarettes made me feel, but even more, it felt special to have people talk with me out of desire to talk, not obligation or assignment from our teachers.

Much like the addictions that formed from these experiences, the liar sells this story that we need lies to help make us feel better, to hide the qualities we don't like about ourselves or others. He wants us to believe that the lies which puff us up and make us out to be someone we are not, somehow, make our lives easier to live. As if stuffing away the hurt into what Jimmy Evans calls our "hurt pocket," helps prevent pain. Some might say that they aren't stuffing the hurt away, that they just choose to walk away, but, truly, they're the same thing, pushing away others and hiding the pain, embarrassment, and disappointment with distance. I think, in that case, the hurt pocket just becomes larger, allowing for more pain to be stored within, causing even more damage and bondage in the long run.

Neither distance nor time heal. They are merely units

of measurement and have no abilities within themselves other than describing how far something has traveled or the unit of progression from one event to another.[30] I found myself in Montana almost twenty-three hundred miles from my father, some fifteen to twenty years after my parents' divorce when God came to me. I was driving my 1996 Dodge Dakota 4x4 on the east side of Flathead Lake, blasting, I believe, Rob Zombie when God told me, in an audible voice, that I needed to reconcile with my father. I was almost at polar-opposite ends of the United States and an absurd amount of time had passed, but the pain and disappointment of those offenses were still as fresh as the day they'd happened. The moment when God spoke this to me I broke down sobbing on the side of the road. He brought that pain back to the surface, not to torture me, but to set me free from it. I had a choice in that moment: either stuff the pain back down or do as God advised me to do. I went home and wrote a two-and-a-half-page letter to my father forgiving him of all the offenses and hurts that I had picked up and held on to. I no longer blamed him for my reactions to what he may have done, and God healed that. Neither time nor distance could heal that pain, only God.

    While healing doesn't come from time or distance, a measurement of time will certainly pass and, sometimes, a large amount of effort will be required for healing to occur. Have you ever been part of a conversation like my opening story, where my conversation with Courtney went wrong and we had to work through some hurt? Real communication and relationship is deep and will take effort and time. To out and just tell someone they don't fit your definition and desire of who they should be is easy. To form a trust-based relationship where people are okay and are encouraged in their differences is not. This is where that addiction to the lie becomes critical mass. It is almost ready to explode, because, if I want friends, it is essential to be open and honest, but if I tell someone something I don't like about them, it may upset them, and I may possibly lose them as a friend. This is a rock and a hard place. Have you ever been stuck here, at that moment where the pain of the lie or reaction of my true feelings is less than the pain of not having friends, feeling lonely, or abandoned?

In an effort to lessen our pain and remove ourselves from between the two hard places, we too often choose the lie, satiating the pain and isolation at the expense of continuing the lie. The lie that we cannot have truly genuine friends; the lie that our views, opinions, and beliefs are not valid; the lie that God has abandoned us, doesn't care about us, or never existed. We are addicted to the lie that if we cover ourselves with a fig leaf no one will notice we are scared and lonely. Deep down inside we know they are lies. I believe that is where the internal conflict comes from in the first place; it's the battle our Father and Rescuer, our Savior, has waged on the death that is keeping us from who He created us to be. Although we know these lies are not the best thing there could be for us, we continue living in them because we just don't believe His Truth yet. The addiction still has its hold.

The Addiction to Lies

What LIES Beneath

Steven Cohen

SECTION 2
The Lies Beneath

Satan is the 'Hurt Whisperer,' because wherever there is pain, you can bet he is there, scheming and plotting, whispering his lies into the core of our hearts and minds.[1]

– Jimmy Evans

Steven Cohen

9
Recognizing the Lie and the Liar

So, what do we do now? Where do we go from here? Let me start off with a different question. What was the first murder in the Bible? Take a second to think that over. As Christians, for a long time, we have been told about Cain's wild jealousy over God's acceptance of Abel's sacrifice but not his own. We have heard how jealousy drove Cain to murder his brother, referring to that as the "first murder." Others might say the first murder was the slaying of the animal God killed to make the coverings for Adam and Eve. The Bible doesn't specifically say how He created coats of skin or that He killed animals, but it is usually assumed that in Genesis 3:21 when "the Lord God made for Adam and for his wife garments of skins and clothed them" that He slayed an animal to do so. This occurred shortly after Adam and Eve had chosen to separate themselves from God, suddenly conscious of their nakedness, covering themselves with fig leaves. *Matthew Henry's Concise Commentary* goes on to draw further conclusions that the killing of these animals was done "for sacrifice, to typify Christ, the great Sacrifice... [making for] them coats of skin, large, strong, durable, and fit for them." He points out that Adam and Eve's attempt to cover themselves was not enough and that a sacrifice had to be made, "such is the righteousness of Christ."

I would contend, however, that the first murder was committed by neither man nor God. I believe it was satan who committed the first murder. His victims, Adam and Eve.

He did not kill them, you might say, but if you look at the origin of the word *murder* and track it back to one of its earliest forms, you'll find the Latin word *mortālis*, or mortal, meaning to subject to death.[31] This is exactly what God told Adam would happen if they ate from the Tree of the Knowledge of Good and Evil. But how does satan come into this? God created the Tree, right? Adam and Eve ate from it, so wouldn't it be their fault?

Let's look at this from the perspective of a common debate occurring today in our society: gun control. If someone is murdered, is it the maker of the gun who is responsible? Is it the victim's fault for not dodging the bullet? Or does the fault lie with the person who made the choice to consciously load bullets into the chamber of the gun, aim it at a person, and pull the trigger?

The skins that God used to cover Adam and Eve with were not the first experience of death they had felt. Again, it seems satan's goal was to point blame at God, leaving the responsibility of the first killing in God's hands, rather than in his own. Adam and Eve felt death when they ate the fruit; they felt the instant separation occur between them and God. The connection to Life was severed and they were subjected to death. I can only imagine the fear and uncertainty that flooded in, causing them to be afraid. They were murdered. Malicious, callous intent to spiritually kill humankind stood behind the discussion between the serpent and Eve.

Jesus even proclaimed that, "he, [the devil, satan, Lucifer] was a murderer from the beginning."[i] This makes me think, maybe Jesus knows something we don't. Is He referring to the Garden as the place of beginning? Or could He be talking about something even earlier than that? What if He is referring to something when Jesus knew the devil as Lucifer, an angel in heaven? Could He be referring to the massacre of one-third of God's angels, filling them with deceit, introducing them to death?[32] It seems likely, as this is satan's *modus operandi*, and the story of his fall is a type and shadow of Adam and Eve's story. Remember, Lucifer, at this point earned his label *satan*, the enemy. He is a deceiver, "a murderer," as Jesus so plainly pointed out, ultimately responsible for one-third of the angels' ejection from heaven.

Regardless of which murder satan committed first, it wasn't God's fault. It is important to discuss the idea of this first murder to show the inconceivable depth lies can have. There is both a tremendous depth to what lies beneath our bound state, as well as to the horrible consequences of believing lies. In both cases we just

---
i   John 8:44

discussed, the punishment was death. Both Adam and Eve, not to mention the fallen fraction of angels, had to find a new home, a new source for their contentment, a new source for truth. No matter what the source or where the home, they fall extremely short of what God had created and designed for all parties.

While satan has no new tricks and his entire arsenal is made up of lies, some lies are hard to see. Some may be disguised in a biblical principle. Most are crafted in a way which places blame on God. So how do we recognize the lie and the liar?

Something pivotal to remember is that we must stay rooted in God's Word and seek His kingdom in the everyday moments. Let the Father reveal His will and His desire throughout the day, not just at appointed or reserved times. While setting predetermined quiet-times is certainly beneficial, if we only talk to Him during those times then we miss out on all He has to say about our encounters outside of our prayer closet.

Once we gain His insight, we should not only come into agreement with what He tells us in our conversations, but we must also give Him the credit, glory, and honor. This doesn't mean every step you take you must exclaim, "Halleluiah, God helped me take another step." It may be that as God gives you a vision of His direction that you praise Him when you get the vision, and, at certain mile markers, revisit the vision, discussing with Him how well His idea works.

Why is that important? Satan's plan includes taking revelation and perverting it so that we think we have the answers and, therefore, become self-sustaining, or we believe that the revelation came from ourselves. In the midst of the revelation of *What Lies Beneath*, satan started whispering to me that everyone was lying, everyone was trying to deceive me and it was my job to point it out to them. I found myself, in a sideways way, calling my eight-year-old son a liar on a regular basis, finding supposed inconsistencies when he and I were talking. God revealed to me that my son was not actually lying to me, but we were experiencing a communication barrier. My, again, eight-year-old son, who had an eight-year-old vocabulary and an eight-year-old ability to express his emotions was having difficulty explaining why he was doing things he knew he shouldn't. He was having difficulty explaining his emotions. He wasn't lying to me, but satan was. He was telling me that my son was and would be forever known as a liar unless I called him out on it. Satan's plan? To ruin my relationship with my son. While my son may have had difficulty talking things through, it was my job to equip him, not rip his heart out by calling him a liar. It is my job to guide him, not confront him at every miscommunication.

Not every breakdown in communication is based on a lie, that in itself would be a strategy of the liar. It is important to work on your communication skills, but it is far more important to work on your communication with the Creator of communication. Ask for His help during those times when you and someone else are not seeing eye-to-eye or are struggling to understand each other.

Sometimes I think that we give satan too much credit. He has been given these titles like, "Prince of this world,"[ii] or "Father of Lies,"[iii] and many of us take that to mean that he has some sort of power over us. While he holds these titles, they function more like a sense of entitlement. I don't want to say that I am in the mind of satan, but if he thinks anything like the selfish, pridefully arrogant person I was for so many years, maybe I know his thoughts more than I want to. Dr. James Richards' book, *Satan Unmasked: The Truth Behind the Lie,* is a great resource on this topic, addressing the most common myths about satan, his power, dominion, and credentials. There are so many myths he has created about himself which have inflated his image to be something much larger than it is; he actually thinks he owns us or has power over us. And, unfortunately, we assume that because there are so many titles

---

[ii] John 14:30
[iii] John 8:44

and myths out there that they must be true, and, with that, his lies automatically have power over us. The only power they have is what we give them. Proverbs 18 is rich with God's wisdom on how this applies to our lives.

It points out that "*death and life are in the power of the tongue,*"[iv] even if we don't boldly proclaim our confessions, but instead whisper or mumble them under our breath. "*The words of a whisperer are like delicious morsels; they go down into the inner parts of the body,*"[v] and have power over us. We are talking about how to recognize the lies beneath, what we believe in our hearts, deep inside us. This is one of the ways lies we have heard get there. We are not zombies under the mind control of satan, but many times we listen to a lie and give it credit, ponder on it, try to make sense of it, rather than simply taking it to God and asking Him what He says. The best way to recognize a lie for what it is, is by seeking the kingdom, seeking the King's truth for His revelation. Some of us are prideful and think that we have the strength or wisdom to discern right or wrong, good or bad, righteousness or evil, and that it is shameful if we can't or don't. But there is no shame in running to God.

> **The righteous man runs [into the Lord's strong Tower] and is safe..., Before [a man's] destruction a man's heart is haughty but humility comes before honor.**[vi]

Considering the sixty-six books of the Bible, how many are primarily about satan? If he is as big and bad as he thinks he is, why does he not get more attention? While he and his tendencies are something we should understand and be aware of, many of us give him way too much credit. While some could argue that this book is all about satan and his lies, giving him credit for the strongholds in our lives, the message here is more about freeing us from the power we have allowed him to have over us, regaining

---

iv   Proverbs 18:21a
v   Proverbs 18:8
vi   Proverbs 18:10 & 12 (emphasis mine)

our lives from the lies we have chosen to believe. It is our choice, many of which were very difficult and emotionally-based decisions, but they are still our decisions nonetheless, NOT his. You see, not only is there not a single book in the Bible dedicated to satan, there is also very little written directly about him in the Bible. Might it be that "God neither wishes to flatter satan with too much publicity nor desires that we become preoccupied with him?"[33] The Bible is God's story. It's His story about how and why He created us, how much He adores us and wants to be with us, as well as the story of how He made it possible for that relationship to exist.

Think about a guide book on hiking the most beautiful place on earth. If it only concentrated on the snakes hiding in the cracks, the sharp, perilous rocks, or the danger of falling from high places rather than the beauty of the destination or the paths and directions to get there, would it be worth your time reading? While that guide would be remiss to exclude some of the dangers to look out for along the way, it would be even further amiss to concentrate solely on those dangers, creating a fear many would find difficult to overcome.

I like the article, "Satan's Part in God's Perfect Plan," written by Bob Deffinbaugh. It speaks to satan's "insatiable desire for prominence, desiring the glory which belongs only to God... [and how] Satan should receive only the attention he deserves." Here are some of the ways the deceiver presents himself and even lies about himself in an attempt to disarm and confuse you:

- Satan, the invisible, non-existent one who is a myth.
- Satan, under cover, works invisibly or through some intermediate agency (1 Chronicles 21:1; Job 1-2; John 8:40-41, 13:2, 27).
- Satan, our ally, who is here to help (Genesis 3:1-5).
- Satan, the fierce, frightening one (1 Peter 5:8).

- Satan, the accuser (Zechariah 3:1-2 and Revelation 12:10).
- Satan, the arrogant one (Isaiah 14 and Ezekiel 28).
- Satan, the tempter (Matthew 4:3 and 1 Thessalonians 3:5).
- Satan, the religious "**angel of light**"(2 Corinthians 11:13-15).
- Satan, the religious, legalistic, hypocrite (1 Timothy 4:1-5).
- Satan, the wonder-worker (2 Thessalonians 2:9 and Revelation 13:11-15, 16:14).[34]

So, with all of these lies that satan uses, where is it that we learn of the first lie? Back in chapter 1, we considered the third chapter of Genesis where satan questions the authority of God. There satan established the path of deception that ultimately affected all of mankind. There we see the first lie experienced in our world. Depending on whether your Bible is organized in chronological or categorical order, where you find the first lie physically may be different, but I would argue that it occurred well before what took place in Eden. In fact, it was well before the fall of satan. That would imply that there were lies in heaven. How does that work? Heaven is perfect, right?

> *You said in your heart, 'I will ascend into heaven, I will exalt my throne above the stars of God. I will sit upon the mount of meeting, in the uttermost parts of the north. I will ascend above the high places of the clouds – I will make myself like Elyon.'*
> *– Isaiah 14:14*

Does a child's failures or attitudes make the parents imperfect? No, I would argue, however, that continual failures or misaligned attitudes might reflect the parents' capabilities, emotional stability, or parenting style. But is that child's decision ultimately his or her parents' decision, or is it their own? We see above in Isaiah that Lucifer, a beautiful and ornate angel in heaven, chose himself over God. Jeremiah 2:11-13 describes this same process,

> *"Has a nation changed its gods – even though they are not gods? Yet my people have exchanged their glory for the worthless things. Be appalled at this, O heavens! Be utterly horrified and dumbfounded." It is a declaration of Adonai. "My People have committed two evils. They have forsaken me – the springs of living water – and they dug their own cisterns – cracked cisterns that hold not water."* (TLV)

The first lie and every lie afterward originated from forsaking Adonai, God of all creation, turning away from Him. The second of the *"two evils"* mentioned in Jeremiah occurs when we take God's place in our lives, building our own cisterns, exchanging His glory and power for our own.

While we do live in this beautiful world with this atrocious liar, the key is recognizing him and the lies he spins. We must also not let our imaginations run rampant, allowing myth to turn into belief, giving him a stronghold in our lives. We must guard our thoughts and keep from giving him permission to rule over us, because once he has permission to rule us, he will. Just because we live in this world where beauty and dangers exist together doesn't mean we have to live fearful. Focusing on the danger only contributes to greater fear, allowing satan's lies to develop a greater stronghold on our lives. We need to be aware of his schemes, not paralyzed by them. When we are aware, we can fight this spiritual battle without our eyes blinded or our hands tied behind our backs, because when it is a fair fight, the fight is no longer fair. There is no competition at all. Jesus has already won and the only way to experience defeat is if you believe that isn't true.

> Free will. It's like butterfly wings: once touched, they never get off the ground. No, I only set the stage.
> - John Milton, The Devil's Advocate

Steven Cohen

10
Discovering the Lies About the Truth Beneath

I chose the word *discover* here for a specific reason. Remember the impact of definitions, not only their meaning, but also how they are created. The words we choose affect the impact made on us. I could have chosen to use the word *find*, but there is more to it than that.

What is it that we do when we discover something? Dis-Covering something is to uncover it, revealing what lies beneath a veil or layer. Archeologists very seldom just walk around and find artifacts or clues to history lying around. They must dig to discover the history they seek, and we must do the same. We have learned to recognize the lie and who has conjured it, but we have to dig to find the when and where, to find the history behind it.

While we have identified that satan is a liar and discussed how he lies, we would be remiss not to address the basis for so much of our trouble and torment. We have revealed a bit about satan, but let's look at the absurd lies spoken about the most foundational truths God created. Many know of Genesis 3 as the chapter detailing the fall of man, but I think that the first nineteen verses, at least, could also be known for their utter disrespect of God's principles. In these verses, seven basic foundational lies were conveyed by the deceiver, received by Adam and Eve, and now flourish throughout the world. Over the next two chapters, we will expose and dissect each of the seven lies found in these scriptures as well as an additional seven I feel God wants to address. All to bring Life and Truth to the root of what lies beneath.

> But the serpent was shrewder than any animal of the field that Adonai Elohim made. So it said to the woman, "Did God really say, 'You must not eat from all the trees of the garden'?"
> The woman said to the serpent, "Of the fruit of the trees, we may eat. But of the fruit of the tree which is in the middle of the garden, God said, 'You must not eat of it and you must not touch it, or you will die.'"

The serpent said to the woman, "You most assuredly won't die! For God knows that when you eat of it, your eyes will be opened and you will be like God, knowing good and evil."
Now the woman saw that the tree was good for food, and that it was a thing of lust for the eyes, and that the tree was desirable for imparting wisdom. So she took of its fruit and she ate. She also gave to her husband who was with her and he ate.
Then the eyes of both of them were opened and they knew that they were naked; so they sewed fig leaves together and made for themselves loin-coverings.
And they heard the sound of Adonai Elohim going to and fro in the garden in the wind of the day. So the man and his wife hid themselves from the presence of Adonai Elohim in the midst of the Tree of the garden.
Then Adonai Elohim called to the man and He said to him, "Where are you?"
Then he said, "Your sound—I heard it in the garden and I was afraid. Because I am naked, I hid myself."
Then He said, "Who told you that you are naked? Have you eaten from the Tree from which I commanded you not to eat?"
Then the man said, "The woman whom You gave to be with me—she gave me of the Tree, and I ate."
Adonai Elohim said to the woman, "What did you do?"
The woman said, "The serpent deceived me and I ate."
Adonai Elohim said to the serpent, "Because you did this, Cursed are you above all the livestock and above every animal of the field. On your belly will you go, and dust will you eat all the days of your life. I will put animosity between you and the woman— between

your seed and her seed. He will crush your head, and you will crush his heel."
To the woman He said, "I will greatly increase your pain from conception to labor. In pain will you give birth to children. Your desire will be toward your husband, yet he must rule over you."
Then to the man He said, "Because you listened to your wife's voice and ate of the tree which I commanded you, saying, 'You must not eat of it': Cursed is the ground because of you— with pain will you eat of it all the days of your life. Thorns and thistles will sprout for you. You will eat the plants of the field,
By the sweat of your brow will you eat food, until you return to the ground, since from it were you taken. For you are dust, and to dust will you return.
– Genesis 3:1-19 TLV

Lie 1: I won't die.

This lie is so critical, which is why I put it at number one. The definition of death itself is what hangs so many people up. Most of us find that either Webster's primary definition, "the end of life: the time when someone or something dies,"[35] or the medical definition, "permanent cessation of all vital bodily functions"[36] to be what we consider death. Like so many others, I read this story in Genesis and struggled with it. I had heard the argument, that it wasn't a physical death, it was a spiritual death, but the struggle within me never resolved. Something was missing. The first time I heard a challenge to the modern medical definition of death was at that Gateway men's conference I talked about in the introduction. It was there where I was challenged with the notion that the death found in Genesis is not just a spiritual death, nor is it only a physical death; it is both.

But Adam and Eve didn't stop existing, they didn't stop breathing, so many people would say that they only experienced a spiritual death. But, if death is the absence of Life and Life is both a physical state and spiritual state, then so is death. Think about what was going on in the Garden. They had access to all of the trees there. They walked in the cool of the morning with God, the Creator of life, Life Himself, and they were all connected; nothing separated their relationship. They had access to the Tree of Life. And they not only had access to it, the Bible never says there was a limit to how much of its fruit they could have. In the book of John, we hear that God has, *"come that they might have Life and have it abundantly."* If God is the same today, yesterday, and tomorrow then we can infer that Adam and Eve too could have had Life abundantly. They could have eaten the fruit from the Tree of Life as much as they wanted.

Most of us have heard that when Adam and Eve ate from the fruit was the moment when they experienced death. However,

I would argue that this death happened moments before the fruit was eaten. In verse 6 it says that,

> *...the woman saw [or believed] that the tree was good for food, and that it was a thing of lust for the eyes, and that the tree was desirable for imparting wisdom.*

Right before she took of the fruit, breaking the Law, breaking the commandment, something worse happened. She believed a lie: God's holding out on us. (We'll address this lie more in the next section.) She didn't randomly, accidentally eat from the wrong tree. A fruit from the *Tree of the Knowledge of Good and Evil* didn't fall from the tree, roll down a hill, and Eve just ate it not knowing what it was. She chose to believe the "death" that the deceiver was spewing out on her. Just as in my story about the first time I smoked, the exhilaration and excitement I felt separated me from what, and from who, I was created to be. I am sure her heart raced and her head spun as she crossed that line, accepting the lie as truth.

Most people at one point in time have or will struggle with God's judgment, how He could send people to hell, how He could break that lifeline between Adam and Eve, how He could allow evil to happen. It is okay to struggle with Him. The Bible is full of stories of God's chosen people struggling with Him. David, Jacob, Moses, and Jonah are merely a few, but in the end we have to come to a point where we realize that God's judgment is based on Truth,[i] not good and evil, right and wrong, or good and bad, only Truth. The way to understand His will and His principles is to seek Him, to trust Him, not leaning on our own understanding,[ii] but, instead, only on His. The Truth just *is*. Just like when we choose to separate ourselves from God, when Adam and Eve chose to break the one and only commandment, there were both physical and spiritual consequences: death.

---

i Romans 2:2
ii Proverbs 3:5-6

… Discovering the Lies About the Truth Beneath

Lie 2: God's holding out on me.

[Love! It's] overrated. Biochemically no different than eating large quantities of chocolate.
– John Milton, The Devil's Advocate[37]

This morning, while driving to a coffee shop to write, I felt bummed about something that happened last night. I'd flown in, late at night, from a week-long work trip where I had worked fourteen to sixteen-hour days. To top off the long week, long hours, and little sleep, when I showed up at the airport parking lot, low and behold in the spot where I left my large, black Nissan work van was a small, blue Volkswagen car. I immediately started calling and texting my superiors, waking them up as I thought we now had another van that had been stolen. (Three had been stolen in the past year.) When I finally got a hold of someone that knew what was going on, he told me that, while I was gone, they had picked the van up in order to have some repairs performed, forgot to inform me, and didn't have an opportunity to return it. But that's not what I was bummed out about.

    I am thankful that earlier as my plane taxied to the gate after landing, God gave me the idea to call my wife and wake up the kids, or at least the one that was sleeping. I asked her to get the kids up and meet me at the office, only ten minutes from the airport. In my mind, it served two purposes: I wouldn't have to drive the van home and I was able to see them all a little sooner. I say God prompted me to, because I had never thought about waking the kids on prior trips. I didn't want to mess with their sleep, but God knew I was going to need a ride home. So, when my van was not at the airport, it was not a horrible burden to have them drive over and pick me up.

    When my bride arrived, I gave her a hug and a kiss and got to hug and kiss my kiddos who were all sleepily snuggled with blankets in the back of our van. It was a nice night in Texas and on the drive home we left our windows open. My very adventurous, fun-loving daughter pinned part of her sheet to the back of my chair and lifted the edges closest to her. FUMP, the sheet caught the air and ballooned up like a dome in the back of the car. She and my son were both giggling and shouting out, "Daddy! Daddy! Look Daddy!" excited to share their experience with me. When I turned around, my response to such an awesome and fun experience for them was, "You need to roll up the window so the sheet doesn't get sucked out." Now while that is true, there is a chance, probably a good chance that her favorite pink sheet could get sucked out the window, what I did sucked all the fun out of that moment. Instead of laughing and giggling and sharing such an exciting time for them, I let my bad mood steal their joy in the moment. While driving to the coffee shop, this weighed heavy on my heart.

Even if the sheet had been sucked out the window, what would have been the worst thing that could've happened? A good story about the time she was having a blast making a dome out of her sheet and it flew out the window on a wind gust? I am sure that, had that happened, we could have simply pulled over and gone back to find it. But I wasn't in the mood for that; I didn't want to deal with the possibility of that inconvenience. The risk at that moment was too great for me to release my control and just have fun.

I justified my bad mood because of the van having been picked up without my knowledge, the thoughtlessness of my company not advising me, and simply feeling tired from such a long work week. And while those are valid reasons, that's not who I am. I am that same fun-loving, excitable, passionate type of person that my daughter is. I like to experiment even if there is a risk of damage.

So, as I drove to the coffee shop this morning, again, I felt bummed out. Like we do too often, I turned that frustration towards God. I felt like He was holding out on me. I felt resentment towards

Him, that He had stolen my fun away. That, for some reason, once I established a relationship with Him, becoming a follower of Christ, all of my adventurous and experimental traits had been tamed or disappeared. I asked God the typical "Why God?" question, with a twist: "God, why?" "God, why is it that I don't take risks anymore? Why is it that following You causes me to lose that part of me?" He showed me that I am simply growing up, that the fun I have now is different, no less fun, just different. I used to "feel alive" hanging off the side of a boulder, roller blading through dirt bike trails, flying over jumps and smacking into trees, flying down the highway in my Mazda RX-7 or on my Suzuki Katana at 140 miles per hour, dancing at clubs until the early hours of the morning, or even consuming substances that altered my state of mind.

 I know some of you may think I was crazy, maybe even just young and stupid, but others of you reading this know exactly where I am coming from. You were doing it too, but something has changed. Now I, and maybe you, feel alive and find joy sharing in new experiences with my family. While the fun and excitement is not as exhilarating, it is still fun and exciting; it's just different. While we are not at the place where I can take my kiddos to do some of the thrills I enjoyed growing up (obviously I will not introduce them to substance abuse or almost tripling the speed limit), God is showing me how I am helping them understand boundaries and limitations, as well as practice safety. Even when doing something stupid, dangerous, or risky, there are practices we can put in place to increase the chances of success and reduce the likelihood of injury or death. Having fun living life isn't about going all-out reckless, careless of the repercussions.

 God is not holding out on us simply because we are not blazing through life, ministry, our careers with our hair on fire. Sometimes we aren't ready for the next step. We are training or practicing; He is preparing us. Then there are those times when we simply aren't made for what we seek. Not everything that looks good, tastes good, sounds good, or feels good is good for us, or was it designed for us.

Satan told Eve that God was holding out on them, keeping Adam and her from enjoying that delicious fruit and from truly living. As if having the knowledge of good and evil was some sort of benefit. "It is not a benefit that we gained the knowledge of good and evil; it's a curse."[38]

While the fruit may have tasted sweet and delicious, the consequences were not worth it. We were not designed to contain that knowledge nor to rely on ourselves. We were designed to be connected to our Father, which is much sweeter than any fruit. When something seems out of place, or we feel lost or alone, we must not rely on our judgment or discernment, the knowledge of good and evil; we were designed to rely on our Father. Like Adam and Eve walked with their Father in the cool of the morning, we are designed to come to Him, to discuss our concerns with Him. He is okay with us having concerns, doubts, and questions. He is even okay with us having resentments as long as we bring them to Him to address.

Thinking back to the Garden, I like to imagine what it was like. One morning, a nagging question came up: Why did God put the tree there in the first place? I even started to wonder if God ate anything while He strolled through the Garden with Adam and Eve. What if the fruit of the knowledge of good and evil was there for Him to enjoy while Adam and Eve ate from the other trees? He didn't need to eat anything, but just imagine Jesus walking in the Garden, plucking fruit from the trees, enjoying all that He had created. Imagine Him, the Father, and the Holy Spirit having a picnic with Adam and Eve. God could partake of all the fruits, including the knowledge of good and evil, because He is capable of handling it. He, and only He, knows truly which is which, so consuming that fruit doesn't affect Him as it did us.

I also wonder how many trees there were, so many fruit-bearing trees that Adam and Eve had access to. They even had access to the Tree of Life, a fruit-bearing tree that actually had *Life* growing on it. Can you picture that? Remember that life is not a heart beating, nor a breathing lung, that might be a little gross hanging from a tree. It's a connection to the Creator of Life. I bet that fruit looked and tasted amazing. Sometimes I imagine it looking like a massive pluot, a hybrid of a plum and an apricot, spotted, with a delicate, smooth skin.

What I find to be amazing is that, in Genesis, we are told that Adam and Eve were allowed to, "freely eat the fruit of every tree in the Garden, except," of course, the one that they really needed, right? No, they are allowed to eat freely from all of the trees that are beneficial to them, all of the trees that they are designed to eat from. In John 10:10, when Jesus speaks about Himself being the Redeemer, Restorer, opposite of the death they had been experiencing, He says something that reflects what we are told in Genesis, "I have come that they may have Life and have it abundantly." (TLV) What does that word *abundantly* mean? In the original Greek, it is the word *perissos*,[39] which can also mean "exceeding abundantly above, more abundantly, advantage, exceedingly, very highly," or my favorite, "beyond measure."[40] We can have Life exceedingly, His Life, beyond measure. Adam and Eve could have had all the Life they could have stood to have and more, yet somehow, the accuser and deceiver made them believe that the knowledge of good and evil was somehow better, that God was somehow holding out on them.

There is a difference between wisdom and knowledge. Had Adam and Eve sought first the kingdom, sought the Father with whom they were so intimate, and asked Him for wisdom, I am sure He would have exposed the death-filled deceptions that the accuser was vomiting on them. I think this is why, when Solomon asked for a discerning or "understanding mind to govern...[His] people... [to] discern between good and evil... It pleased the Lord that Solomon had asked [for] this."[iii] Solomon asked God for His wisdom to discern what He saw happening between His people. Solomon did not lean on his own understanding, He trusted in the Lord. He asked for God's wisdom regarding governing and being the King of His people.

I think it will please the Lord if we do the same thing. No, we may not be kings over Israel, but we have our own dominions, or spheres of influence, He has placed us in. When we ask Him what He desires for us and His children around us, I think it pleases His heart. And as He sees that our heart's desire is aligning with His, for His children and not our own benefit, and that we can handle the additional responsibility and honor of more blessings, He pours them on.

> *It pleased the Lord that Solomon had asked this. And God said to him, "Because you have asked this, and have not asked for yourself long life or riches or the life of your enemies, but has asked for yourself understanding to discern what is right, behold, I now do according to your word. Behold, I give you a wise and discerning mind, so that none like you has been before you and none like you shall arise after you. I give you also what you have not asked, both riches and honor, so that no other king shall compare with you, all you days. And if you will walk in my ways, keeping my statutes and my commandments, as your father David walked, then I will lengthen your days.*
> *– 1 Kings 3:10-14*

His desire is for us to have a life beyond measure, free from comparison and expectations, free from our knowledge of a situation, reliant on His wisdom and discernment. It is as William P. Young, author of *The Shack*, describes: we are designed to live

---
iii   1 Kings 3:9-10

a life of expectancy rather than one of expectations. As Psalm 139 illustrates, God is everywhere. Therefore, everywhere we go, we can expect that He will show up in ways only He can. We can release the expectation that He will do what we expect Him to do. As we become un-blinded, unshackled, unbound, recognizing the liar for who he is and the lies for what they are, we can start to see the abundance of life He has truly given us. When we stop concentrating on the things we don't have, we start to see all that we do have, creating a thankful heart. God's not holding out on us. We can live with expectancy beyond measure.

Lie 3: I have the potential (and right) to be like (or equal to) God.

What does it mean to be like God? Many movies try to portray gods, but they are very limited, typically based on Greek mythology. To be the One, true God, having all power, possessing all knowledge, present everywhere simultaneously, spanning all time is much greater than our minds can even comprehend. That might be why Greek mythology and our stories and movies of god-like characters are so limited, having only one or two superpowers. We cannot imagine the totality of what omnipotence, omniscience, and omnipresence unlimited by time or space is truly like. Omnipresence alone is mind-boggling based on our concepts of time and space. It is not having the ability to travel through time or teleport through space, my wife's favorite superpower. Instead, it is being present in every space, in every moment, both in and outside of the measure of time.

Perhaps we like to think we can create our desired circumstance through sheer control. As a general populace, we certainly like to think we have the right and ability to answer to anything for everyone. And, though we elevate multitasking on a pedestal as the new normal for our lives, our ability to do more than one thing at once, much less be in more than one place simultaneously is simply beyond our capabilities. Try typing two emails with completely different contexts and emotions on two different devices simultaneously. Try running track in Australia while swimming across the Hudson. Or even simpler, try to talk to your spouse about important decisions while texting your boss about work. To have meaningful conversations, our attention must shift back and forth and, obviously, we are limited to one space and one time.

We were not made to be equal to God. We were made in

the image of God. An image is like a picture or snap shot. Think about the limitations of a snapshot, a two-dimensional glimpse of a subject, at a certain point in time, in a particular location. While an image does allow us to see certain parts of that subject, it also limits our perspective. Even with newer technology 360-degree cameras, there still exists a limitation on perspective and time. While it allows us to see more of the surroundings, we are still limited by the view from the lens. If a person faces us, then we cannot see their back. An easy way to think about how we are made is to consider those snap shots. There are certain traits that we, the image of God, will exhibit at any given time. At the same time, there is such a vast array of information we cannot tell people about through our representation of God. This is why, when people judge God based solely on what they see in people, it doesn't expose a flaw in God, it simply limits their view of Him.

For many years, I justified my atheistic belief based on the hypocrisy of Christians. I like how Robert Morris, Pastor of Gateway Church, argues how it is impossible for someone to be an atheist. He reasons that for someone to know with certainty that there is no God, it means they must have all knowledge that exists on that subject, resulting in their being omniscient. Pastor Morris continues to strengthen the point through a study that reveals how the smartest human is capable of obtaining only 1-2% of all knowledge available, making it impossible for someone to say with any certainty or surety that there is no God. Having lived as an atheist for many years, I agree with his statement. I can see now how much of God I missed out on due to my limited perspective. Knowing what I know now, I would say I was at best, like Pastor Robert points out, agnostic or oblivious to God. At worst, I was anti-Christ or anti-God. But, either way, I could never say that I was 100% positive that there was no God.

In June of 2002, I found out that I could, with all confidence and certainty, say that there is a God and that He sent His Son to be our Savior. That realization did not come because I gained all the knowledge in the world, but instead because I met Him. Or, I should say, He met me in a time and space that I needed Him most, when I cried out to Him, sitting on my bed, needing to know if He was there. That realization came partially as a result of the actions of one of His children, a coworker of mine, who acted out of a desire to be like God, but humbly understood that he was not equal to Him. You see, if we were made to be equal to God, we would not need a Savior; we could save ourselves or save others.

In Genesis, satan lies to Eve by telling her the reason she is not to eat from the Tree of the Knowledge is because she would become *"like God, knowing good and evil."* But are we really designed to know good and evil? Throughout the Bible, scriptures tell us not to judge, that we are not the judge, and that God gave that right to Jesus. So why would we want to know good and evil if we are not intended to judge?

It is almost inevitable that along with the knowledge of good and evil comes judgment. But without the knowledge of good and evil, what would we have? Love. Without our judgment of others, we would simply love them, regardless of who they are, what they look like, what they did, are doing, or might do in the future. We would simply love them. Isn't that what God does? Could that be what God created us to do? When we believe that we are someone's judge, we step out of our design and take on the role of the distributor of judgment. In reality, we were only supposed to eat of the Tree of Life, enabling us to see who He created, rather than who our judgment says people are.

There is no one like God. To this day, satan continues to play the "God's holding out on you" card, but God isn't holding out on us. He is simply giving us what we are capable of handling at any given moment. I find the book of Job to be an awesome resource for understanding how GREAT He is. In Job 38, God makes a point to Job, that He is God, and that Job is not. It's not a crushing argument to break Job's back and keep him in submission, but perhaps God was trying to break a lie Job believed.

> Then the Lord answered Job out of the whirlwind and said:
> "Who is this that darkens counsel by words without knowledge?
> Dress for action like a man; I will question you, and you make it known to me.
> Where were you when I laid the foundation of the earth?
> Tell me, if you have understanding.
> Who determined its measurements—surely you know!
> Or who stretched the line upon it?
> On what were its bases sunk, or who laid its cornerstone, when the morning stars sang together and all the sons of God shouted for joy?
> Or who shut in the sea with doors when it burst out from the womb, when I made clouds its garment and thick darkness its swaddling band, and prescribed limits for it and set bars and doors, and said, 'Thus far shall you come, and no farther, and here shall your proud waves be stayed'?
> Have you commanded the morning since your days began, and caused the dawn to know its place, that it might take hold of the skirts of the earth, and the wicked be shaken out of it?
> It is changed like clay under the seal, and its features stand out like a garment.
> From the wicked their light is withheld, and their uplifted arm is broken."

By the words in this passage you might get the idea that Job thinks he is God. And, although it looks like that is what God feels as well, notice that He doesn't smite Job. God doesn't just kill him off for doubting, or puffing himself up. He does, however, point out that He is God. It may seem sarcastic, but God is trying to expose Job's arrogance, that he believes he is all that and a bag of sheep clippings. (A common saying back then, I am sure.) God met Job where he was at, to expose a lie he had believed that allowed Job to believe that he and his problems were much larger and more important than God Himself. God is not holding out on us.

      This thought that God is holding out on us brings us full circle to the lie that we are equal to God, that we deserve or could even handle everything that He is and has. We feel that we need more than He gives, that we haven't received our fair share. But when Truth enters in to decimate this lie, this mentality, we can begin to see how we are mere images of God, not duplicates of God, but snapshots. We're given the holy responsibility of revealing Him, representing the portion of His Love He has given us to the world. What an honor and privilege. How beautiful it is to care like He cares, to love like He loves. How could we ask for anything more than that?

Lie 4: It is better to be my own source of knowledge rather than to rely on God.

*Better to reign in hell than serve in heaven, is that it?"
"Why not? I'm here on the ground with my nose in it since the whole thing began. I've nurtured every sensation man's been inspired to have. I care about what he wanted and never judged him. Why? Because I never rejected him. In spite of all his imperfections, I'm a fan of man! I'm a humanist. Maybe the last humanist.
– Kevin Lomax and John Milton, The Devil's Advocate*[41]

Back in Genesis 3:4, "the serpent said to the woman, 'You will not surely die. For God knows that when you eat of it your eyes will be opened, and you will be like God, knowing good and evil.'" We know that he, satan, was trying to make us believe that God is holding out on us, but it goes deeper.

The quote from the character John Milton, who portrays satan, exposes his intent and strategy: to deceive us into believing he actually cares for us, that he wants what's best for us. Through this conduit of false concern and care, he pours a lethal concoction of death, persuading humanity that knowing good and evil is somehow a benefit. He continually attempts to convince us that we are not only capable, but are designed to ascend above God, designed to be worshiped, capable of being our own source. He wants us to believe that by taking on the responsibility of being like God, something we were never intended to do, that we will receive our true power, our true inheritance. He implies in that one sentence that our God is holding out, keeping us from becoming something bigger, something better, and, when we are our own source, we no longer need God.

One major epidemic here in the United States, and throughout much of the developed world, is obesity. Food was designed by God to be fuel for our bodies, but in many ways it has become something else entirely. It has become our comfort, our source of pleasure, entertainment, and even identity based on what eating style or preference we have. Vegans, Vegetarians, Paleo People (who eat no dairy, bread, or sugar and only organic fruits, veggies, and meat), Pegans (Paleo Vegans), See Food eaters, who eat everything they see, and the list goes on. The WHO, World Health Organization, claims that, in 2016, 2.5 billion adults, 41 million children under the age of five, and 340 million children ages 5-18 are overweight and a substantial percentage of those are obese. As a supporting argument to how dangerous obesity is, they compared obesity to malnutrition (or being underweight) and found that more people die due to obesity than at the opposite end of the spectrum.[42] To "fix" the problem, we see all sorts of solutions, including fad diets, food pyramids, even some genuinely healthy active and nutritional living styles. But even the best activity plan or eating habit can have detractions. Vegans, who don't eat meat or dairy, can easily consume too many sugar-spiking carbs and hormone-modifying soy products. Carb-free diets tax the kidneys. Fat free diets often leave us lacking in the essential fats we actually need to function correctly.

    What about the diet in the Garden? We know there was a Tree of Life available to Adam and Eve. What other trees were there? I can only imagine the variety. There may be that apple tree so often pictured when describing the Tree of Death, maybe avocados, pears, plums, and peaches, oh the peaches. What if there was a tree of joy or peace? It would be fantastic to have all of the fruit of the Spirit just hanging on a tree. Revelation 22:2 gives us a beautiful picture of what could be exactly this:

> *On either side of the river, the tree of life with its twelve kinds of fruit, yielding its fruit each month. The leaves of the tree were for the healing of the nations.*

What detraction would there be to eating the fruit of the Spirit? How could eating Life not be perfect for us? I wonder what its chemical and nutritional makeup was. I am pretty sure that it was a low-glycemic, protein and nutrient-filled super-food. I bet health-minded people would practically crawl out of their skin to promote it. Foodies, people who enthusiastically enjoy food (on the verge of worshiping it), would be ecstatic about the taste. "It's the perfect blend of every flavor desired and the perfect essential nutrients to keep our bodies running at their ideal and peak performance for thousands of years. It provides 100% organic, non-GMO, gluten and leaven-free truth for our minds." However, while I believe the fruit in the Garden was designed to nourish our minds and bodies, I think our souls were created to feed off the time spent with God.

Unlike a common belief today, God did not simply create the universe, get the world spinning, and drop Adam and Eve off in the Garden, saying, "There you go; be fruitful and multiply. You've got it from here." While He *did* tell them to be fruitful, multiply, and take dominion over this place He gave them, God also walked with them, talking with them in the cool of the morning.[iv] He designed us to live in relationship with Him, to rely on Him, and to allow His essence to fill our souls the more time we spent with Him.

Instead, as if this knowledge of good and evil, or good and bad, somehow benefits us, we continue to eat it. Instead of walks in the cool of the morning, feeding our souls, being filled with Life through the fruit of its tree, we eat of the fruits of our labor. We work the ground and provide for ourselves based on the knowledge we now have.

Being our own source begs the question: what do we worship? Are we worshiping the created or the Creator? While driving home one morning after a workout, I heard an old song, that, back in the day, I'd grown tired of hearing the "far right" conservatives denounce as "satan's music." It reminded me a lot of

---

iv   Genesis 1:28

Mama Boucher, Bobby Boucher's mom, in the Adam Sandler movie, *Waterboy*. She referred to "foosball," school, and even Ben Franklin as the devil.

But isn't everything out there that we worship, other than God, satan's desire for us? Are those things of the devil or just our worship of them? The whole reason satan was cast out of heaven was because he wanted to take worship away from the only One who deserves it. It's not that we're necessarily worshiping satan, putting him on the altar, bowing to him, saying he is so great, or tattooing pentagrams on our foreheads. But our worship is misplaced when we worship what he wants us to worship, which is anything other than God. In the Garden, satan wanted us to know, in the same way that God knows, the difference between good and evil, because then we would be so concentrated on everything other than God that we would forget the character of God. By concentrating on everything else, we would forget that He is who we should actually be worshiping.

Even if we worship "good things" like the Bible, we are under the influence of satan's desire. The Bible is a culmination of God's words, works, and His desires for our lives, but it is not the Creator Himself. It is the inspired Word, meaning that it was spoken by the Holy Spirit for men to record. Think about that. Everything in existence is spoken out of the mouth of God. And that's how the Bible was created. The Bible says that, "from Him and through Him and to Him are all things."[v] In 2 Timothy 3:16, it very clearly states that all Scripture is, *"breathed out by God... profitable for teaching, for reproof, for correction, and for training in righteousness, that the man of God may be complete, equipped for every good work."* It is a tool to bring God's people into relationship with Him, to bring glory to Him, and to help guide His people in worshiping Him.

What it does not say is that Scripture itself is to be worshiped. If we hold the Bible up and take oaths to it or we bow

---

v   Romans 11:36

down to it, thinking that because it is a *word* of God that it *is* God, we risk becoming legalistic and losing all of the power the Creator actually possesses over our lives. When we embrace the ink and paper, the oh-so-familiar leather spine, or sewn-in-place marker instead of the One who spoke the words, wrote the words, inspired the words, created the words, created us and everything that we come in contact with, we are worshiping the created, not the Creator.

The knowledge we have gained from teachings and experiences pales in comparison to His wisdom. Earlier, I referred to a statistic Robert Morris uses when discussing the existence of atheists, that even the most intelligent human has gained and retained only 1-2% of all attainable knowledge. Think about that. I am not sure how statisticians even quantify the total amount of knowledge. Paraphrasing Donald Rumsfeld, "There are the known knowns, the known unknowns, and the unknown unknowns."[43] So, not only do we know there are things we don't know, but there is so much that we don't even know we could possibly know. But if there is 98-99% of knowledge still available to me through some other source, it would be wise to connect to that source. It makes sense that the Creator of everything would have that knowledge, information, and wisdom. We were never created to be our own source. He always intended and desired for us to be connected with Him.

Lie 5: There is shame in nakedness/vulnerability and I must hide in order to protect myself.

Wow, this is so important to grasp. Recently, in a conversation with another group leader at church, I realized how deeply this lie has penetrated the church, society, and humanity as a whole. We were discussing the idea of having a small group of people of all different ages, races, genders, and stages of life gather to support each other, to be transparent with their struggles, and to work through the struggles and successes together. I was taken aback when the church leader suggested that I be careful with that train of thought because, "Men won't talk about issues when women are in the room." He was suggesting that there is too much shame and embarrassment in our lives to overcome. That we, as people, have feelings too different to understand. That we, as people, somehow have never felt the same pain, shame, joy, love, passion, and weakness that every other created person, even of the opposite gender, has felt. The implied meaning was that people's vulnerabilities and weaknesses must be kept hidden. The lie that has transcended throughout culture is that we are to be "strong like bull"[44] and that admitting our need for help is simply an admission that we are weak or somehow less of a person than those around us.

    I would argue that needing help is part of the way we were designed. We were not created to be God; we were created to be dependent on Him who created us. We were created to be in relationship with others. Man was created to leave his mother and father and join with his perfectly opposite match, even before there was a mother and father. We were created to talk things through, to share our experiences, fears, and emotions with others.

    A stigma about seeking counseling has created a barrier

for so many people. It says that if you need counseling then you are broken or crazy. In the majority of cases, that is simply not true. Going for counseling is simply looking for help, guidance, assistance, or training to overcome difficulties or struggles we have come across. Basically, counseling is teaching on the backside of experience. As parents, we strive to teach our children how to handle circumstances before they happen so they understand, or at least have an idea about, what might come along with their experiences. But what about when we experience something we have not been trained to handle, or simply experience something that is overwhelming? Why do we find shame in that? Why is it that we are proud of our accomplishments, but shame overwhelms our shortcomings? My wife and I have taught our kids that it is okay to ask for help, but it is also important to ask others if it is okay to help them. One reason for this is that many people are bound by a thought that they must do everything themselves, otherwise they are a failure, they are incapable. But just like in lie #3 (that we are not to be God) we are not made to be or do *everything*. We are all parts of the body, right? If we are all designed to handle certain aspects of life, what if my design is to help you through difficulties, to come alongside you to strengthen you, to lift you up out of the muck and mire so that you can be the person God designed and desires you to be? That is what He has designed and desires for me to be.

  To do that, however, we must be transparent. We have to be vulnerable. In one discussion, my wife came to talk with me about sexual intimacy and how we had not been on the same page for months, if not years. We both came into our marriage having lost our virginity many years prior, but we strived to honor God by trying to keep our courtship and engagement pure. While physically we never had sex before marrying, there were times when we both failed to keep our minds pure. That being said, two to three weeks into our marriage, I hurt her. We had waited over two years to have sex and, once married, there was little to no holding back. Until that day arrived when I was exhausted from work and not in the mood. (Yes, that happens. Men, it is okay to not be in the mood. The stigma that we are simply walking penises just waiting to have sex is a lie. The stigma that we find our manhood in how much sex we have is a lie.) Back to my point. I hurt my wife by turning down sex, and for the next ten years satan bombarded her with thoughts and lies that she was a burden to me, that I did not want her. It was not an original lie; I am pretty sure it is simply the same lie that immobilizes so many people. The fear of rejection. The fear of being alone.

I use this example for multiple reasons. One is that it is transparent. I have heard statistics which commonly say that half of marriages end because of sexual issues. I am pretty sure that is not the case. The sexual "issues" are actually communication issues manifested in one of the most intimate acts humans can experience with each other. But to experience this intimate act the way it was designed and God desires it to be, there must be two things: the first is nakedness and the second is vulnerable communication. If, in the midst of sex, your partner just starts looking the other way with lack of emotion on their face, it could leave one reeling in doubt or confusion. Thoughts or feelings that could come from that range dramatically: they don't want to be there, they aren't enjoying that intimate time with you, they are thinking of someone else. Ouch. Without communication, you could miss out on the fact that they may not want to be there because of some horrible news they heard or that they are dealing with some other stress that is preventing them from being in the mood. I use sex as an example only because of how close and intimate it is.

Paul talks about sexual sin being one that affects your own self more than anything else. In the example above, what if it was simply that the tacos you ate at lunch left a lingering aroma that was hard for your partner to handle? Or your partner thought they heard a child in the hallway and was simply trying to concentrate for a moment to figure out if it would be appropriate to pause for a moment?

When you first read this as an example, what ran through your mind? Did it match the reasons just mentioned? Might it benefit you to ask, to be vulnerable in all of your weakness? It is not shameful to admit that we are hurt, it is simply realizing that we are emotional humans. We are not perfect, nor are those we are involved with. So there are going to be times when clarification needs to be made, but unless we are vulnerable, that gap cannot be spanned.

It is the same way with our Father and Creator. There are times when we feel as if He has taken His eyes off us, times we feel alone or awkward. You might even feel awkward that I am talking about sex as a parallel to having an intimate relationship with God. Sex is a physical, enjoyable act of bringing two people intimately close. No, we are not to desire sex with God; that is what the hedonists in Sodom and Gomorrah desired. But we are to desire such a great intimacy and vulnerability with Him that we can come to Him, bare and naked, physically, emotionally, and spiritually, to reestablish the relationship He first desired and created in the Garden.

Lie 6: God is a horrible judge.

For God did not send His Son into the world to condemn the world, but in order that the world might be saved through Him.
– Jesus

Judgment. We live in a world full of it, yet we long to be free from it. We are quick to judge, but hate the results of judgment, unless of course those results are in our favor. The artist, KB, summarizes it this way,

> They tell me not to judge,
> but they mean don't be offensive.
> If I judge you as cute,
> you call it wisdom.[45]

Previously, I referenced one of the most powerfully freeing books I have ever read, Dr. James B. Richards' book, *How to Stop the Pain*. It addresses the pain and bondage we experience, which result from our judgments of others, not the judgments from others' judgment of us. Others' judgment of us is their issue, but our fear of judgment will wreak havoc on us, causing pain and anguish in our lives.

As we have discussed, we were not created for judgment, nor are we created to judge. We were created for life-giving relationship, which can be and often is ruined by judgment. Instead of loving someone regardless of their faults, our treatment of people and our ability to receive affection from others is often dependent upon an opinion we have of them or their actions.

My father's primary love language is giving gifts. He finds deep satisfaction in giving gifts. I think it is partially because he grew up with very little and he doesn't want others to go without like he did. For a long time, I kept a running list in my heart of unforgivable offenses my dad had made against me. I held that list against him. I shared it with him one evening while we rode in the car with my brother. Well, I didn't share it, I unloaded it on him. The primary offense was that after my mom and dad divorced, he seemingly moved on without my brother and me. We only saw him every other weekend while his new wife and step-children could be with him all the time. It didn't seem fair and I made the judgment, right or wrong, that he loved us less than them.

Because my love language is quality time, it didn't matter how much stuff he bought us. I was hurt and my expectation of the time he should spend with me was not met. It came to a point where I resented the gifts he gave, and eventually I even told him from time to time not to give me anything. It felt to me that he, at times, was trying to buy our love which, I am sure, was like a slap in his face. He was simply trying to show me that he cared in the way he knew best, through gifts, and I was rejecting his love.

Shortly after my father and I restored our relationship, God revealed to me that my dad gives because he can and because he loves people, not in order to manipulate or control them. Sometimes his gifts come from left field and make no sense to those around him, like cutting up a king-size comforter to take to downtown Atlanta in the middle of winter. I used to think it was crazy and offensive that he would cut it into smaller pieces, but that again was my judgment keeping me from seeing his heart to help as many people as he could. I later realized it was not only to help as many people as he could, but also to lighten their load, while still giving them something to keep warm. Sometimes, it even seems to me that he is merely rummaging through his own unwanted stuff to get rid of, but I see now that he simply wants to give whatever he has to those he loves. That is how he gives of himself; that's how God made him.

Soon after my reconciliation with my dad came my reconciliation with the Father, not just my dad, but the Father of all fathers, our Creator. This was the Father that Jesus speaks of when He says, "no one comes to the Father, except through me."[vi] It was an awesome revelation when, shortly after that, I saw how my dad was showing me one aspect of our Father's Love. Gift giving. In John 3:16, one of the most commonly quoted scriptures, we see His desire to give gifts.

> *For God so loved the world, that He gave His only Son, that whoever believes in Him should not perish but have eternal life.*

Jesus is speaking about His Dad here. He was talking with Nicodemus about how to see the kingdom of God. Jesus goes on in verse seventeen to say what I opened the chapter with,

> *For God did not send His Son into the world to condemn the world, but in order that the world might be saved through Him.*

Like I realized about my dad, God also finds deep satisfaction in giving gifts. Gifts free from manipulation and judgment about whether we deserve them or not. He gives gifts because it is part of who He is and He desires to shower us with abundance. He is *all good*, not like the saying from the late 90's and early 2000's where people tried to cover their hurt or offense by pronouncing this platitude over the situation or their offender. He is truly ALL GOOD. And while He is all good, He also knows good and evil. He knew that He did not create us for the knowledge of it. He knew it would ruin our lives, usher in death, and sever an intimate bond with Him. That's why He told us not to eat from that tree. (Had Adam only come up with a catchy tune to keep Eve from the tree, we may be in a different situation. *Eve, Eve, Eve of the Garden, watch out for that tree.* Sung to the tune of "George of the Jungle," a cartoon originating in the late 1960's.) I digress.

When Adam and Eve chose to rely on themselves as the

---
vi   John 14:6

judges of good and evil, the fear of that same judgment from good and evil was introduced as well.

> **For with the judgment you pronounce you will be judged, and with the measure you use it will be measured to you.**[vii]

The world must have looked different right after the fruit was consumed. Adam and Eve suddenly knew that they were naked; they saw everything around them with a different set of eyes. They immediately saw imperfections in the area around them, whether they actually were imperfect or their limited minds merely tried to grip and grasp for an understanding of this new reality, they could not tell the difference. The fields, viewed as perfect just moments before, may have suddenly seemed full of grass that was now too tall, needed to be mowed, or was not the exact shade of green they preferred. The wind that blew through their hair and across their bodies to keep them cool and refreshed, may have swiftly become an annoyance, as it tangled Eve's hair. As they looked at each other, I wonder if it was at that moment when the world first heard, "Do I look fat in this?"

I am not sure how drastically it affected them as they looked at each other, but something had definitely shifted. When they heard God coming, Adam and Eve hid from Him out of fear. They were naked and afraid, but afraid of what? I believe they were afraid, not because being naked is good or bad, but instead simply they suddenly had the ability to know the difference. They were no longer tethered to the love and wisdom of their Father. The ability to judge things on their own created a fear of being judged. They could see imperfections, which meant so could God. The difference is that God's Love loves despite our imperfections. But once Adam and Eve were separated from God, autonomous and self-sufficient (or they thought they would be), their love became dependent on a measure of perfection.

---
vii Matthew 7:2

> *For with the judgment you pronounce you will be judged, and with the measure you use it will be measured to you.*[viii]

Judgment is defined as forming an opinion, estimate, notion, or conclusion based on circumstances presented to the mind.[46] So as we perceive things, we make judgments about them. As we receive information, we create opinions. Everyone has opinions, right? Everyone has made judgments, many of which are made prior to coming to an understanding of who someone is or was created to be. Those are called prejudices, assumptions made about someone or something which are based either on your experience with something similar or your lack of prior knowledge about them. Too often we think our prior experiences dictate our impending future when, in fact, those pre-judgments many times become self-fulfilling prophecies. Racism is evil; it is a lie that a select few have believed to be true about ALL people of a certain color. It is no different than the lies that ALL Muslims are evil, ALL gay people are trying to ruin the world we live in, ALL Christians are hypocrites, or ALL Buddhists are calm, loving, and peaceful. Racism and any other intolerance is simply an extreme level of prejudice, or pre-judgment, of ALL members of a certain group of people, a belief that each person in a given group will be the same.

I do want to say that it is okay to have a preference. I used to say that I like my woman to be like my coffee, creamer white. That is not saying that anyone darker than creamer is bad in any way; that is simply my preference. And being that I am going to be married to this woman for the rest of my life, I would like to be pleased with her appearance. Needless to say, my wife's complexion is creamer white with a few thousand speckles of melanin, and I am very pleased with looking at her every day.

We were all created uniquely in the image of God, whether we wear that image openly or have chosen to hide it under a cloak

---

[viii] Matthew 7:2

of lies, we all still bear His image in a unique way. He created us that way: unique. So, if we are all unique, how can ALL people within a particular category be the same? The answer is easy: we can't. We simply aren't the same. And we were never designed to handle or carry the load associated with judgment anyway, which is why we do so horribly at it. Judgment continues to poison us from the inside with the knowledge of good and evil every time we partake in it.

We were designed to be in relationship with our Creator. His image (which is *not* the stereotypical picture of a white-bearded, old man) is in us. If you consider the diversity of humanity, you will see shades and attributes of not only the Father, but also of the Son and the Spirit. It's beautiful how the movie, *The Shack,* portrays God, the Father, as an African-American woman for the majority of the story and a Native American male at the end. Beautiful, because we are able to encounter deeper attributes, not merely of skin color and gender, but of personality and His heart as well.

God is one-in-three and three-in-one. Written on our hearts, the Son is our Savior. Without Him we will never see the kingdom of heaven; without Him we will not come to know the Father. Our knowledge of good and evil brings us to a likely and twisted conclusion: that God is a horrible judge. After all, if He cherishes us all so much, why doesn't He let us see Him clearly? This is where the lie begins.

The judgment so many people make about His statements like we find in John 3:3, "Truly, Truly, I say to you, unless one is born again he cannot see the kingdom of God," is that not everyone can be born again. As we have seen in some of the previous lies, we often conclude that either He's holding out on us, we're too dirty, or He simply is a horrible Judge.

It is specifically for those who think that God is a horrible, unfair judge, that God reveals Himself to be fair and just. He allows the relativist, the skeptic, and the person who was never presented with the Gospel to be his own judge.

> *For all who have sinned outside of Torah will also perish outside of Torah, and all who have sinned according to Torah will be judged by Torah. For it is not the hearers of Torah who are righteous before God; rather, it is the doers of Torah who will be justified. For when Gentiles, who do not have the Torah, do by nature the things of the Torah, they are a law to themselves even though they do not have the Torah.*[ix]

Those who have never heard the Torah (the Word of God given to Moses) are not held to the same exacting standards as those who have. While the standard of perfection is the same, those who have never heard the Torah have a different perception of perfection. They will be judged as they have judged. They are judged by their own conscience, which is not their own knowledge or interpretation of good and evil, but instead is an inner gift from God, a deposit of His wisdom and guidance imparted through the Holy Spirit and their willingness to receive it. A conscience guided by the Holy Spirit can be rooted in and transformed by Life. The Holy Spirit talks to everyone who will listen, guiding their beliefs, transforming their heart in order to bring them into relationship or deeper with God. Some will say otherwise and place God in their little box, limiting in their minds what He can and cannot do based on a limited understanding of who and how powerful God really is. This belief limits them to the knowledge of good and evil and is rooted in death.

Our judgments made against God and each other eventually come back on ourselves. In Jesus' statement, "Truly, Truly, I say to you, unless one is born again he cannot see the kingdom of God," from John 3:3, Jesus is talking with Nicodemus, a Pharisee and Jewish leader. After that statement, Nicodemus, like many of us,

---

[ix] Romans 2:12

was wrestling with Jesus' mind-bending reality that we must be born again to see the kingdom of heaven. Nicodemus was thinking literally and was baffled as to how he is to, "enter a second time into his mother's womb and be born,"[x] a second time. He must have felt pretty hopeless, or he might possibly have felt like Jesus' requirement was ridiculous, insatiable, and unfair. Nicodemus, in his older age, had likely seen many of his friends die, seen those closest to him dedicate their lives to God. Then Jesus, revealing Himself as God, seems to say it was all for nothing because a person could not satisfy this requirement to reenter their mother's womb.

I've struggled with the question that if it was just as simple for Jesus to come and people to believe in Him, then why did He not do that generations before so that all of those people who had suffered, all of those who had tried to earn their way to Him through their works, would have come to know Him so much sooner? Why did He even kick Adam and Eve out rather than just forgive them on the spot? If they were his children, made in His image, how could He sit and watch His kids destroy themselves for thousands of years? How could He let evil reign? If He was a just Judge, how could He? Much like the third servant in the parable of the minas from Luke 19, I wasn't a good judge of God's character.

> He said to him, "I will condemn you with your own words, you wicked servant! You knew that I was a severe man, taking what I did not deposit and reaping what I did not sow? Why then did you not put my money in the bank, and at my coming I might have collected it with interest?"

That word *severe*, in the original is *austeros*, meaning grim, strict, or exacting.[47] It is where we get the word *austere* from, meaning "uncompromising."[48] Prior to knowing Christ as my Savior, if I had truly believed Him to be so uncaring, yet powerful, why did I

---
[x] John 3:4

not fear Him, like those who live beneath a dictator? If I had known Him to be a severe, uncompromising person, why would I not want to simply do as He said to please Him so I could be left alone?

> *For with the judgment you pronounce you will be judged, and with the measure you use it will be measured to you.*

Those judgments were exactly what kept *me* from coming to *Him*. What kept me from my Savior weren't *His* judgments, but *my* judgments. Had I not pushed those judgments aside, trusted Him regardless of my understanding of them, been born again, and surrendered my will to my Savior, those judgments would have been my measuring stick. On the day of my judgment, if I still lived in bondage to that measuring stick, those judgments would be used against me, to judge me, not out of His horrible judgment of me or my character, but instead from my horrible judgment of His perfect Truth. While there are laws throughout much of the Bible, Isaiah 33:22 gives great insight into the dynamics of those laws:

> *For the Lord is our Judge; the Lord is our lawgiver, the Lord is our king, He will save us.*

He is not a horrible Judge out to stick us with the repercussions of our failures and actions. He gave us those laws, again, not to just give laws to judge us by, but because we are His people. We are His children, He is our King, not so that He can rule over us, but instead so that He can save us.

The Bible in its entirety shows us the love God has for us, His children. John Mark McMillan's song, "How He Loves," covered by David Crowder Band, paints a stunning picture of this revelation. I suggest listening to this song if you can, but if you can't, here's the opening verse and chorus:

> *He is jealous for me,*
> *Love's like a hurricane, I am a tree,*

*Bending beneath the weight of His wind
and mercy.
When all of a sudden,
I am aware of these afflictions eclipsed by glory,
And I realize just how beautiful You are,
And how great Your affections are for me.*

*And, oh, how He loves us, oh,
Oh, how He loves us,
How HE LOVES US ALL.*[49]

If we do not know Him, Jesus, as our Savior and Lord we will not be able to know the Father, receive the Holy Spirit, or feel His tenderness and affections for us.

God is not a horrible Judge. He speaks Truth. He speaks reality. But, too often, when He speaks and we try to interpret His words as law, attempting to make sense of His reality within our own limited capability, we fall so short of understanding how superb He is. We try to make rules conform our lives to His reality when He simply wants us to come to Him to show us how that is to happen.

I wonder if the Ten Commandments would have ever been written had the Israelites simply approached God, listened for Him, sought His words. I wonder whether the Bible would have even been needed had the fruit never been eaten, had we stayed in communion with Him from the beginning. I wonder what our view of Jesus would be today if He had not had to die on the cross for us. I think our view of God would be drastically different; simply the perfect image of Love.

Lie 7: It's not my fault.

Chewbacca and Princess Leia glared at Lando as the hyper drive failed. Lando responded, "They told me they fixed. I trusted them to fix it. It's not my fault!"
– Lando Calrissian, The Empire Strikes Back[50]

As a child, this would have been my most-used defense, second only to, "It wasn't me!" Both statements are very similar in that they are made in an attempt to avoid taking responsibility for our actions, placing them instead on someone else. As child, I watched *Star Wars: The Empire Strikes Back* more than eighty times. One character, a swindler named Lando Calrissian, through his statement above, affirmed that it is okay to blame other people. Although he was just a character in a movie, he was still a grown man presenting a belief to my impressionable, young mind.

Can I blame the writers and producers of Star Wars for my desire to not take responsibility for my own actions? Well, that would not be taking responsibility for my own actions, wouldn't it? But what about the values we are taught as kids? If we are taught ways to approach situations and we are supposed to submit to the authority over us, doesn't that mean we should do as we are taught and told? Maybe, but that doesn't mean we will not be held responsible for those actions. We still must take responsibility for them.

Children of Christians are often taught while growing up that blaming others is the way to explain our deficiencies. But it's not worded like that most of the time. Instead the lie is subtler and is usually phrased, "We sin because we were born into a sinful world, which began when Adam and Eve ate the fruit of the Knowledge of Good and Evil." Therefore, we believe lies such as, "It's not my fault," "I was born this way because Adam and Eve sinned," and "I live as a fallen person in a fallen world." Statements like these make it sound as if we are okay with being stuck and we are good with it being what it is. In the Garden, we see this blame game playing out as well; Adam and Eve, unfortunately, did not set a good precedent of blaming themselves rather than others. Instead, they had just eaten the fruit, hidden, and covered themselves with fig leaves because they were afraid, when God asked them, *"Who told you that you were naked?"*[xi] Their response, *"She made me do it,"* *"He made me do it."* Adam blamed both Eve, for giving him the fruit, and God, for giving him the woman in the first place. Eve then blamed the serpent for deceiving her.

The subtlety of what lies beneath is that those statements are, for the most part, fact. The serpent *did* present a very convincing argument to Adam and Eve which deceived them into eating the fruit. God *did* give Adam "the woman" so he would not be lonely, and she *did* give him the fruit to eat. Remember that facts are not always truth. The truth here is found in the part that they left out, the lie of omission. The reality was that they chose to believe the serpent over God's Word. Adam chose to stand by and let his bride, his woman, the woman God gave him, listen to the serpent's lies and even let her eat of the fruit. He then chose to go off the deep end with her and eat it too, just because she gave it to him.

Blaming others protects us from feeling that we are responsible, but it also prevents us from taking responsibility. It makes us the victim and condemns us to bondage. Andy Mineo's song, "Vendetta," identifies the real problem:

> *You wanna know the real problem in America? Always has been and always will be, me.*
> *If you had any other answer*
> *you've been deceived.*

We cannot gain freedom and forgiveness from the mistakes we make if we don't think we make them, if we blame others for

---
xi   Genesis 3:11

what we are responsible for, or if we never confess that we have made them. When we refuse to confess, or simply openly and verbally agree that we have made a mistake, we have judged that our failures are bigger than God's forgiveness. They are bigger than the love He or those around us have for us.

There is a common statement in our house, "Mistakes are okay and expected; lying about them is not." I mentioned before that I wonder what would have happened had Adam and Eve confessed to God that they had eaten of the forbidden fruit. I wonder what would have happened if they had come running to God afterwards instead of hiding, if they had admitted making a horrible mistake, a detrimental choice by believing the serpent's lies, owning up to that horrible decision. Most of us have been programmed to blame satan; much of this book even points to him as the father of lies and the originator of many of our problems. But it really comes down to us making the choice to believe what he is saying. We must take ownership of our own choices and mistakes. God tells us in His Word that we are to take every thought captive.[xii] We are not in control of what enters our mind, but we are in control of what stays there, what is allowed to burrow in and make its home.

The artist NF's song, "Mansion," speaks powerfully to this topic. Verse three illustrates where so many of us find ourselves:

I'm trapped here,
God keeps saying I'm not locked in
I chose this,
I am lost in my own conscience
I know that shuttin' the world out
ain't solvin' the problem
But I didn't build this house
because I thought it would solve 'em
I built it because I thought it was safer in there

[xii] 2 Corinthians 10:5

> *But it's not, I'm not the only thing that's livin' in here*
> *Fear came to my house years ago,* **I let him in**
> *Maybe that's the problem,*
> *'cause I've been dealing with this ever since*
> *I thought that he would leave,*
> *but it's obvious he never did*
> *He must have picked the room*
> *and got comfortable and settled in*
> *Now I'm in the position*
> *it's either sit here and* **let him win**
> *Or put him back outside*
> *where he came from, but I never can*
> *'Cause in order to do that*
> ***I'd have to open the doors***
> *Is that me or the fear talking?*
> ***I don't know any more.*** *– (Emphasis added)*

It is our choice how we are going to handle what comes in our mind. If we are going to entertain it and give it a room to sleep in, then how long is it welcome there and what we are going to do if it stays past its welcome? While it is our choice, it is through God's power, wisdom, and love that we get to see the resulting reality of our choices.

In our house, we try to be diligent, being quick to identify when we are believing lies of the enemy. This is not always easy and can cause some hurt feelings. But those hurt feelings are often another symptom of the greater issue, the lie beneath, that somehow the person *exposing* a lie is at fault for making the person *believe* the lie. Many times, when we do not realize we have believed a lie, we are too quick to defend it and not fast enough to step back and examine it. In reality, the reason we feel bad is the misalignment with God's vision and desire for us.

At times, we confront each other about lies we have seen embraced. These conversations are not guilt trip sessions. Nor are they a platform for blaming our emotions and feelings on another's actions and choices. When we blame others for our own choices and emotions, it becomes a difficult cycle to escape because we are stepping into the very trap we've laid. I still struggle with this from time to time. We truly have to seek God for His wisdom, His guidance, and His protection as we dive deep into this spiritual war. It is a spiritual war we wage; it is not against the flesh. It's not a war against evil, it's a war against Good and Evil, at least our knowledge of it anyway.

War is uncomfortable. And having someone point out that a belief, especially anything dear to your heart, may actually be a lie doesn't make it easier. But we need to be open-hearted enough to receive it, go to God about it, own up to it, and then give it to Him. That is the way it was designed to be. We are not created to bear the burden and weight of our shortcomings and failures. We are to take on the burden of His yoke, which is light and easy.

In a recent conversation, a friend asked me how we, as broken people living in broken families, should handle our family issues. Our cousins, brothers, sisters, mothers, fathers, children, in-laws, and exes, as well as all of the drama that comes along with them, can be overwhelming if we let it. And that is the point, if WE LET IT. Before I knew it, I answered his question with a question, "Well, that depends on how stuck you want to stay." I surprised myself with the answer and knew that it was something God wanted to talk about.

This isn't some Jedi mind trick, waving off worry, concern, or even decades of offenses. It is, however, an incredibly simple, yet challenging answer. You handle those people and situations with love. We are to love our neighbor. This is not an emotional or sexual feeling, but rather, a heavenly, affectionate love. After all, God *is* Love. This becomes simple when we seek Him for how He sees everything and everyone around us. Again, in the movie, *The Shack,* it was remarkable how our heavenly Father was portrayed,

Discovering the Lies About the Truth Beneath

by Octavia Spencer as *Papa*, in such an awe-inspiring light. Papa would simply start praising people whom Mack (Sam Worthington) thought would be exceedingly far from Him. But we are all His children and, even if we choose to walk away from Him, His love for us never wains. It is our choice, our responsibility, our duty, our honor, and can and should be our pleasure to be a part of His Life.

We have an awe-inspiring Creator and we have been made in such magnificent ways, many of which we do not understand fully. He gave us safety mechanisms to survive trauma and pain. Much like traditional war, those defenses should not be taken down until the threat is gone. This may be why, in Ephesians 6, when Paul describes putting on the armor of God, he says that we are to, "*stand firm...[and] above all take up the shield of faith with which you will be able to extinguish all the flaming arrows of the evil one.*"[xiii] We are to stand firm in our faith, not in ourselves or in our ability to make it through. A few verses earlier, in verse 10, we are encouraged to, "*be strong in the Lord and in* **His** *mighty power.*"

If you have been a victim of trauma or are experiencing continual horrific acts, please know it is not your fault. Those incidents occurred because the same enemy that is out to steal, kill, and destroy you is also out to steal, kill, and destroy the person who is doing those things to you. I am not making excuses for their actions. I simply hope to cast light on a dark area for both you and them.

We should not take responsibility for other people's thoughts, actions, or emotions. Their actions are not your fault. Taking on the burden of others is not the intent of this section of the book. We are responsible and accountable for our own actions. We are to take captive our own thoughts. And we will experience our own emotions. Our enemy wants to trap us in lies based on the lies others have believed so that it becomes a web, sticky and

---

[xiii] Ephesians 6:16

difficult to escape. But remember, "The wicked one is trapped in the work of his own hands."[xiv] We can be set free from that web.

There is hope for freedom and restoration through our Savior and Redeemer. He knows what you have been through and He knows the defense mechanisms He armed you with to cope with trauma. Like a fortress, He has created you with layers of walls and protection. It is possible to keep up the outer wall while you lower your defenses to Him. He wants to heal your wounds and protect you more than you know, but He won't force Himself on you. It must be your choice to let Him in. When you are ready to come out from behind the inner walls, or even simply your chamber door, He will be waiting with arms wide open ready to lift that burden. Christ says in Luke 4 that,

> the Spirit of the Lord is upon me, because he has anointed me to proclaim good news to the poor. He has sent me to proclaim liberty to the captives and recovering of sight to the blind, to set at liberty those who are oppressed, to proclaim the year of the Lord's favor.

My hope is that all people come to know the intimate, fervent passion of our Savior, that both victim and offender are saved from our enemy, and that we can all celebrate and proclaim how great His favor is. When we choose to have Him standing in front of us as our shield, we will do more than strive to survive; we will thrive.

[xiv] Psalms 9:17b TLV

Discovering the Lies About the Truth Beneath

Gentleness is not weakness. Self-Control is not self-condemnation. Peace is not passive. Patience is not sloth-like. Joy is not just feeling happy. Kindness is not merely acting kind. Goodness is not being perfect. Love is not lust. Faithfulness is truly rewarding.

Steven Cohen

11
Lies Upon Lies

God revealed to me the quote above as I prepared to teach a class called *Hearing God* at Gateway Church in 2015. This impressed on my heart that there is an ongoing attack on the gifts of the Spirit. Our enemy seeks to redefine those gifts and what they look like. These attacks neither limited to only the gifts of the Spirit nor to the seven lies found in Genesis 3 which we looked at in the previous chapter. In addition to those seven foundational lies spoken in Genesis, in the coming sections I will address seven additional lies many of us face. Although I cannot address every lie in our lives, I hope that through these examples the bondage of these lies loosens, if it is not completely stripped off of you, allowing you to continue to see what lies beneath the struggles you encounter while also seeking God's design and desire.

Lie 8: I have to clean up before I can show up.

> *You're hopeless, you Pharisees! Frauds! ...Just like unmarked graves: People walk over that nice, grassy surface, never suspecting the rot and corruption that is six feet under.*
> – Jesus, Luke 11:43-44 (The Message)

The lie that we must be righteous and clean before we can have a relationship with God is one of the most commonly held beliefs I have heard during my time in ministry. It's not limited to only the initial meet-and-greet with God, but also the daily walk with Him. Many people feel that they need to iron out their issues in order to have a solid relationship with God. They can't be angry with Him, they can't be upset, they can't have sins they still struggle with.

This lie is one of a few that, thankfully, I didn't believe before I began an intimate relationship with Jesus, surrendering to Him as my Savior. Although I didn't believe it, many people do and, tragically, it prevents them from experiencing God's heart, His forgiveness, and salvation. However, just because I didn't believe it before coming into a relationship doesn't mean this lie hasn't been used on me. Many times, I have chosen to believe that, somehow, I can clean myself, prepare myself, create a righteous version of myself by covering my imperfections to impress my Heavenly Father.

This is the same Father who watched His Son die a painful, torturous death. This is the same Son whose Father sent Him to conquer the lies we believe. This is the same death that allows salvation not to be dependent on us, but instead only by grace and faith in the power of the death, burial, and resurrection of Christ.

This is the same lie that says we don't need God, that, somehow, it makes sense to place the requirement of an unattainable righteousness on us, the unrighteous. One ridiculously funny and gross example would be when an infant has, what we call in our house, a blowout. The combination of urine and diarrhea is just too much for their diaper, really for any diaper. The result? Nastiness all over place, seeping out the sides of the diaper, down their legs, up the back, and occasionally up the front of their shirt, and sometimes even making it up to their hair.

That's us. Every day, sometimes many times a day, we have blowouts. And, as loving parents, though we may not enjoy the mess, we still clean it up, rejoicing at our clean baby, lavishing praise on them. But the love didn't stop when they were covered in poo. We, like God, see beyond the mess, knowing that our baby is under all that nasty. That's how God sees us. He knows what's under our mess, and He is just waiting to lovingly clean us up and pour lavish affection on us. How ridiculous would it be to assume that an infant could change himself after something like that?

The heart behind the deception is, likely, that if we must be righteous and clean before coming to know God personally and that we are capable of cleaning ourselves up, then why do we need to know Him? His death means that He is the only one with power over the death we consume and power to restore Truth, Life, and Love in our lives.

This deception doesn't simply stop the day we come to know Him for ourselves. I have, many times, tried to impress God with my efforts at school, at work, at church, and even at play. And, while I am sure He sees the heart, I am also pretty sure He's not jeering me on from the sideline, saying, "You almost made it; try harder. You're not good enough. Once you get it right, then let's talk." Instead, I believe He is cheering us on, saying, "Nice try, son. Come with Me and let's do it together. I'll take care of the stuff you weren't designed for." The moment we each believed in Jesus as our Savior, His grace came into us and we changed. If the greatest change came about because we simply believed, why not continue in that same belief? Or, as Paul said in Galatians 3:3, 'Are ye so foolish? Having begun in the Spirit, are ye now made perfect by the flesh?"51

In a timely message "#Struggles-Following Jesus in a Selfie-Centered World," Craig Groeschel, of Life Church in Oklahoma City, talks about how we have found ourselves in a "filtered world," presenting a "filtered version" of us, communicating a filtered or "controlled message" which prevents us from experiencing true, biblical relationships. Adam and Eve experienced something vastly different. As we've discussed, they found themselves naked and afraid, but, remember, that moment occurred not too long after having been made from the dust of the ground and from the rib of man. Because of sin, fear seeped in soon after Adam and Eve's walk in the cool of the morning with their lovingly pure and righteous Creator. Have you ever thought about what was said during those strolls? Likely, I have not given it enough thought, but those conversations probably weren't much like our prayers today. They may have included sports and weather, like the cheetah races and the elephant power lifts or how it was always a perfect, sunny 78 degrees. I imagine that every one of the conversations included God telling Adam and Eve how much He enjoyed their company, how important they were to Him, filling them with Truth, Love, and Life. So, after having experienced an authentically pure and perfect relationship with their Creator, with their fall into self-reliance, they received the knowledge of good and evil and suddenly felt that they had to "filter" their presentation to the God who created every intricate and intimate part of their bodies.

This lie doesn't only apply to our relationships with God, however. How many times have you shown up to a meeting or a first date in your comfortable jeans? My wife hates, not just strongly dislikes, but hates, my comfortable shorts. It's probably because only a small percentage of the remaining threads barely hold them together and don't hide much. You can see parts of my pockets. Nothing indecent shows through, but it's still something I would not wear to work or church. I have worn them to the car parts store and to the local DIY warehouse. So, what's the difference? Why is it that I feel comfortable wearing my own skin in those locations? Is it because of the commonality my threadbare shorts share with those environments and the people in them? Everything is dirty and informal, so it's okay to dress like that. But if we think about it, isn't that what God is asking of us? He wants "our weary and downtrodden."[i] He wants us to be raw and, as we just discussed, vulnerable. He doesn't want our best efforts. He wants our belief and trust in Him that He will make the changes in our lives, our circumstances, our hearts, and even our wardrobes that He sees fit, when He sees fit.

> *What this world needs is a Savior who will rescue,*
> *A Spirit who will lead,*
> *A Father who will love them in their time of need,*
> *A Savior who will rescue,*
> *A Spirit who will lead,*
> *A Father who will love,*
> *That's what this world needs.*
>
> *What this world needs is for us to care more about the inside than the outside.*
> *Have we become so blind that we can't see?*
> *God's gotta change...[our] heart before He can change... [our] shirt*[52].

    In what ways have you been trying to impress God? Is it through your appearance, behavior, service, education, church attendance, or giving? Many people feel unworthy, and in reality we are. But that simply reveals how exquisite our Father is. We as a church have failed to squash this mindset of unworthiness. Although we say the words, "Come as you are," the stigma of Sunday dress has made many of us think that we must impress God with our appearance and works in order for Him to approve.

---
[i] Matthew 11:28-30

We behave as if the Creator of the universe is somehow impressed or in awe of how well we match or how shiny our shoes are. He created the sun, the stars, the universe, the very molecules that make up our clothes. He created the physics behind how our eyes perceive color. He created the light that bounces off threads woven together which allows our eyes to interpret what we see. He created the designers who tell us what current trends are. He is not impressed with our efforts, but is impressed with us, regardless of whether we are having a good day or are in the midst of a blowout. He is impressed with us because **He** made *us*. There is nothing we can do to change that. He loves us.

Lie 9: I am stuck in the past.

The children now love luxury; they have bad manners, contempt for authority; they show disrespect for elders and love chatter in place for exercise. Children are now tyrants, not the servants of their households. They no longer rise when elders enter the room. They contradict their parents, chatter before company, gobble up dainties at the table, cross their legs, and tyrannize their teachers.
– Commonly Accredited to Socrates via Plato

Every generation has been witness to truly horrific acts and catastrophes. When I was young, these included Mount Saint Helen's eruption and the Oklahoma City bombing. More recently, we have seen tragic hurricanes in the Gulf of Mexico and Caribbean Sea and horrible hate crimes both involving and targeting law enforcement across the United States. While natural disasters seem to unite our country with a common cause, hate crimes seem to unite our divisions, greatly polarizing our opinions. Social media typically explodes with divisive rhetoric. This polarized perspective is not limited to one biased media outlet or another; it also comes from some people you would least expect.

The early part of the 2010's was a painful time in our nation as many law enforcement officers, for whatever reasons, exerted lethal force in many questionable situations, primarily on our brothers and sisters of color. As a result, many people understandably experienced an astounding amount of pain and uncertainty regarding the safety of their own and their family's lives. Some individuals and groups even took to the streets with action and retaliated. I am not debating the motives or mindsets in this space and I do understand that this may strike a nerve in many people who reading. But please understand that my intent is for us to hear God on all topics, especially the sensitive ones, the ones that hurt most, as those often are the ones that get us stuck most.

The entire situation was an attack on freedom, liberty, and the sanctity of life, all life, the very threads our society were founded on. Those who serve to protect it were also under attack. As stated earlier, prejudices and stereotypes caused an astounding amount of pain. People had only the information provided by the media, which often was based on limited information, leading them to judge the actions of others. This judgment ran rampant without waiting for, seeking, or desiring the facts of the matter from either side. The worst part was that many of our beloved friends and family felt as if they were not loved or, even worse, that they were hated or being judged simply by the pigment of their skin or by their occupation.

Now, I am not going to pretend ignorance of the problem of racism, but I will not subscribe to the notion that any complete race is racist, that in itself is a prejudgment placed on millions of people I do not know. I challenge you right now to imagine a race of people who are racist. If a group of people came to mind, then that is a prejudgment, a prejudice in your heart. There are a select few who are truly racist, who have believed lies, and bear an intense hatred and judgment about others based on their differences. Racism is a problem, but it is not our only problem by any means. It is also not a problem limited to only Caucasians and African Americans as it is commonly portrayed in mainstream media. There is not a single ethnic group on this earth that has been immune to racism.

One of the points I tried to make with one of my friends (let's call him Phil) during that volatile time was simply that the issue at hand was not simply a black/white thing. I was trying to convey that I believed it was a Truth thing. I attempted to make the point that (tell me if you have heard this yet) when we seek God's Truth in situations like the one our nation was in, His Love for His children around us gives us both a different perspective. We then gain freedom from the lies the accuser has attempted to spin.

The conversation didn't go well, for a few reasons. Part of the failure was because it took place on social media where tone, inflection, and facial expressions could not be received. It also failed because of my friend's hurt, pain, and his perception that I was not sympathetic to the situation. He was right in believing that I was not sympathetic, although I was empathetic. (Sympathy would be the taking on of someone else's emotional state, but empathy is understanding how they feel that way without being overcome by it.) Nevertheless, since barriers stood between what I hoped to communicate and what was being heard, I ended up apologizing for my responses, eventually deleting my contributions to the thread. I realized, with the help of some great godly counsel from another friend, that this was not the time. The wounds were too fresh and many of the people reading my posts were being hurt even further by the lens they were reading my comments from. Even though my goal was to point them to Christ and God's Love, they didn't know me or understand my character or genuine care for them as God's cherished children. Without that, no matter the comment, pain can easily be produced.

I do appreciate how, despite our failures, ..."in ALL things God works."[ii] Even though this interaction stressed my relationship with Phil, it brought about a conversation between an acquaintance (let's call him Jim) and myself that was very beneficial to both of us. In my conversation with Jim, he and I shared both of our viewpoints, which allowed us to better understand where each of us came from, as well as the lenses we were looking through. Jim shared a story with me that helped shift my understanding. A man went shopping at Home Depot with his wife, nine months along in her pregnancy. (I was surprised to hear that she was even willing to go to Home Depot at nine months pregnant.) The wife became tired as this supposedly short shopping trip turned into a few-hour

---

[ii] Romans 8:28 (Emphasis added)

marathon. During that vortex of time, known as a trip to Home Depot, the wife became so fatigued that she sat down on the floor, right there in the store, as her husband continued to shop. Though I fail to understand why, when he realized what she had done, he became upset and berated her in the middle of the store.

A few days later at their small group, which my friend Jim attended, the husband and wife both gave their sides of the story. Some of the men present agreed with the husband that there was simply no amount of fatigue that would make sitting down in the middle of a store acceptable. (I still could not follow why this was a problem as I have sat in the aisle of many a Home Depot, granted not from exhaustion.) Jim shared that he thought the men who stayed quiet were simply trying to stay on their wives' good sides, indicating that the men were likely all on the same page. But he then pointed out that ALL of the women understood where the wife was coming from. They were all mothers. Collectively, they made a simple, yet powerful point: the men were never women, would never be women, and could never understand what it felt like to be a woman experiencing that kind of exhaustion. I would agree that most men would never know how carrying a baby inside of them feels, especially at nine months along, while walking through a store for hours. They would never understand how, instead of walking through endless aisles of the store, a pregnant wife would much prefer for her champion, her hero, to get a flat-bed cart with a lawn chair on top, allowing her to rest her achy, swollen feet, while guiding her through the store and providing some ice cream to snack on. And although the men in the story still did not approve of the pregnant wife sitting down in the middle of the store, they too had to agree that their wives had valid viewpoints.

Jim used this story to compare the husband's perspective and my disagreement with the viewpoint Phil, and many other people of color, had about the tragedies in the headlines. Because I am not a person of color, I simply could not understand the burden that they feel.

    I, like the men in his small group, didn't agree with how things were being handled. In my case, I disagreed with how the media reported the stories, seemingly very one-sided. The fact that there was very passionate, hurt and hate-filled vocal judgment proclaimed from both sides without discussion also stirred the pot of disunity. But Jim's argument was powerful. I do not understand what it feels like to be a person of color, so perhaps the burden they felt was real and acceptable. However, it still didn't settle in my heart. So, during my quiet time the next morning, I asked God about it, seeking His will and His desire for my friends, my brothers, my sisters of every color, who carry this burden of hurt based on the history of discrimination and the current pattern of hatred toward them or those with shared ethnicity. God's beautiful heart shone through our conversation. He also showed me that His original design for childbearing was not painful; it was not a burden.

    Had Adam and Eve chosen not to separate themselves from their Creator, this thing called *pregnancy* would have looked much different. Imagine what a pregnant woman in the Garden would look like, would feel like, probably nothing like she does today. Imagine fruit from the trees supplying the perfect nutrients to prevent morning sickness. She would inhabit the perfect environment to produce rest and rejuvenation. She would encounter the perfect, genuine heart of God speaking His encouragement, tenderness, and love over His daughter. Pregnancy was never designed to be such a burden; women were not designed to carry that burden. Simply knowing that they were not designed to bear that burden doesn't mean the burden goes away. But if they put that burden on God and rely on Him to get them through, it surely lightens the load and, many times, can even change the burden into a blessing. It's a matter of perspective and the lens looked through. When we see situations how God sees them, Truth and Love prevail. The same goes for any of our brothers and sisters who find themselves burdened with history being repeated.

We should *never* ignore the past, no matter how painful it was, because that means we never get healing from it. We need to realize that we are designed to mourn so that we can get past the pain. Mourning for what was lost allows healing to begin. The mourning process is not a time to simply soak in sadness and welcome a spirit of depression. Nor is it limited to only the passing of friends and family. Jesus said, "blessed are those who mourn,"[iii] not because He desires for us to be stuck, unable to move past our pain. This surprising statement reveals how He wants us to heal from pain. Yes, we most certainly mourn the loss of loved ones, but we can also mourn other losses.

Personally, I was stuck for quite a while. Changing jobs, moving three times in two years, having two kids, leaving a church we were highly involved in, launching and closing a business, finishing my undergraduate and starting my master's degree, and losing the ability to have more natural children all at approximately the same time was stressful. But even worse is that I never mourned my losses.

My wife and I lost strong friendships when we moved. We had also just lost our newlywed status. And possibly the hardest experience of that time was losing the ability to have more biological children after two life-threatening and complicated pregnancies. I did not have the opportunity to process and mourn before I was forced to move to the next thing. Everything kept piling on and, eventually, I noticed that I hadn't laughed, truly laughed, in months, maybe even years.

We can identify that we are stuck by a lack of mobility. Well, that's obvious, right? But it's more than merely physical motion. It's also when we lose the ability to move from idea to idea, when

---
[iii] Matthew 5:4

we lose the ability to let God direct our thoughts, emotions, and desires. My joy was stuck somewhere in those very difficult events. It took God's love penetrating this realm, as scripture says, cutting through sinew and bone[iv] to get to the heart of my hurt; and He restored my Joy. Yes, I cried, but it wasn't crying that freed my soul; it was my Savior.

    I tell you this story as an encouragement that you don't have to be stuck or bound by the lies of the past, you don't have to be shackled by the hatred of others or by the lies they have believed. If you find yourself feeling stuck in an endless cycle of hopelessness and despair, seek the kingdom. Ask God where He is at in the midst of that circumstance and see what His design for that situation is. Ask Him for His Truth of the matter. Maybe His design is to work through you to help others through their thick fog of emotions to find Him. Maybe He wants to work through you to raise people above what they think is insurmountable, to help pull them out of the muck and mire they feel stuck in. Maybe He simply wants to have some experiences with you, to bring you joy, peace, patience, kindness, faithfulness, gentleness, self-control, and, most of all, love. Yes, those are the fruit of the Spirit that we are to exhibit, but remember that they belonged to Him first, and sometimes all He wants is to share them with you to set you free.

[iv] Hebrews 4:12

Lie 10: Lies won't affect me.

> *But I am afraid that as the serpent deceived Eve by his cunning, your thoughts will be led astray from a sincere and pure devotion to Christ. For if someone comes and proclaims another Jesus than the one we proclaimed, or if you receive a different spirit from the one you received, or if you accept a different gospel from the one you accepted,*
> *you put up with it readily enough.*
> *– 2 Corinthians 11:3-4*

"It's only a little, white lie," she thought as she spared her friend's feelings. "It's just a small exaggeration; without it I wouldn't get the promotion," he thought, justifying his words. She was trying to be polite, even encouraging, to her friend. He was trying to be a better provider for his family. But they both came at a cost.

Is one type of lie costlier than the other? Does a little "white lie" have less of an impact on people than a "black lie?" Is there actually a difference between the two? Most would say that a white lie is meant for good and a black lie is intended for bad. After all, the definition for a white lie is, "a minor, polite, or harmless lie."[53]

However, had she simply shared her true feelings with her friend, it would have encouraged open conversation. The sting of her true feelings would have been felt for moments, but the gaping wound caused by lies and deceptions may not be discovered for years, perhaps not until it's too late.

This is, likely, my last *Devil's Advocate* quote. Hopefully, these references give you an idea of how intense this war is.

> *You sharpen the human appetite to the point where it can split atoms with its desire; you build egos the size of cathedrals; fiber-optically connect the world to*

every eager impulse; grease even the dullest dream with these dollar-green, gold-plated fantasies, until every human becomes an aspiring emperor, becomes his own god...and where can you go from there? As we're scrambling from one deal to the next, who's got his eye on the planet? As the air thickens, the water sours, even bees' honey takes on the metallic taste of radioactivity... and it just keeps coming, faster and faster. There's no chance to think, to prepare; it's buy futures, sell futures...when there is no future. We got a runaway train, boy.

– John Milton, The Devil's Advocate[54]

Although this quote is certainly not in the Bible, it does provide a vivid glimpse into how quickly this deadly "stage" is set, as well as the intentions satan has for the small "innocuous" lies he tells. While I do not condone watching this movie, I have seen it many times. It was released at a time when I was looking for every reason to hate God. As you can see by these quotes, it is pretty intense. And although satan can be intense, the movie portrays him to be a lot more powerful than he is. In this passage, John Milton (the character representing satan) connects the dots between all of the lies, egos, and fantasies he has plagued our world with. His intent, just like in the Garden, is to create distrust and misbeliefs that separate us from God, meaning that our dependence is on ourselves instead of on Him who created us. That way we strive and struggle on our own, and satan and his demons can move on to the next, no longer having to interfere. Death becomes self-perpetuating.

We have visited Romans 1:25 a few times now, but this time I want to go back a few verses to see how the people described arrived at the point of trading the truth of God for a lie.

They exchanged the glory of the immortal God for an image in the form of mortal man and birds and four-

> *footed beasts and creeping things. Therefore God gave them over in the evil desires of their hearts to impurity, to dishonor their bodies with one another. They traded the truth of God for a lie and worshiped and served the creation rather than the Creator, who is blessed forever. Amen.*
> *– Romans 1:23-25*

We don't start out worshiping people. Maybe we just wish we had a car like Mr. Jones, or perhaps his house. But in order to have that, we first have to have his education and his job, and eventually we decide it would be a lot better if we were simply him, or for that matter, if we never existed.

When we know Christ as our Savior, it is not we who are dead. The Bible says in Colossians 3 that,

> *Your old life is dead. Your **new life**, which is your **real life** – even though invisible to spectators – is with Christ in God. **He is your life.** When Christ (your **real life**, remember) shows up again on this earth, you'll show up too – the **real you**, the **glorious you**. Meanwhile, be content with obscurity, like Christ.*[v]

Remember, that when our identity is skewed, and we find ourselves believing some of the core lies lined out in this book, our desires start to become misaligned with God's.

Each little lie we tell and each little lie we believe affects us greatly. They all compile into a larger state of being, a larger state worshiping something we were never intended to. We were not created to worship the created. Everything that the created, which are our worldly surroundings, tells us to worship needs to go.

> *And that means killing off everything connected with that way of death: sexual promiscuity, impurity, lust, doing whatever you feel like whenever you feel like it,*

---
v   Colossians 3:3-4 MSG

and grabbing whatever attracts your fancy. That's a life shaped by things and feelings instead of by God...[vi]

This scripture penned by Paul to the people of Colossae starkly contrasts the quote from *Devil's Advocate*. A life shaped by God is not one that revolves around emotional decisions, desires, or material possessions. Those are the things that need to be killed off. Paul continues:

> Don't lie to one another. You're done with that old life. It's like a filthy set of ill-fitting clothes you've stripped off and put in the fire.[vii]

Don't go get them; you will get burned and, even if you don't, what's the point?

> Now you're dressed in a new wardrobe. Every item of your new way of life is custom-made by the Creator, with his label on it. All the old fashions are now obsolete.[viii]

Satan will try to tell you that following God is out-of-date, but, in truth, his lies are obsolete. Jesus paid the price; He has dominion over us and this world. The days of religiosity are gone and we get to live in a relationship with our Creator.

> Words like Jewish and non-Jewish, religious and irreligious, insider and outsider, uncivilized and uncouth, slave and free, mean nothing.[ix]

And, here is the best part:

> **From now on everyone is defined by Christ,** everyone is included in Christ.[x]

[vi] Colossians 3:5 MSG
[vii] Colossians 3:9 MSG
[viii] Colossians 3:10 MSG
[ix] Colossians 3:11a MSG
[x] Colossians 3:11b

We are defined by Christ but just know that lies can and do affect you, no matter the size, shape, or color. They are simply death in disguise, waiting for you to reach back into that fire and drape their charred mess all over you. There is no need for all of the shiny, carnal things this world offers. Be content with obscurity in the world around you, knowing that you cannot go unnoticed by your loving Creator. Enjoy and embrace His new wardrobe of love for you.

Lie 11: I am my family.

Family – Always Room for One More

Early in my wife's and my courtship, we discussed our shared desire to adopt. That's where the statement, *Always Room for One More,* comes from. It is the family vision God gave us as He continued to reveal the desire on our hearts to have a large family. God has since shown us that this vision is not limited only to adopting more kids, but it also applies to the kid down the street, our children's spouses, our grandchildren, their friends, their families, and many more. God gave an expanded vision to my wife, that there is always room for one more hope, dream, and love, which are all parts of this thing called *family*.

But what happens to that vision when our family doesn't seem to fit our understanding of what family ought to be? What happens when we have more than enough, can't handle any additions, or are simply out of room physically and emotionally? What happens when we are good where we are? Isn't there something to be said for contentment?

Part of my desire for a large family comes from my memory of family reunions with my mother's side of the family. She is one of five children, four of whom married and then had between two and five children each. Those numbers added up pretty quickly. The cousins, as we call ourselves, used to be a tightknit group. We would play, hang out at the beach, go to the park, and play various sports together. Some of my most vivid memories are of our huge dinners, whether at Grandpa's favorite buffet or eating Nanny's *dynamite* meatballs. During one of my favorite moments, one of my twin cousins accepted a dare to plant his face in a cake while we ate dinner. That was not well received by the parents, but the cousins enjoyed it thoroughly, as you can imagine. While some memories were great, others weren't. There was drama in our family; there is in practically every family.

I remember sitting at the end of my driveway, hugging my brother for what seemed to be an eternity, as a consequence of our fighting. My parents were not too pleased to come home and find my younger brother's broken elbow. Countless bloody noses were issued on the way to school. And verbal and emotional battles occurred as a result of a few strong-willed members of our family butting heads.

This thing called *family* ends up being both one of the greatest blessings and one of the hardest challenges in our lives. Whether it is through birth, adoption, marriage, or simply deep friendship, we all have experienced family. Sometimes we strive to deepen, strengthen, and bring our relationships closer. Other times we can't get away fast enough.

Just before I turned nineteen, as my mom and step-dad were leaving the house for vacation, I announced that I would not be there when they came home. I am sure they would tell you they were both relieved and saddened. We were not the perfect family, nor were we the worst, although I thought so for many years of my childhood. But even in the brokenness, even in the times I wanted to run away, even in my desire to commit suicide, or sniff substances to numb my pain or alter my perception of the world, they were still my family. It's because, even in the most apparently broken families, there is something spectacular to be said about familial bonds. And conversely, sometimes even in the most beautiful families there is tremendous bondage.

Growing up, we listened to Harry Chapin's, *The Cats in the Cradle* on a regular basis. It was and is, to this day, one of my dad's favorite songs. In the song, a little boy who, like boys should, greatly desires to become like his daddy. His dad, caught up in providing for his family, fails to recognize that reality, and, in doing so, fails to provide for the emotional needs of his son. As the little boy grows up, the relationship gap widens and eventually desires shift. The dad retires and his desire to spend time with his boy grows, but now, his son doesn't have time for him, since he is working to provide for his own family. It is a sad portrayal of the brokenness within many familial relationships today.

When I asked my dad why he liked that song so much, he said it was a reminder of a hope that that story would never come true. His relationship with his dad was not a good one. Whenever I ask him to tell me about his father, there is still hurt and pain which make it difficult to discuss. Ironically enough, prior to my father's and my reconciliation, our relationship wasn't that different. We were not too far off from the story line of that song. Hurt and disconnectedness, bitterness and business ruled our relationship. At one point I, like so many, thought like my dad did, "I hope that doesn't happen to my family."

Early in our marriage, we lived in Parker, Colorado, just outside of Denver. Soon after our son was born, God really impressed on Court's and my hearts to move back to Texas. God had certainly been working on me because I hated Texas. The flat land, the shrubs called trees, and the two seasons: summer and a cooler summer, which was called winter didn't stir up much interest for me. Growing up in Atlanta, I was accustomed to trees, hills, and four distinct seasons, with color changing on the trees. While living in Denver, we experienced a mixture of desert land, magnificent mountains, gorgeous trees, and, again, four seasons. We were entrenched in our church, would go hiking on the weekends, and had even just bought our first house. It was exactly what we wanted, planned for, and envisioned for our family. We did not plan on anything else, until one December, God began softening my heart towards that flat, brown land we now call home.

While visiting Court's family that Christmas, as we drove down a hilly, country road in Argyle, TX, I turned to Court and let her know something had shifted and, for some reason, Texas had started to feel like home.

Yes, the trees and hills were shorter and the summers longer and hotter, but God started showing me the beauty of the sunset, the beauty of a land He created. Then, one day in my quiet time, God let me know it was time. The one-word reason He gave when I asked why He would want us to move, "Family."

So, a few months later, with our house still on the market, we were on our way. The plan was that we would stay in a relative's guest suite until we could save up enough money to buy another house. We were welcome to stay there until we found a place more suitable. We had a six-hundred-fifty square-foot, one-bedroom space to house my wife and me, our newborn son, and two fifty-pound dogs. Our suite had its own kitchen and living room, even a small patio overlooking a beautifully landscaped backyard. It was great, although it was a bit crowded. We had family right next door who were loving, built-in baby-sitting. Overall, it was a sweet deal.

However, just a few months after our move, we experienced some communication issues with the relatives we were staying with. Intentions and motives were not expressed or interpreted well by either party and, one evening, I found myself outside having a frank discussion with the Holy Spirit. I didn't understand it; we had heard Him speak so clearly. I paced back and forth, venting out my frustration, "God, *You* told us to move here. *You* told us to come here for, 'family.'" He replied, "I never told you *what* family." I stopped dead in my tracks. "What?" This was the only family that we could stay with. How could we have misinterpreted what He said? We had taken His one-word answer and made it our own. We had been relying on our family to do only what He can do: build true relationship.

Just days later, we moved our little family into a two-bedroom apartment not much larger than our previous suite, but at least it was ours. A place to call our own, a place to build our family right across the parking lot from some of our best friends. While we cared for and were so appreciative of the family members who opened their doors and welcomed us into their house, we felt pressure to conform to their lifestyle and expectations, whether it was intended or not. We felt guilt and shame for not being able to contribute more or spend more time with them, because we needed to concentrate our limited free time on developing our own family system.

With that being said, our family, like yours, is imperfect. Family often comes with a lot of baggage. I want to be clear that I am not just referring to the family members we stayed with, but in every relationship, every member, every family, we all have our expectations, our hurts, and our contributions. Sometimes those bags can look very similar and, like at the baggage carousel at the airport, picking up the wrong one is easy to do. What makes it worse is that we don't realize what we have until we start to unpack it. We take on habits, skills, and traditions as well as quirks, attitudes, and offenses, which may or may not be part of our design.

While we are a part of our family, and family is critical to our existence, our family is not *who we are*. Yes, family can shape certain aspects of how we perceive and how we communicate with and relate to others, but it doesn't determine who we are. Our Father is the only one who did that. He dreamt of us before existence existed. He knit us in our mothers' wombs. One day, God gave me an image which revealed how that knitting happens. Scientists have discovered DNA strands and attribute them as building blocks of who we are. God showed me that, while there is so much more to us than DNA strands, Scripture gives us a peek into what it looked like as God put us together, as He created us. He, both literally and figuratively, knit us together.

We are not limited by or bound to the success or failures of our family. Scripture tells us that when we enter the heavenly realm we will be able to recognize those from this life, but it is unclear if we will know family as family. But because the Bible says that we will not have spouses in heaven, or we will be beyond marriage,[xi] we could infer that the familial bonds and lines will be blurred or broken as we are all truly grafted into His family. And while God created this physical mechanism of reproduction to help produce more of us, and makes countless references to that familial structure, He also breaks it apart, saying family will fight and war over Him and their relationships with Him. Jesus Himself denounces His relationship with His mother and brothers, proclaiming that those who believe in Him were His family.[xii]

While we as people are reproduced into this thing called *family*, God is the Creator and Author of that story. Through His perspective, we will spend eternity as one true family, no longer divided along or limited to genetic lines. Our family will be restored to one family, His family, from the one true Father.

If we are one family in heaven, and we truly desire God's will on Earth as it is in heaven, then, while here on Earth, there should be no lines of division. We are to love everyone within our sphere of influence regardless of how they feel about or treat us, even those who hurt us the most, which, many times, includes our family members. That kind of love is only possible when we allow God's heart for someone to be revealed to us. Many times, this will require forgiveness, not to release those who have mistreated us from justice or responsibility, but instead to release us from the bondage tied to that judgment and shame.

When we allow that release, we allow our vision to be transformed by God's perspective, into His Truth about who we are as well as who they are. The call to forgive "seventy times seven," or four-hundred and ninety times (maybe even more in some cases), is just a reminder to keep looking for what lies beneath through the lens of Love.

[xi] Matthew 22:30 Message
[xii] Matthew 12:50

Lie 12: I have no Father.

Kids have a hole in their soul in the shape of their dad. And if a father is unwilling or unable to fill that hole, it can leave a wound that is not easily healed.
– Roland Warren

While I could quote from one of the many statistics on the fatherless epidemic, I won't because, like facts, statistics don't always tell the whole story. But I will say that the effects of fatherlessness cannot go unnoticed. As Mr. Warren stated in this chapter's opening quote, when our dad isn't around, for whatever reason, we become wounded, missing something critical to the way God designed us. That woundedness comes with the increased likelihood for both children and adults to participate in criminal or deviant behavior, sex and pregnancy outside of marriage, substance abuse, and a barrage of other detrimental activities which is staggering.

While the numbers behind a statistic can usually be proven, reality may not always be revealed. Is it a fact that those making those choices did not have a father in the home? Maybe, but at the same time, was that the reason they ended up in those situations, or was it something deeper? Statistics don't explain what lies beneath; they simply expose a pattern that may need to be looked at. For example, we are told in the Bible to take care of orphans and widows[xiii] for a reason. Statistics definitely support the principle behind God's desire for us to serve those in need. We are to show them the essence of God that they are missing. Christ sacrificed Himself so we could all experience that.

Jesus addressed fatherlessness, or having been adopted by the wrong father, when He spoke with the Jews in the synagogue in John 8. Although we considered this earlier, it deserves another look for its relevance to this topic. The truth is not that we have no

---
xiii James 1:27

father; it's that we have replaced our true Father with the father of lies. Do I blame the people cited in these statistics for their situation during childhood? No. Plain and simple, we have no right to be their judge. That also means we cannot judge why they are in that situation either.

I, myself, have a dad; two if you look at the reality of things. I saw my birth father every other weekend after he and my mom divorced. I also had a stepfather, although he was gone most of the time too, traveling almost constantly for work. Although I had two dads who took care of me, I still felt like an orphan.

God showed me that the day I prayed for Him to heal my cat, an orphan spirit started to influence me. I didn't hear, see, or feel my Heavenly Father; I felt as if He didn't exist. I had no dad. I had accepted that God didn't respond because He either couldn't hear, didn't care, or didn't exist. But no matter the reason, I felt that He left me stranded during a time of complete desperation and brokenness. You may have felt that same way at some point. That is what this spirit of abandonment does.

The statistics of fatherlessness don't determine whether it is solely due to their fathers being absent that these children ended up where they were. While the facts may point to that, it seems to be a prejudicial statement, prescribing that those with no earthly father are destined, or at least are highly likely, to live a lesser life. As if a godly woman, a mother who is relying on the Father, cannot point her children to their true Father.

I do not want to make excuses for men who walk away from their family, but what if that broken dad had stayed around? Is there any guarantee that the children's lives would have been any better? What if, instead of the father choosing to leave being the problem, that his leaving was God protecting His children? We cannot know and are not designed to be that judge. What if that father staying would have been worse than him leaving? Saying that we know the answer is simply us relying on our knowledge of good and evil. What if the father's absence was not by his choice, or it was a result of being influenced by a spirit of abandonment himself?

God showed me that when I believed that lie, I tried to take my pain and protect against it ever happening again. I believed that I could not stand the pain of not hearing God respond, not sensing His protection, and not experiencing His provision. My fear of pain seemed insurmountable, so I built walls that I would not let anyone into. And the entire time, God had His arms wrapped around those walls, protecting me, just waiting for me to take them down.

Part of the key to the previous lie, *I am my family*, was figuring out that our earthly parents, our earthly family, really aren't where we come from. Nor are they who we are destined to be. Like so many people today, that leaves us yearning, desiring to know to whom we belong. Like a fatherless generation, we may be missing that guidance we desire. What are fathers supposed to do for their kids anyway? In Proverbs, it says that parents are to raise their children in the way they should go. They are supposed to guide their children into a relationship with their heavenly Father. But what if their father doesn't know *the* Father? Again, what if their earthly father was allowed to leave because having him around might cause more harm than good? While the statistics may be staggering, if we consider people without a relationship with their heavenly Father and the resulting consequences, they are far graver.

Looking back, the hurt and pain which resulted from not hearing, seeing, or feeling my Father in a time of need caused me to feel abandoned. I don't compare my situation to those who did not have a father in the house, because I can never know what that feels like. I can, however, say that, even with three loving parents, I still felt fatherless. That feeling expressed itself through self-hatred, carving, threats of running away, and thoughts of suicide. I wasn't worth God's attention, my parents' attention, anyone's attention, so I had to create something that would grab and deserve their attention. I started stealing, smoking, drinking, using inhalants and, eventually, harder drugs. As I had no perceived value, it didn't matter what happened to me. I had no one to protect me, so I had to call off relationships before they became too deep for fear of getting hurt.

When we look at statistics, we assume that, based on the numbers, we know the problem and solution. We take on the roles of prosecutor, judge, jury, and executioner. We also support the lie that, just because our earthly dad was not present, we do not have a Father who cares for us, listens to us, provides for us, or loves us. That is what satan wants us to believe, but it is a complete lie.

I had been a believer for years when God gave me this revelation. While He had previously identified that moment as a child when I walked away from Him, He had not revealed the hurt and pain that I still harbored against Him until that moment. I wasn't ready; like in Matthew 13, the tares were growing next to the wheat. Had He plucked the tares before I had started writing this chapter, the wheat may not have been stored here in this book, feeding you, encouraging you.

While God was revealing this to me, He had a larger plan: to tell you that He loves you. He is the perfect Father. He is here. He is your Dad. You are His son. You are His daughter. And you have a Father who cares for you more than you can imagine.

Lie 13: Everything is relative.

No culture in history has ever embraced moral relativism and survived. Our own culture, therefore, will either be the first, and disprove history's clearest lesson, or persist in its relativism and die, or repent of its relativism and live. There is no other option.
— Peter Kreeft[55]

Relativists may be closer to the truth than they think. Many people have asked me how I escaped the terribly dark place my heart was in, experiencing a stark reversal in such a short period of time. Many times, I have attributed it to my all-or-nothing passion, but that has never felt like the right answer. After all, I am not the only one who has experienced unbelievable transformation. And not everyone who has had that experience shares my fiery personality. So, what is the commonality there? Obviously, it's God. But not all people who come into a relationship with Christ abandon the darkness for the light as I did. There is something else. Part of it, I believe, is this relativist thing.

As a diehard atheist, I believed wholeheartedly that absolute truth did not exist. Truth was relative. (You may already see the conundrum I was in.) If we truly believe that nothing is absolutely true, then we make an absolute statement. NO THING, contracted together, becomes *nothing*, which is a negative absolute. But it is still an absolute. Therefore, through our assertion of the non-existence of absolute truths, we are in conflict with our own belief system. Lecrae, a hip-hop artist, wrote about the fallacy of this relativistic thinking in his song, "The Truth (After the Music Stops)":

*You're killing yourself.
If what's true for you is true for you
and what's true for me is true for me,
what if my truth says yours is a lie?*

Is it still true?

And while we think that this statement may catch a relativist off guard, allowing us a mic-drop moment, it won't. It is a thought-provoking conundrum, but it is not the end all argument in a debate with a relativist. While it may end the conversation, it may do so in a way you did not intend. Blocking an opportunity for discussion only strengthens many relativists' argument that Christians don't care enough to listen or empathize with someone, especially when the believer is convinced that the relativist's beliefs are a lie. Had Lecrae posed that question to me during my time of disbelief in God, my answer to Lecrae's question would have been, "Yes, it's true for you." As we learned earlier, it is okay for you not to believe a lie that someone else has believed. But for someone who doesn't believe truth exists, it makes it even more subjective, frustrating, and confusing, fostering a careless attitude represented by statements like: "Who cares? That lie is their truth." Or, "Let them believe what they want to believe."

You may have heard one of those statements or spoken one yourself. Alternatively, your head might be spinning right now trying to make sense of this madness, frustrated even with the simplicity of truth and how this seems much more complicated than it should be. You may also be baffled as to why others cannot see how easy truth truly is. It is simple, though only once we go to the source. We first have to be willing. If we are not willing to look at the possibility of God, we will never accept the reality of God.

Without God, there is no truth. That is the easy Christian tenant. But for someone who isn't Christian, how does this relate? If someone is not willing to walk with God, then they have no truth to reference, complicating the matter. If they have walked away from God, the faith they once stood on, now lacking, redefines their identity and everything becomes relative to self-perception.

Although I do not believe as I once did, there is validity to the mindset that "everything is relative." Remember that, especially in the most intricately woven lie, there is truth. Sometimes even more truth exists in a lie than falsehood. Looking at creation, everything was designed to be relative from the beginning. To understand, let's first look at the definition of *relative*. There are close to a dozen definitions regarding ways that *relative* can be used, but they all come down to its root word, *relate*. *Relate* also has quite a few variations of its definition depending on its use. I guess it's all relative to how you use it (pun intended), but all variations boil down to the concept of *connectedness*. One definition of *relate* is "to bring into or establish association, connection..."[56] Another is "to be connected by blood."[57] We will come back to that nugget shortly.

Relate, or this intricate connectedness, comes from the Latin word *referre*, which means to carry back or bring back.[58] Think of a referee (despite how much many of us dislike them); they try to hold everyone accountable to play a game the way it was originally intended to be played. Referees try to bring the game back to its original intention, or creation, not our own rules and desires that emerge along the way.

What "relativists" don't see in their, often self-proclaimed, identity as a relativist, is that the One who created them is calling them back. They are so much closer to the Truth than they know. Being omnipresent means that He is right beside us, including and especially relativists. As a matter of truth, He is just as close to a relativist as He is to a pastor of any church.

Every time a relativist says, "It's all relative," they are correct; Truth is relative to what you believe about it and they have believed a lie about the Truth. Jesus is "the Way, the Truth, and the Life!" He also said that "no one comes to the Father except through me."[xiv] So Jesus, the Way, carries us back to the Father and establishes a connection. He reconnects us by His blood and sacrifice. He gives us our lives back, the lives we were intended to have in the Garden,

---

xiv John 14:6 "Emphasis Mine"

connected in relationship with our Father, the Creator. He gives us Life, He is the Truth, and the He is the only way.

How I changed from dark to light was not through my passion, nor was it simply growing up, as my mom declared just weeks after I came to know my Savior. It, instead, was through His passion for me. He has that same passion for you. God is so passionate about every one of us, even our perceived enemies. Even though many of us have believed lies about our connectedness to Him, we are all His children. We are all just one decision away, one hole in the veil between our world and the kingdom of heaven, from real, absolute truth.

All we need is the Author of Truth.

Lie 14: I'm not worth it.

What's a penny worth? One cent, right? Did you know that it actually costs more than one cent to manufacture a penny? Over the past few years, the cost has fluctuated from 1.4 to 1.6 cents in order to make this coin which is only worth 1 cent.[59] But how much is a cent worth? Where do we get that value from? A complex algorithm beyond my current comprehension determines how much a penny's value is compared to other currencies and materials around the world. But how much is it *really* worth? Some might answer one one-hundredth of a dollar, but how much is a dollar worth? What is the value of anything? What is *anything worth*? Without an agreed upon scale used *to* value something, we have no way to assign *a* value to it. The value ends up coming down to what someone is willing to sacrifice, exchange, pay, or accept in trade for an item.

Growing up, I wanted to be like my big brother, Gary. I wanted to be like him so much that, one day, when I found a pair of glasses on the side of the road, I picked them up and put them on so that I could look like him. My step-father, Mike, trying to protect me, popped the lenses out of the glasses so I wouldn't ruin my eyes looking through some random prescription lens. He truly had my best interest at heart. I wore the lens-less glasses for weeks.

In my family, growing up, we were not destitute, but we were also not wealthy. When all of my teeth finally grew in, they were not straight at all. My right canine protruded out from the front of my gums instead of downward like they are supposed to. I was extremely embarrassed to smile, and feared judgment from the other kids I tried to befriend. Desperately, I pleaded with my mom and step-dad for braces, unaware of their exorbitant cost. Mike replied to my pleadings; they were not going to pay for braces just so I could be like my brother who had his braces removed a few months earlier. My step-dad compared my desire for straight teeth to my desire for glasses. I didn't need glasses. My vision was perfect at that time, but my teeth were not.

My perceived value, was not the same as *his* perceived value. My value for braces was determined by my desperation for acceptance, my dire *need* for relationship. He saw it as something else. He saw it as a large sum of money that would be spent to satisfy a fly-by-night, whimsical request so that I could be like my big brother. I do not remember how long it took for me to plead my case before I finally got braces, but it did eventually happen when our perceived values came into agreement.

Many of us struggle daily with our valuation, what *we* are worth. We hear tragic stories from all over the world about people sold into slavery for miniscule amounts of money. Then, as employees, we work daily for the vision of others, for a wage assigned to us by someone who has determined the value of a person with our skillset and talents. But that does not determine our value. Some of us have a net worth in the billions of dollars and others are in the red by millions, but that does not determine our value. Where do *we* get *our* value from?

The Christianese answer you may be expecting to hear is *God*, and you are correct. But what does that mean? Consider this: What value would you place on a house that you spent an unimaginable amount of creativity on? One that no one else could create, one that could not be seen anywhere else in existence, one that would reflect who you truly are deep down? Where would you place that house? What would the property surrounding it look like? If there were no financial limit, what would you be willing to pay to have that house exactly where you wanted it, exactly what you wanted it to look like, knowing that it was and always would be truly yours for eternity after you pay that price?

The house is us. When we know Christ as our Savior, we are His temple. The Holy Spirit dwells in us. Our Father, the *Creator,* designed us to be a home for His Spirit. He poured a portion of

What LIES Beneath

Himself into the creativity of the universe, to establish the perfect landscape, the ideal setting for His house, for us. The price? You may say God has all the resources in existence and didn't have to pay a penny. But He did. What was the cost? His Son. Such a high price, yet so worth it. He loves us so much that He sacrificed His only Son, so that we may have everlasting life. *Life*.

I will leave you with this. During a sabbatical in the Appalachian Mountains, I walked through the hills. Progressing through a shaded area beneath the trees, I wondered what I would talk with my wife about when I got home. I had come all this way to get away and hear from God, to have some long-needed time with Him, and to write. And while I had made a lot of progress in this book through God's insight, I had not had that intimate time I was expecting to have with Him.

On my walk, God pointed out the first stop I was to make. I had just started to make an excuse for Him not talking, as if to tell Him it is okay if He didn't want to talk to me. I had just started to say to God, "I love hearing Your voice for others, and it's okay if You....," when He interrupted me with, "You ARE worth it." I was all ready to excuse Him for not talking with me, and He drops a bomb like that. I was not ready for something as deep and meaningful as the Creator of the world, telling me "You are worth it." Taken by surprise, "Huh?" was my response. It was the deepest thought I could spark at that time. As if He would have been impressed with anything else I could have come up with.

He continued, "You are worth the time, you are worth the sacrifice, you are worth meeting with. You ARE worth it." I looked immediately to my right and saw a tree laid down from a severe windstorm a few years ago. A few branches stuck out from a bend in the tree, yet He invited me to have a seat. I broke off one of the branches, thinking it doesn't look very comfortable. He simply invited me to "Just have a seat," in a warm and welcoming tone. As I did, realizing how comfortable the log was, He met with me.

The Holy Spirit spoke to both my heart and mind, reassuring me of my value, confirming that I was worth Jesus' suffering. We had an intimate conversation and, as I looked up from the shadows, there was a clearing in both the trees and the clouds, the shadows gone, a light beamed down right in front of me. It was surreal, like the cover to a cheesy Hallmark Easter card, but so wonderfully, intimately more. This answered my final question about how He could make something happen even in the darkest of times. He is light and He was assuring me of that.

Standing up, I proceeded hiking through the hills and trees, sharing a few more moments like that with Him, one of laughter, a few in tears, and others simply spent enjoying His company. It was amazing. I came to another log and He asked me, again, to sit. This time, when I sat down, I felt Jesus' presence to my right. I leaned in and it felt as if He did too. Shoulder to shoulder, I got to sit with Jesus on that fallen tree.

It felt weird at first. I wondered for a moment, "What would it look like if someone came up from behind," it felt like I was leaning so far over. But those thoughts were fleeting as my joy became unrestrainable. I was sitting on a log, side by side, shoulder to shoulder, with my Savior. He didn't say anything. For a moment, I closed my eyes and my joy came pouring out in a flood of tears and convulsions. I felt that I should be falling off the log, but He reassured me that He had me, and the flood continued. I am not sure how long we sat there, but I am so grateful for that time. Through our time together, He told me that no matter what anyone else tells me, no matter what happens in life, I was worth it and He loves me.

We gain freedom when the valuation we give ourselves aligns with His. Although our perceived value may be based on our jobs, others' opinions of us, or even our own, our true value is not. God created us and He is the only one who knows and can place true value on us. And while one might want to keep an encounter like I had to themselves, I am sure the reason He met me there in that moment, was not just for me, but was to be relayed to you as well. *You are worth it.*

Lies Upon Lies

What LIES Beneath

Steven Cohen

SECTION 3
Here Lie Your Lies

HERE LIE YOUR LIES.

Here lie your lies, no longer in control,
a graveyard of bondage
telling of freedom experienced,
a freedom no longer chained.
Here lie your lies, no longer in control,
a graveyard of pain
proclaiming the joy discovered,
a joy no longer contained.
Here lie your lies, no longer in control,
a graveyard of death
testifying of the life inside you
the life revealed, no longer restrained.

We've identified the structure to lies, the root to many common lies we believe, and the flipside to those, Truth.

In this section, we will illuminate the Life and Love living within you, creating a graveyard of death, not to go and revisit, but to memorialize ways you have been broken free.

Steven Cohen

12
What Lies Beneath Your Disbelief?

What LIES Beneath

Disbelief is not merely the opposite of *belief*. Google dictionary gives two definitions for *disbelief*. The first is "the inability or refusal to accept that something is true or real." The second is "the lack of faith in something." The lies I want to address in this chapter are those that may not be easy to see because they hide beneath statements like, "It doesn't make sense," or "There's not enough proof." Statements like these keep us from believing not only in the fullness of God, but also in the fullness of the design and desire He has for us.

However, the dichotomy of belief and disbelief is not as clear cut as we may think it is. I recently watched a video of a very popular pastor praying over teens at a high school. One teen's vision was restored, young men and women were physically healed and, even more importantly, they were shown the personhood of Jesus. But while the video played, disbelief reared its ugly head. Because I was not physically there to witness the scene, because I was not that young man who had his sight restored, doubt and disbelief crept into my mind.

Doubt and disbelief are not bad within themselves. After all, doubt caused me to seek answers from a believing friend who bought me my first Bible. That doubt and seeking helped me find my Savior. Doubt and disbelief are not bad, but what we seek to overcome them with and the roots they develop within us very well could be. In my case, the doubt and disbelief that ruled my early and formative years were deeply entrenched in the lies of satan.

I know God heals physically because I have proof. A ruptured disc between my L4 & L5 vertebrae, from a rollerblading accident when I was 18, protruded into my spinal cord causing pain and periodic loss of control of my legs. This continued for more than a decade, into the first few years of marriage. I was preparing to have surgery to repair the disc and fuse the vertebrae together when one morning in a worship service, while pouring out my love, adoration, and thankfulness, surrendering to my Father, I felt a cold swipe across my lower back. After the service, I went home and told Courtney what I'd experienced. My healing was later confirmed when my surgeon informed me that he would not perform surgery as there was nothing to perform surgery on. I have the MRI results still in my file cabinet, and when I see them from time to time I'm reminded of my Creator and Healer meeting me, healing me, and loving me.

And then, there are days when attacks from the enemy try to instill doubt into my belief. The lies he used on Adam and Eve, "Did He really say?" are replaced by, "Does He really heal?" I watch as my wife struggles with type 1 diabetes, many times feeling helpless as she inserts an insulin delivery system into her belly every three days. I see friends needing transplants and operations to fix brokenness in their bodies. Our family lost both my stepfather and nephew to cancer within a few weeks of each other. Satan tries to use that loss as a platform to ask, "Does God really heal?" And while I have seen many people who are not healed for whatever reason, I have also witnessed and played a part in many others' healings. I have the choice to forget about the times God has healed, forgetting what He has done, concentrating on what He hasn't done, and welcome in disbelief and doubt. Or I can concentrate on remembering what He has done, being hopeful of His faithfulness, and staying thankful for His love.

Many years ago, God showed me the gaping spiritual and emotional wound that existed in my soul. It has since been healed and redeemed, but it took Him showing me and speaking His Life for that to happen. And, while it is healed, that doesn't mean our enemy doesn't try to test it or reopen the wound from time to time. This gash in my soul was a lie deep-seated early in my childhood. Many times, these foundational lies are the hardest to find, but exposing them can often be the most freeing moments.

In chapter 3, I shared the story of my childhood prayer for my cat, Kissy. Experiencing not only her death, but also the lack of obvious response from God was crushing. At that moment of such great emotion, satan attacked me, a wounded child, with a lie intended to prevent me from ever knowing my Father and Creator. He attacked with a lie designed to keep me from knowing God's true character. With a simple statement, "God doesn't listen; He doesn't care," doubt regarding a God I never knew entered my soul. Before people ever told me about my Father, satan wanted to give me his version of the story. He didn't want there to be a chance of me ever discovering the truth.

The years of my youth were based on this lie: not only doesn't God listen, but no one listens; no one would ever listen to me. I did not realize until recently that satan chose this lie because God created me to be a teacher, a communicator. Satan chose that lie in an attempt to hinder me from becoming who I was created to be, who God dreamed of when He thought of me before the beginning of time. That is why it caused so much pain and toil; this lie spoke against who I was, against my very identity.

Many of us have believed this root lie. While it may not have been the antithesis of your identity, it is still detrimental and, in many cases, debilitating. The thought that there is a God who doesn't listen or care, who sits in the sky merely going through the motions prevents us from getting close to Him, reaching out to Him, or trusting Him. It easily creates what Christ referred to as "lukewarm"[i] attitudes towards God's existence. After all, if He is there, but doesn't listen or care, why should we?

In a time of wounding, brokenness, or weakness, you too may have had that same lie spoken over you. Considering the circumstances, it sounds right. It sounds too true to be ignored. So, I listened. I let that lie burrow down deep in my soul, influencing me in ways that continually took me toward a downward spiral, further and further from what God could have ever wanted for me.

Later that lie went from, "God doesn't listen; He doesn't care"

---
[i] Revelation 3:16

What Lies Beneath Your Disbelief?

to what satan had planned all along, "God doesn't even exist; He never did." During that shift, my hurt turned to disbelief, my hurt and heart turned cold. I said things like, "I just can't believe in a God that would let me hurt like that." and "If God exists, why would He let there be pain and death?" Very likely, you or someone you know have said something similar.

Although this part of my life was the tipping point, the crescendo of my disbelief in God, it was only one layer.

When we uncover what is below one layer of pain we cannot become complacent and satisfied. Below this attack existed even more elemental problems, such as a lack of spiritual foundation from my parents, and even their parents, who lived lives of bondage, hurt, and despair. They themselves lived with doubt in Jesus, which was based on their own hurt and the lies believed throughout their lives. What lies beneath will go many layers deep and may seem to never end, but God will meet you where He needs you to be, where He wants to heal you, where He wants to set you free.

So, before we go on to our next section, keep in mind that this is a journey and a conversation with God that should continue for eternity. It is not something you should endlessly pursue because one could exchange a pure pursuit of God with this insatiable desire for "why" and "what lies beneath." Instead, this message should simply provoke the question, "God, what do you say about that? What is your truth about what lies beneath?" allowing, in His timing, for His Truth, His Healing, and His Love to pour into you.

Let's take just a few moments to put this into action. We are not called to be listeners, but doers, right? I suggest for you, in a moment, to put the book down and talk with your Father, listening to God. If you have never done this it may take a few moments to quiet your mind, but He is like a lion and can speak over and through all the other noise. If you find yourself sitting in an airport or train station where substantial noise surrounds, don't fear. If your mind is racing, simply let Him calm it. Ask Him to still your concerns and worries. This prayer does not need to be complicated; it can be as simple as, "God, I want to hear from You. Please relax my anxiety, let me experience Your peace, shalom, and let me hear from You."

Go ahead and take that time now and use the space below to write what you may hear or feel.

Next, ask Him, "Is there an aspect of You, God, that I don't believe to be true?"

"Is there anything that I have not been able to trust You with?"

"God, can You show me what lies beneath that?"

Can You show me Your truth about that situation?

Don't worry if you don't hear anything right now. He knows you; after all He created you. Again, this is a journey, not a race. Continue seeking Him later today and throughout the week. Just seek Him and continue to ask those questions.

Self-help is no help at all. Self-sacrifice is the way, my way, to finding yourself, your true self. What good would it do to get everything you want and lose you, the real you?
— Luke 9:24-25 (The Message)

Steven Cohen

13
What Lies Beneath Your Belief?

By now, we have established that just because we believe something doesn't mean it is truth. One of my favorite stories about my wife's and my relationship took place a few weeks after our courtship began. Keep in mind, Court agreed to this courtship knowing that my intention was not merely to date her, but to purposefully get to know her with the intentions of marriage. To set the story between Courtney and me, first I need to provide some background.

Shortly before establishing my relationship with Christ, I was engaged to an older woman, older by about eight years. At that time, she was, self-admittedly, a backsliding Christian. I had no idea what that meant then, but we lived together for almost two years, frequenting the local bars and clubs, getting drunk, spending way more money than we had, accruing massive amounts of debt, living what I thought to be "the dream." Out of what seemed to be left field, my fiancée broke off our engagement when she felt a deep conviction that she could not marry a "non-believer." This happened two years into our relationship. I offered to go to church and appease her conviction as it didn't matter to me. Since there was no such thing as God, according to my beliefs at the time, to darken the doors of a church was, to me, like attending a social club. What I didn't understand was that it wasn't merely a social thing for her. The conviction came from something deeper. Although she was backsliding, the Holy Spirit still worked through her to get to me. Plain and simple, the engagement was off. Our relationship ended and she found her own place. I gave her all of our furniture except, like a typical bachelor, the couches and entertainment center.

After our separation, I told some of my friends that I was done with women of her kind. "No more older women," I said. "I am going to find a 20-year-old, blonde-haired, blue-eyed woman who has never been mixed up in the bar scene." It may have come out as a joke, but in my heart, I meant it. I had no idea how I was going to find a woman who had never been mixed up in the club or bar scene since that was almost the only place I went to find women. But that was my heart's desire and I know now that the Holy Spirit was speaking to me, creating that desire. What I didn't know was that, soon after I made that statement, I would come into a relationship with Christ, ironically because of that entertainment center I didn't let go of.

My ex-fiancée left a copy of her *Creation Science Evangelism* video tapes inside. I am not sure if she did it on purpose, or if she forgot they were in there. But, one day, I figured I would watch them. The evidence they presented blew away my beliefs about the creation of the world and my understanding of how humanity had evolved. Desperate for an explanation, I asked to borrow a Bible from a friend. Selflessly, he instead bought me a Bible of my own. God was wooing me like I had never noticed before and, in June of 2002, I surrendered my will and gave my life to Christ. I started my relationship with Him on fire, becoming involved with the local church. Very quickly, God put me into leadership, to many people's chagrin. One of those people, I might add, was Courtney. However, that's a different story.

One evening, at a small group where I had been asked to help, I looked across the room and saw a beautiful, young woman, probably in her early twenties. There was something special about her, so I asked God to "please make me the man that would deserve a woman <u>like her</u>." That young woman was Courtney. We had a few more encounters after that, and one day, during prayer, God told me she was my wife. Apparently, He had not informed her, because the first time we talked about dating, I let her know that I wasn't interested in dating, that God had told me she was to be my bride, and I was interested in courting her as such. She seemed to be a little skeptical. (She'll tell you otherwise, but I remember the look on her face, which seemed to say, "...Umm sure, we can date a little." Now I could have misinterpreted her facial expression, but I doubt it.)

A few months later, Courtney was accepted into Denver Seminary to pursue her Masters of Divinity. Thinking ahead, as she likes to do, she saw the distance between Dallas and Denver, the work load, and our limited time together and came to believe that our relationship couldn't work. When we met one evening, she told me that she was ending our relationship. I, at that moment, had the choice to believe the lie being spoken to me: that God doesn't care, God didn't really tell me she was my bride, I just made things up in my own mind to satisfy my own desires. Or, I had the choice to refuse the lie. I simply replied to her, "One of us isn't hearing God right now. Go home and pray about it and we will talk later." As I stated earlier, this was the beginning of my wife's and my relationship...what do you think happened?

I figured it would be best to let you hear this story from my wife's perspective, so I asked her to insert the following section. My wife, author of *Refining Identity, Chronic Healing, The Sacred Shadow*, the *InTentional* book series, and *Where Your Beginning Began,* is obviously a writer as well, so the opportunity for her to write in my book was accepted eagerly. Here is her perspective:

> When Steve looked at me with this intense way he has and said, "I want to court you," as in the direction of marriage, I was taken aback. That was something I'd never experienced before. I was surprised, honored, excited, and overwhelmed... basically all of the emotions. I had all of them. But knowing that he was being so intentional with this helped me have a long-term perspective on our relationship as well. I didn't have to wonder (as I had with all of my previous relationships), "What does this mean?" for every action he took. I knew exactly what he meant. He intended to make me his bride someday.
>
> So, when I looked ahead and saw the reality of my move to Denver coming in about a year, I thought that having a long-distance relationship would only end in hurt,

so it was better to let go now before I'd fallen head over heels in love. I believed it was for the best. I believed I was using my God-given common sense. I believed that this decision was the most loving one for both of us in the long-run.

But, when I attempted to break it off and Steve made that simple statement, "One of us is hearing God and one of us is not. Go pray and figure out which is which and we'll talk," that pierced me. It challenged me. I wondered, "How could I not be hearing God?"

The next morning right after waking, I laid in bed and prayed. I asked God to help me know if I'd heard Him or if I was just doing what I thought made the most sense. Immediately, He very clearly told me that Steve was right and that this was a man I should not let go. He told me not to be afraid. Six months later, God made it clear to me, personally, that this man would be my husband.

God took my beliefs, many of which were simply wrong, and tweaked and bent them until they aligned with His reality. But I could have stuck with my beliefs. I could have broken it off with Steve. And then I would have missed out on so many plans and blessings God was just waiting to smother me with.

I am so thankful that God spoke to Courtney's heart that morning. I had already heard Him, so I was confident of the outcome, but she also had a choice whether to listen or not at that time. Had she chosen to stick with her beliefs rather than seeking God, I likely would have been disappointed and hurt, but my love for Courtney would not have changed simply because she was believing a lie, just like our love for each other doesn't change when either of us believes one now. We simply continue to pray that His will be done in our hearts as it is in heaven.

We need to examine our beliefs and disbeliefs, comparing them to what God says. Because our beliefs are just as influential as our disbeliefs, we need to make sure they align with truth. Yes, they are two sides of the same coin, but they both have separate and powerful effects. It wasn't Court's disbelief in me or our inability to be the perfect couple which convinced her to break our relationship, but a belief that it was better, more humane, more sensible than having to work hard and be intentional about our relationship. It is important to cross-examine, discussing both sides with God, allowing Him to point out what lies beneath, replacing lies for truth so that we can experience His Love.

What Lies Beneath Your Belief?

Lies are a little fortress; inside them you can feel safe and powerful. Through your little fortress of lies you try to run your life and manipulate others. But the fortress needs walls, so you build some. These are the justifications for your lies...Whatever works just so you feel okay about the lies.

— Papa, The Shack[7]

Steven Cohen

14
What Lies Beneath Your Justifications?

What LIES Beneath

We can justify anything. From a shift in our schedule to allow for time to serve at a homeless shelter, a purchase made beyond what our budget allows, to the heinous murder of millions of people in an attempt to eradicate an entire race. When we justify something we are declaring it righteous.[60] Good or bad, we can justify everything we do. Hitler had an ideology that allowed him deceive others, convincing them to murder almost an entire race of people. And while that may be the most heinous in our collective memory because of the sheer number of people impacted, it is just one instance of justifying the lies of the enemy. We see atrocious acts almost daily on the news and social media. In one way or another, they have all been justified.

Jesus said hate was the same as murder, lust was the same as adultery. If that is true, then we, the billions of people who have committed murder and adultery in our hearts, are just as guilty of atrocities as are Hitler and Stalin. I am not trying to compare the murder of millions of people to the choices we make every day, but I do want to illustrate how they come from the same place. Many times we ask, "How could someone think or do that?" But, in reality, we do the same thing. We make a judgment or we believe a lie that could result in the same actions we are judging that person for. And we feel justified in our actions because we know our circumstances, we believe we have a good, possibly even a great, reason.

Have you ever been cut off in traffic? If I were a betting man, I would bet that if you have a driver's license and utilize it at all, you have had someone come into your lane quickly and unannounced, causing you to slam on your brakes, afraid that the person behind you isn't going to stop in time. How did you feel? Likely anger or frustration was involved. There's a good chance you were offended, as your personal space was violated, or you felt that your property and your life were of little meaning to the offending party. You may have even felt a bit righteous as you judge them for not considering your well-being or your loved ones. You judge their disregard for the rules and lack of responsibility for not using their blinker or giving proper notification of their intent to change lanes. Undoubtedly, you're fearful as you brace for impact from the vehicle behind you. Think about it: When that happened, how did you react? Did you ask God how you could express His heart for His child in that car? Or did your emotions possibly turn to anger? Did explicatives fly? If not out of your mouth, then within your heart and mind? Do you hate people who cut you off? I recently saw a public service announcement billboard that read:

> *Even people who text and drive hate people who text and drive.*

Sounds hypocritical, right? And that is exactly what justification is, hypocritical: doing something that doesn't align with our true beliefs. We say we think one way, and act as if we are above, don't struggle with, or are not guilty of that justification, while our heart is really somewhere else. How can you hold standards and yet justify your violation of those standards without being a hypocrite? This is exactly why Jesus called out the Pharisees and teachers,

> *You hypocrites! Isaiah was right when he prophesied about you: "These people honor me with their lips, but their hearts are far from me. They worship me in vain; for their teachings are merely human rules."*[i]

These teachers told everyone else what they needed to fix, showing them how to behave, but disregarded the brokenness within themselves. They justified that disregard through a bloodline, an inheritance. They appeared righteous, "like whitewashed tombs, which look beautiful on the outside but inside are full of dead men's bones and everything unclean."[ii] But, as James Richards points out in *Satan Unmasked*, "We should never look at what is right with us to justify wrong actions." He goes on to say,

---
i   Matthew 15: 7-9 NIV
ii   Matthew 23 27 NIV

> *The moment you justify your actions from some basis of greatness, you are corrupting your wisdom. Corrupting wisdom always begins from a basis of what is right. You will look at the truth about you and say, "Because of this, I am justified in pursuing that. Because I have done all of that right, I am justified in doing you wrong"... In other words, you begin to build until you ultimately build beyond truth. When you reason beyond truth, you have corrupted truth, [you have believed a lie.]*[61]

As for our opinion of the delinquent driver who cut us off, we need to seek God's heart for our opinions of others and be cautious not to murder them in our hearts. Jesus says it this way,

Everyone who hates his brother is a murderer, and you know that eternal life does not reside in a murderer.[iii]

As if me calling you a hypocritical murderer who uses Jesus' words to *justify* wasn't enough, I want you to think about the following situation. (Understand, I am not speaking this over you. I simply want you to mentally put yourself in this situation for a moment and when we are done you can pray a cleansing prayer that wipes any lies and demonic spirits from your thoughts.) You haven't had a date night in almost a year, because one of your children has been horribly sick and you've had to work longer hours to pay the medical bills. You're looking forward to tonight because a friend has volunteered to babysit and you have plans to catch a play with your spouse. Your spouse is waiting for you at the theater and the doors close in fifteen minutes and won't reopen until intermission halfway through the play. Your GPS says you're fourteen minutes away, just enough time to park and run into the theater as long as you have no delays. You had planned plenty of margin, but your boss kept you late at work, and now you might be forced to miss possibly the only date night of the year. As you get

---
[iii] 1 John 3:15

What Lies Beneath Your Justifications?

on the entrance ramp for the highway you see there is a space, just big enough to fit your car, although it leaves no room in the event someone has to slow down or stop for any reason. The line of traffic behind this spot is endless and the next opportunity looks to be possibly a minute or two back. What do you do?

What if the situation was a little more serious and your spouse is just fed up with the lack of attention and this was the last straw before filing for divorce? What if the situation was desperate and, instead of meeting your spouse at the theater, you are rushing to the hospital across town as your child was being care flighted as the result of an accident at school? What does it take to justify doing something that's wrong which almost all of us hate when it happens to us?

Texting or talking on a cell phone without hand-free devices has become illegal in many states and municipalities because of the higher risk of an accident. Almost every driver has encountered someone stopped at a green light while on their phone. Most of us have seen the car swerving across lanes as the driver fumbles to text someone with both hands. Recently, I even saw a guy with a phone on his dashboard watching a movie while he had another phone in his hand, presumably texting, all while in rush-hour traffic. Have you ever considered why we do things we know are not good or safe for us or those around us? Whether it's what we eat, a financial decision, something work related, a spiritual practice, or even how we drive, you may have noticed that our justifications seldom align with the reality of the situation. Sometimes they just happen because that is how we have always done it, or *tradition*.

> *Tradition is an incredibly powerful tool [in the justification of our lies.] It becomes part of our emotional fabric through a very simple process. Once we accept a certain opinion, the mind seeks to find equilibrium. In other words, if you believe it to be true, the mind seeks to prove it's true.*[62]

What LIES Beneath

In the above examples about driving, which one would you say is worth putting your and another human's well-being at risk? Would you cut into traffic if you knew the result would be an accident and the death of a newborn thrown from their car-seat? What if it was your child? Would you continue to smoke if you knew it would leave your spouse with the burden of supporting the family alone, abandoning your children? Would you choose to continue working that job that, by leaving your children without a father or mother figure, would cause them years of mental anguish?

In the past, you may have given an explanation that just doesn't make sense or made an argument in an attempt to sway someone else's opinion to match your own opinion that just doesn't hold water. Those are indications that there is a lie beneath that justification.

When our beliefs don't align with truth, it seems we will do nearly anything to justify our actions, even if it makes us the fool. If our opinion is expressed and others know why we do something, we are satisfied. Regardless of what God says, we strive to make our viewpoint known. But in doing so, we are truly fooling ourselves, especially when it comes to God.

> *In unrighteousness* **[not living in, by, and through the wisdom, power, and love of God]** *they suppress the truth, because what can be known about God is plain to them—for God has shown it to them. His invisible attributes—His eternal power and His divine nature—have been clearly seen ever since the creation of the world, being understood through the things that have been made. So people are without excuse—for even though they knew God, they did not glorify Him as God or give Him thanks. Instead their thinking became futile, and their senseless hearts were made dark. Claiming to be wise, they became fools.*[iv]

---
63 Matthew 23 27 NIV

Truth has no need for justification. There is no reason to justify or prop it up, because it simply is. It is reality. What gives it legs, propping it up, is itself and the God who spoke it and stands behind it.

In the examples above, they seemed like hopeless situations that had no good way out. Many times, we find ourselves in similar situations through no fault of our own, and I am not trying to pass fault or blame. Blame is simply judgment and justification. But many of the situations we find ourselves in are results of us not aligning ourselves with what God says about us, about who we are supposed to be. Who you are, a son or daughter of God, needs no supporting structure. While we are to build our lives on the Rock, Jesus, who we are needs no support other than the reality of God's Word. You are His son; you are His daughter.

The catch is that we must know something is truth so as not to fall into the trap of justification. One of the greatest indicators that we are not in truth is when we attempt to justify our stance. Don't be afraid to take that to your Father. It is okay to wrestle with God; in fact, I would encourage it, just as Jacob did.v Don't simply take others' words for how great God is. Don't just believe because your parents did. Find your blessing; find His/your truth.

When we are aware of our own state of mind and heart, when we have empathy for someone and understand that we too are in that same place sometimes, it allows us to make room for mistakes. When there is room for mistakes, when the pressure to perform is off and we do not need to look as if we are whitewashed, we no longer have to justify our actions, justify our*selves*. We are free to experience and extend the mercy of our Creator. We are free to love.

---

v Genesis 32:22-32

Hey, yeah you
In the back of the room with those
concrete shoes
It's okay, to cut loose
Oh, it ain't about how you move, but
what moves you
We're so consumed with what we
think we're supposed to be
That we stop living like we know
that we're free
We've got reason to get up
Reason to get down
He done traded our sin for joy
And now, that joy wants out

– "Happy Dance" MercyMe

15
What Lies Beneath Your Actions?

Over the past few chapters we've learned to examine two sides of the same coin, our beliefs and our disbeliefs. We've considered that there is a difference between the two. And we have explored how satan will craftily attack us by creating doubt and disbelief in the totality of God and the goodness of His created. While doing so, satan also attempts to flip that coin over in order to have us believe that we know best, that we can be God, and to make us believe that is why God gave us rules, to keep us down and bound.

Remember in Genesis 3, when satan arrives on the scene thinking he's all smooth. The Bible even says he was crafty. It says, "Now the serpent was more crafty than any other beast of the field that the Lord God had made." Now pause here: where's the lie? What's the pattern or symptom? Ask God to show you what lies beneath just this one revelation. Remember, take small steps, otherwise considering what lies beneath can become consuming.

What about the lie that satan thinks he should be god? What about the lie satan has whispered to you, that he is all powerful like God? While the Bible says he is crafty, meaning smooth and cunning, why do we take that and amplify it to mean that he is a smooth and cunning warrior with all might and power, capable of ruling over us? Why do you think satan enacts all the evil he does? As a reminder, the meaning of *evil* we used earlier in the book is not just the opposite of *good*, because that is bad, but instead is anything that stands against God. The liar, the father of all lies as it says in John 8, has believed a lie himself and he wants you to believe the same lie, that he is God-like. If he can get you to believe that he is much mightier than he is or he can instill fear and confusion as to what he is and isn't, then, as the artist NF refers to in his song "Mansion," we will invite fear into our lives, giving it a nice, cozy place to stay, influencing every decision we ever make, never kicking it out, while fear and confusion as to what is God and what is not overtake us.

If satan has bought the lie that he is supposed to

be god, what fruit do you think is going to be produced from that lie? What actions do you think he might perform? Would he act out of character, maybe attempting to make others believe what he believes? How does he deal with being misplaced from the throne he thinks he deserves? Would he try to drag others down with him? The saying, "Misery loves company," comes to mind again and he has to be unbelievably miserable; he was in heaven and then got kicked out. He feels that heaven should have been his. How jealous would he be to see Adam and Eve in the Garden of Eden? Those children that God breathed Life into, roaming through this beautiful heaven-like paradise, reminding him every day of what he lost, what he desires so deeply. How could he exact revenge? How could he even the score?

Satan said to the woman,

> ***Did God actually say, 'You shall not eat of any tree in the garden'?" And the woman said to the serpent, "We may eat of the fruit of the trees in the garden, but God said, 'You shall not eat of the fruit of the tree that is in the midst of the garden, neither shall you touch it, lest you die."*** [i]

We could spend days on this section alone, but we need to move on and discuss what some of the symptoms of a lie beneath are? Did doubt sneak into Eve's mind as a result of satan's challenge? Why was Eve adding to what Adam told her earlier in the Garden story? Whether it was an exaggeration or just Eve's skewed memory of what God told Adam, I think we need to give Eve a little grace. Keep in mind, Eve wasn't around yet when God gave His guidelines and ramifications for eating from this tree. Who knows, perhaps Adam added the little extra about touching the fruit just to make sure that Eve stayed away from it. Sometimes what lies beneath has good intentions. Although well-intentioned, we are all imperfect and need grace. We must not seek our

---
i   Genesis 3:1-3

knowledge first, but, again, we need to seek first the kingdom of God.

Why did Eve feel that she had to defend herself? Are we kept accountable by satan? Is he our judge? So, why do we often feel that we must defend ourselves to people who are not in authority over us? What about the lie that we need the acceptance of others in order to be fulfilled as the creatures God created us to be? Peer pressure is a real thing. It's not just a public service announcement to help aid in the war on drugs. Examine this, how do you think Eve felt while this all happened? Put yourself in the situation, what was it like? Remember: empathy, not sympathy. Do not simply analyze Eve, her motives, and situation from the outside, placing blame on her for the death of the world. That's judgment, something we are not designed or equipped to do. It is easy to place blame on Eve and to build a hatred for satan. But take a moment to put yourself there in the Garden.

Close your eyes and picture the situation. (Well, you will have to wait to close your eyes until you have read this, but once you do, let your imagination take you back to the Garden.) You are in the most beautiful environment on earth. The air is thick with a refreshing, vitalizing aroma, it's like breathing *Life* in vapor form. The colors are the most brilliantly vibrant, tantalizing colors in existence. The sky shines with all colors of the spectrum, as there was a different atmosphere at that time. Even the most beautiful blue sky today doesn't compare. The flowers, shaped with great creativity, colored by the paint brush of God, emit the fragrance of their sweet nectar within. The trees stand tall with the strength of their Creator. Beams of Life cast through the branches and leaves, creating great contrast between the shadows and the pockets of light. Nearby are fields of grass, freshly mowed by the teeth of livestock roaming freely. The hides of animals glisten in the light as they frolic around in utter delight at the creation God has placed them within. And there, this beautiful snake, its skin a blanket of intricately woven scales, in a pattern of great complexity and beauty. This word used for serpent in "the original Hebrew, 'nachash'... is often used as a figure of speech to describe someone who is cunning and in opposition to God's order. When this same word 'nachash' is used in the Hebrew as a verb, it actually means 'to enchant, fascinate, bewitch or of one having and using occult knowledge.' In Isaiah 14:12, the enemy is called 'Day Star' which is the Hebrew word 'helel' meaning 'Shining One.'"[63] I am not sure how large this serpent was, but I would think it was much larger than a garter snake, maybe even the size of an anaconda. But no matter the size, it was not ugly or alarming.

    At that moment, the serpent strikes up a conversation, which may have even been normal in that place, for animals to commune with Adam and Eve. They were likely the first animal whisperers, as God created them to rule over the animals. But then something off-putting happens, the serpent says to you, "Did God actually say?" How does that make you feel? You are in this safe place that God designed and created for you and something comes along and tries to take that safety from you, tries to take that security, casting doubt in what you know to be true. That feeling of doubt and insecurity, the defensive attitude that accompanies it are all the result of a lie, something lies beneath it. And if we are not sensitive to that feeling of doubt and insecurity, we will act out of our beliefs or disbeliefs.

> *But the serpent said to the woman, "You will not surely die. For God knows that when you eat of it your eyes will be opened, and you will be like God, knowing good and evil." So when the woman saw that the tree was good for food, and that it was a delight to the eyes, and that the tree was to be desired to make one wise, she took of its fruit and ate, and she also gave some to her husband who was with her, and he ate.[ii]*

[ii] Genesis 3:4-6

Even the most knee jerk, "spontaneous" reaction is not simply based on the information in front of us, but it is actually based on our beliefs and disbeliefs. At some point in that conversation, Eve and Adam alike had to have believed the lie. Otherwise, they would not have acted on it.

A way to identify lies is to look at the fruit being produced by the person. In Matthew chapter seven, we are told that,

> **A healthy tree cannot bear bad fruit nor can a diseased tree bear good fruit.**[iii]

Now, realize that people are people and human at that. People have emotions because we were given them by God. We currently live with this curse of the knowledge of good and evil. We, like you, make mistakes. You may see someone who is angry and think that's not compassionate, but you need to ask the Holy Spirit whether that person's anger or your judgment of their anger is the issue; which is not aligning with what God desires at that moment? What if it's both?

Our perception of others is not always reality. What if the emotion you interpreted as anger was extremely passionate joy, exuded in a different way than you understand? Have you ever seen a sports fan screaming passionately, celebrating a goal, a 9th inning walk-off home run, or a game winning field goal? Have you ever seen someone weeping with joy as they finished a marathon for the first time, or just witnessed the birth of the child they were told they could never have? That is why it is so important to get counsel from the Holy Spirit and bear the fruit of the Spirit.

Even as I write this at almost 3 a.m., having come home from a night out with the guys during a work trip, I see the lies and misery being hidden by the guise of "fun" or "a good time." No doubt, many of you immediately think that, because of the hour,

---

[iii] Matthew 7:18

What Lies Beneath Your Actions?

I may have closed down the bar and was probably consuming alcohol. By the grace of God, I was not even tempted and did not drink a single drop of alcohol; it was just water for me. That is not to say that I had not been in a similar situation, consuming mass quantities of alcohol, in my past. But tonight, it was different. It was the first time that I can recall since coming to know Christ as my Savior where I was out that late with a group of guys who most likely do not know Christ, or at least are not showing evidence of that relationship. I watched as they consumed the fruit of the lie they believed: that they need a substance to change their state of mind, to allow them to have fun.

As I looked around the bowling alley, I saw hundreds of people's spirits inebriated, deceived to believe that, somehow, intoxicated actions were more fun than sober ones. Deceived to believe that, somehow, living in a manner that glorifies our Creator and honors His design for us is somehow lame and less entertaining. I had a great time playing foosball, pool, and corn hole (bean bag toss for those not from the South). I was joking, laughing, and having fun until the guys became inebriated. My defenses went up as theirs came down. Things were starting to be said that did not glorify their relationships with their wives and did not exhibit the people they had expressed a desire to be.

They were no longer being themselves. I used to defend my drinking by saying it allowed me to be me. Because my defenses were down, I was just being the fun, free-willed guy my defenses prevented me from being when sober. What I didn't realize was that, when my defenses came down, it simply made me susceptible to the lies and attacks of the enemy. In a military sense, when your enemy's walls come down, it's only a matter of time before their demise. That was almost always true for me. What I believed to be true, that I needed alcohol to be myself, was a lie, but because I didn't know that, I continually made myself susceptible to even more lies, more death.

While our actions are not only susceptible to substances that alter our perception, that is what I struggled with the most. We are free to choose, we are free to act how we please, but that is not His desire for our lives.

> *Looking at it one way, you could say, "Anything goes. Because of God's immense generosity and grace, we don't have to dissect and scrutinize every action to see if it will pass muster." But the point is not to just get by. We want to live well, but our foremost efforts should be to help others live well.*[iv]

> *We were "called to freedom," A freedom that, although it can be used for carnal pleasure, we are "not to use …[our] freedom as an opportunity for the flesh, but through love [we are to] serve one another."*[v]

We were called to Love.

---

iv   1 Corinthians 10:23-24 Message
v   Galatians 5:13

What Lies Beneath Your Actions?

Ah, that is the risk of faith...Faith does not grow in a house of certainty...but my life inside you will appropriate risk and uncertainty to transform you by you own choices into a truth teller, and that will be a miracle greater than raising the dead.

— Papa, The Shack[1]

Steven Cohen

16
The Lie Is That They Are Your Lies

What LIES Beneath

For years, *The Matrix* was my favorite movie. It illustrated the intricacies of the world, our minds, our deceptions, our delusions, and the assorted paths we take to traverse through, or be set free from them. It revealed the repercussions and consequences for our actions and showed how, when we depend on something (in the case of the movie, technology), it will take over and rule us in a way we were never intended to be ruled. *The Matrix* helped me think more, it helped me see things from an alternate angle. And while it is not linked to *The Shack*, my new favorite movie and book, *The Shack's* storyline picks up where *The Matrix* left off. No, Neo does not traverse out of his futuristic technology-based setting into a suburban one. Nor does *The Shack* have visually stunning epic war scenes, but *The Matrix* exposes *a* problem and *The Shack* reveals *the* solution.

The solution, as simple as it sounds, is that God loves us. Regardless of our failures, He loves us. Even if we have believed the lie that He doesn't, He still adores us. He loves us so much "that He gave His only Son, that whoever believes in Him should not perish but have eternal life."[i] He did not save us because He needs us, but instead because He enjoys us.

The problem is the deception we suffer from, whether we realize it or not. In *The Matrix*, millions of people are unknowingly deceived into being bioelectric energy sources for a massive computer. You may say that "*unknowingly deceived*" seems redundant, but you can be knowingly deceived. Sometimes it just *feels* better, or is easier, to believe a lie. Denial of reality, much of the time, is easier to deal with, but it is never freeing. Joe Pantoliano's character in *The Matrix, Cypher,* exhibited that decision when he chose to give up his freedom by going back into the matrix because he missed the luxuries of the virtual world. One of his petitions to the agents, as he negotiated the location of the rebels for his return into submission, was that he wanted steak.

---

[i] John 3:16 ESV

The Lie Is That They Are Your Lies

Have you ever known something to be a lie, but you've gone along with it anyway? Has anyone placed a label on you that you knew to be untrue, but it wasn't worth arguing against, so you didn't reject it when it happened? We have all picked up someone else's lie. No lie is our lie. Satan is the father of all lies. If he is the father of all lies, that means we can be the father of none. Although satan wants us to adopt them as our own, lies are his children, the product of his deceit. Believing a lie is nothing to be ashamed about. The shame comes from the labels and judgments of others, not from simply being imperfect. We make mistakes, we are all imperfect when we look at each other through the lenses of good and evil, but, thanks to our Savior, when we are looked at through the lens of truth, we are the magnificent beings God created us to be.

In Max Lucado's *You Are Special*, a children's book about Punchinello and a race of wooden people, the Wemmicks, he illustrates this principle. These little, wooden people constantly judge each other, placing stars on those who are more favored and do well and dots on those who fail. We see how people's judgment of us as good or bad, successes or failures, sticks with us wherever we go. The key to the story is that, "the stickers only stick if you let them...if they matter to you.[64]"

The problem is not that others judge us. The problem is when we go along with those judgments and lies, accepting them instead of seeking our Creator (portrayed in the book as the character Eli, the woodcarver) and how He created us. By accepting the lies, or even by neglecting to reject them, we let them affect our identity. When we allow lies to stick, they go along with us. The longer they stick to us, the more we think they are true, and the more we think they are ours to deal with. However, like the dots that stuck to Punchinello, the lies start to fall off the more and more we hear our Creator and Father's truth about us. The lies are not ours. They are not us. The more we come to Him, our Father, Creator,

Savior, Counselor, and King, the more the lies fall away. And, as those lies fall away, the person we were created to be is revealed, made free, and restored.

Just as *The Shack* offered the solution, God's unconditional love for us, so we see too in *You Are Special* how God's heart for us isn't dependent on our failures or the opinions of others. The solution is His love, whether in *The Shack*, in the world of the Wemmicks, or in our day-to-day reality. The lies we believe have never been intended for us, but His Love always has.

The Lie Is That They Are Your Lies

What LIES Beneath

Steven Cohen

SECTION 4

What Lie's Beneath

What is Truth?
- Pontius Pilate

Steven Cohen

17
Recognizing Truth and the Father of All Truth

What LIES Beneath

Pontius Pilate stood face to face with Truth incarnate. Not as a Jew or Christian, but as a Roman governor, Pilate questioned the Son of God, the One through whom the universe was created. He had the chance to talk with God face to face and his response in the end was "What is Truth?"[i]

Our Father is the Father of Truth. This is not like the antithesis to the evil satan. I am not talking about a Tom versus Jerry, Batman versus Joker, Dallas Cowboys versus Philadelphia Eagles (I'll let you decide which one is evil there), He-Man versus Skeletor, Wile E. Coyote versus Road Runner, Bugs Bunny versus Elmer Fudd, or any type of rivalry we could think of. God is the Creator of all while satan is part of the created; there is no competition. Satan is not a challenge; as Richards points out:

> *Christ is no longer in a battle with him [satan]. That battle has been won. And as we shall soon see, our battle is not with him [satan], but with our beliefs. It is time to give up all fear of the enemy. Let us give up our vain attempts to cast him down. Instead, let us accept his consummate defeat at the hands of our Lord and Savior [Jesus]. Let us rejoice in Him and be glad.*[65]

While there is a battle for our minds and for our souls, there is no battle for domination or kingship of the spiritual or heavenly realms. Our Creator created everything, even Lucifer, the angel we are describing when we use the words *satan* or *the devil*. Think about that. How easy is it for us to believe the lies satan spits out? Why are we susceptible to feeling the feelings we feel that separate us from God? The truth is that we were created with the ability to choose, with the ability to decide what we want to believe, what we want to worship, and whether we want to align ourselves with our Father and Creator. Lucifer and the angels had that same choice too.

---

[i] John 18:38

While God, Yahweh, the Great I Am, is the Father of us, He is also the Father of all Truth. There is nothing without Him, but even in the void and vacuum created in His absence there would be proof of His existence. Just the sheer presence of the vacuum points to the fact that something must have been there to create the pull, draw, attraction, or awareness of something else. I believe this is what creates the gnashing of teeth described in Scripture, which refers to a person being cast from God's presence. It is the awareness of His reality, but the absence of it. It is the burning desire of all burning desires that can never and will never be quenched.

All of creation points to Him as the Creator. If all of reality could not exist without Him, then there is no truth without Him either. Remember: truth is reality, but our reality is not truth. Truth is reality, not our perceptions of it. Truth is not right or wrong, good or evil, or even the judgment called "fact" that we place on things we believe are irrefutable. And our part in this is not to judge His truth to see if it is right or wrong. Our part is simply to accept it, apply it, and spread it to those around us.

> *We renounced the hidden shameful ways—not walking in deception or distorting the word of God, but commending ourselves before God to everyone's conscience by the open proclamation of the truth.*[ii]

Back in chapter three, "The Birth of a Lie," we discussed how there was a choice, as in *The Matrix*, to listen to the truth or continue to listen to and live the lie. Part of that choice is not just how it affects you, but also how it affects the one telling or relaying the lie. When someone tells us a lie, we again have a choice. That choice is to accept the lie as truth or to understand and reject the lie and its effect on you. There is also the option and opportunity to ask God His Truth about the death and deception that causes that person to rely on lies, why they feel they should, what I like to

---
ii 2 Corinthians 4:2

call, "re-lie," or retell the lies they have heard or created over and over. Back in chapter eight, we discussed our addictions to the lie. Remember that those people you experience, those who are within in your sphere of influence, may have been placed there to help you. But on the flip-side, they also may have been placed there for your help. As you start to hear God's Truth about your life, your actions, and your identity, you become freer, and, as it is said in freedom ministry[iii][66], "Free people, free people." Once we accept truth, we apply it. And then, as free people, we spread truth to help free people.

With the help of our Creator and His truth, we could, much like Christ did in John 8:44, call out the lies in others' lives for what they are, lies.

> **You are of your father the devil, and your will is to do your father's desires. He was a murderer from the beginning, and does not stand in the truth, because there is no truth in him. When he lies, he speaks out of his own character, for he is a liar and the father of lies.**

Now, before we go out and stand on the corner of the square wearing a sign that tells people they are liars and have believed lies, we need to listen for God's lead. He has such a great fondness for and understanding of His children; He will know what to talk to them about and when. That is what prophecy is about, listening to our Creator, accepting the truth, applying it, and sharing it. Advising someone that their father is satan and they are following in his footsteps might come across in an unintended fashion, hindering even your best intentions. This is multifaceted as, obviously, this is a story from Christ's time on earth. We cannot compare ourselves to Him, nor can *our* advice have the power or revelation it does when Christ gives it, unless of course *we* are relying on *Him* to provide that revelation to *us*. Empathy and compassion are two invaluable traits. Keeping these traits primary

---

iii   A kingdom-focused ministry designed to help you become truly free in Christ.

in our focus will help us deliver words from God to His people with a heart of love rather than one of judgment.

The truth He asks you to deliver may be a similar revelation to Christ's, advising the Pharisees that their father was satan (the father of all lies), but the important part is that we lean into what He reveals regarding what we are to spread to others. That it is not our will, but His. Paul wrote, as some of his last words:

> *Proclaim the Word! Be ready when it is convenient or inconvenient. Confront, rebuke, encourage, with complete patience and instruction.*[iv] *(emphasis mine)*

Keep in mind, that like you and me, many times in our lives those we are led to talk with may not be seeking the Father for His truth about their situation at that moment. Asking permission to share something you feel led to share with them, instead of just blurting it out, is a good way to show honor and respect. Sometimes you may be led not to say anything at all, but instead, to simply refuse to believe the lie someone else has chosen to believe. It is okay to discuss, or as the aforementioned scripture says to "confront" them about why you aren't going to believe it. When we do so, we need to speak with honor and respect, which is the "rebuke" portion. Too often we read this word *rebuke* as if it gives us permission to rip into someone for their stupidity or rebellion. And although rebuke in English does mean to "criticize sharply," in the original Greek, it is the word, *epitimēson*. *Epitimēson* is comprised of two words, *epi* and *timaó*.[67] *Epi* means on or upon.[68] *Timaó* means to value at a price or honor.[69] So, when we rebuke someone, we are to do so with honor, valuing them, respecting them as the person God created them to be. If we are truly seeking what God says about them, it is extremely unlikely that He is going to tell you to tear into them, ripping their heart out. This is supported by the next step, to "encourage." How hard would it be to encourage someone after ripping into them? Remember

---
iv 2 Timothy 4:2

honor. Seeking God and what He wants to tell them is the best encouragement someone could ever receive. Even though some people may not seem to receive what is told to them, a word from their Papa, their Father, the Creator about how He sees them plants a seed of Life. Remember all of this is to be done "with complete patience and instruction."

Or you may simply choose to not "re-lie" whatever they are saying to another person. It is your choice not to buy into the death and deception being sold to you. When we buy the lie that others are selling, it reinforces the lie, further entrenching their belief that death and deception is reality. By you not buying into their lie, you can affect not only the life of the one telling it, but also those that satan is hoping and counting on you to spread that death to.

There is a belief that you should "fake it 'til you make it." That in itself has deception in its heart. I understand the meaning behind the statement, but again, do we want to create a foundation of lies or start with a clean slate, a solid foundation and build up from there? The deception here is the fake it part. We all struggle with things, but this thought of *fake it 'til you make it* is an attempt to deceive others into believing that you don't struggle. Yes, in adversity you should continue on, striving for success in whatever challenge you face. But to fake it, to try and prove that you are not struggling, is death to others. What happens when they watch you faking, thinking that you have it all together, while they are struggling? You don't have the opportunity to build them up because they have shame and doubt building in their lives. What if you watch someone else make something look easy? You probably don't see the hundreds, if not thousands, of hours of preparation and practice they have put into making it easy for them. Just thinking about the "make it" portion, I feel the Spirit leading me to reveal the deception and lie there as well. It is not something that is just one and done.

The imagery portrayed in the movie, *The Shack*, where God

("*Papa*") helps "*Mack*" begin to forgive the man who brutally killed his young daughter is so powerful, yet tender. Mack was struggling with the thought of no longer hating, not even knowing where to start in that healing process, when a ladybug, the calling card for the serial murderer in the movie, landed on Mack's hand. As Mack's anger for the man rose, his hand started squeezing around the little insect. Papa simply leaned over his shoulder and told him it starts with Mack first saying that he forgives the killer. Just saying the words has unfathomable power. After a few moments of struggling with getting the words out, Mack started to open his hand. When he finally said the words, the ladybug flew away, symbolizing the release of Mack's burden of unforgiveness. Just as in our lives, forgiveness is only the beginning of the process. Mack then admitted he still felt hatred and anger to which, Papa replied,

> ***Son, you may have to declare your forgiveness a hundred times the first day and the second, but the third will be less and each day after, until one day you will realize that you have forgiven completely.*[70]**

That's not faking it until you make it; that's struggling through a process.

Once we succeed in one thing, we should press on to the next goal or desire God has for us. In this freedom process, that is finding the next lie we have believed and pressing into God to reveal reality, gaining even more freedom, growing closer to God and the design and desire He has for us. Paul, later in 2 Timothy 4:7, states the famous line, "For I am already being poured out like a drink offering, and the time of my departure has come. I have fought the good fight, I have finished the course, I have kept the faith." Strive on or struggle until you succeed doesn't have such a catchy ring to it, but at least it reveals the reality of the situation. Maybe a summary of Paul's statement would be better, fight on to the finish.

Where does this conversation even start? Well, when we start this journey, it is not easy. The lies we have lived with for so long influence us in ways we have never imagined. Even when we get free from one lie, a similar lie may be influencing us in another area. Instead of faking or lying to ourselves that that lie is gone, fight through. Press further into God to reveal the source. Sometimes we can reveal a symptomatic lie that is being told or believed which is based on another lie hiding somewhere deeper in our foundation. And although we have received freedom from the addiction of smoking, we may still deal with the addiction to porn. Freedom from "addiction" may rely on gaining freedom from multiple things that have spurred on an addictive personality or spirit.

Personally, I struggled with many addictive tendencies and issues. A few of them were miraculously overcome one July evening just weeks after coming to know and accept Jesus as my Savior. As usual after a social outing, I was drunk, smoking up a storm. It would not be unreasonable for me to smoke a pack of cigarettes in a single night like this one. A group of friends, coworkers, and I had gone to a Texas Rangers game at the Ballpark in Arlington, TX. At the end of the game, after a number of souvenir cups of beer, we proceeded to a local bar, letting the liquor continue to flow. I cannot remember where we were exactly. I have even gone back to the area to try and find where we went, but too much had changed. I just remember sitting at the table, feeling drawn to look out the window. The view was beautiful, being an upper floor of a small building. The dark navy sky was accented with the glistening of street lights below and stars in the distance. I wasn't sure why I went to the window, but while there I heard a recognizable voice. It was the same voice I'd heard in Montana. This time the voice said, "This is not what I have for you." And, despite my drunken state, I felt a deep burden for His desire for me. As a new believer, I had no idea what that meant or looked like, but I knew I wanted it. Keep in mind, this was not a long conversation, it all happened within moments of my arrival at the window.

My response was simple, my soul responded with something like, "Okay, I want what You want, show me." In an instant, I was completely sober. I turned around from looking out the window and saw what I can only describe as a vision of the spiritual realm, the darkness, the hurt and pain of all of those I had arrived with. It was overwhelming. I knew something had changed in addition to my now-sober state, but I could not tell what. I threw down some money to cover my bill and told my friends I had to go. Eighteen years after my introduction to alcohol, ten years of bondage to it, and twelve and half years after my bondage to cigarettes began, I was free. My body physically changed. I no longer craved or desired alcohol or a cigarette. I no longer needed them to be social and have fun. I could be who He designed me to be without the chains of a bottle, beer can, or cancer stick hanging from my mouth.

My mind also changed, but that didn't mean satan wouldn't try to test it. A few weeks later, I was having a horrible day at work. I was under pressure to make a few big sales to get my numbers up for the month and no one was buying that day. I went to the break room and my old mindset kicked in. Approaching a coworker, I asked for a smoke. It is so amazing that we as a people are so quick to accept each other's defeat and congratulate them in it. In their snarky tone, they mocked me, "I thought you quit," as they pulled out a cigarette and obliged my request. I snatched the cigarette, "Shut up and give me a light." I stepped outside and lit up the cigarette, expecting to inhale a rush of nicotine to help relax my body when my lungs turned to fire and I quickly coughed out the toxic fumes I had inhaled. What was that? Then a rush of nausea came over me, almost dry heaving. This was not like the rush I'd felt in the boy's bathroom from that first smoke. My body had truly changed. It was rejecting the chemicals that did not belong, reminding me of the words God spoke to me. He had something so much better for me. It seems that God wanted to redeem and restore that first smoke with His truth about me. He is, after all, the Father of truth; who better to help us become who we were designed to be? He wants to do the same for you. He wants to help you recognize Him, His Truth, and who He created you to be.

Recognizing Truth and the Father of All Truth

I was formed from the soil,
I got dirt inside of me.
But I was born to be royal,
I was made for glory.
Take me back to the garden, take
me back and walk with me.
For your presence, I am longing
...Lord take me back
to your kingdom come.
- "Back to the Garden" David Crowder

Steven Cohen

18
Discovering the Truth Beneath

Throughout this book we have talked about hearing God: asking Him what He says about the situations we find ourselves in and who He intended, desired, and desires us to be. All of that is to help us discover the truth beneath.

Early on, I said that this process can become much like the mystery of the chicken and the egg and that we need to dig until we find Jesus. In my wrestling with God, struggling through my history, He has been so gracious. Sometimes He has been found just a few layers down, because I wasn't ready to deal with the deep, dark stuff below. Sometimes, we don't need to dig up the death for Him to obliterate it, we just need to rely on Him to do so. If He feels it's necessary for your healing, I am sure He will reveal it in His timing. He knows there are lies we have believed and death that has entangled itself in and around the very fabric of who we are. Death's goal is to attempt to strangle and choke us out, but God wants to let us know, He has got it handled. He brought me to this passage in Matthew:

> *The kingdom of heaven is like a man who sowed good seed in his field. But while the men were sleeping, his enemy came and sowed weeds among the wheat and went away. Now when the stalk sprouted and produced grain, then the weeds also appeared.*
> *So the slaves of the landowner came and said to him, "Master, didn't you sow good seed in your field? Then where did the weeds come from?"*
> *But he replied, "An enemy did this."*
> *Now the slaves say to him, "Do you want us, then, to go out and gather them up?"*
> *But he says, "No, for while you are gathering up the weeds, you may uproot the wheat with them. Let both grow together until the harvest. At harvest time, I will tell the reapers, 'First, gather up the weeds and*

> *tie them in bundles to burn them up; but gather the wheat into my barn.'"*
> *– Matthew 13:24-30 (TLV)*

    Jesus lets us know in this parable that as we live in His kingdom, here on earth, there will be trials and challenges we go through. Our desire is for everything now to be as it is in heaven, without pain, toil, or strife, where we are always in His presence. While our souls cry out for that time to come and come soon, we are not there yet. Sometimes we get caught up in the earthly realm we are in, wondering how or why bad things happen to us and those around us, those we care for. But, although we were created in and from the elements of this world, we were not created for this world; this world was created for us. The stuff we have judged as "bad" may have caused discomfort or pain, or may not have brought the desired results we preferred. But, again, we were not created to be that judge. God our Father created us to live in relationship with Him. He sowed good seed. The liar planted the weeds.

    Even when we know there is no question as to where the weeds came from, sometimes we find ourselves overwhelmed or worried and feel as if we need to do something about the thistles. But our Father knows the schemes of the enemy. He is not intimidated, worried, or panicked about them.

    Sometimes He simply permits the tares and thistles, or lies, to grow alongside His Truth until it is ready to be revealed and harvested. He does this not because it is *not good* to tear out the lies, but because He doesn't want His Truth currently growing inside of us to be uprooted and thrown out as well.

    Earlier, I told the story of the first time I remember God speaking to me as I drove through Montana. That moment when He told me to reconcile with my father took place six years prior to my salvation. Satan's lie that I had believed as a child, that God either didn't care, hear, or exist is the same lie that continued to grow throughout the years. It wasn't just that He couldn't speak. That day God spoke to me, an atheist and sinner, audibly, over my blaring radio, and although I did not realize it was Him for years to come, His Truth, Love, and Reality spoke to my soul and changed me. Many years later, in a conversation with Him, He revealed to me that it was Him speaking in my truck that day, shattering my concepts of His ability, or inability, as God to speak. The lie that kept me from knowing Him intimately for so long was being pulled up.

You may find yourself asking, "Why does He wait so long?" You may wonder why He would let us sit in torment, but when you do, you do so with a limited perspective. A person trapped under a car can only see the car on top of them. They cannot see those working, positioning supports and safeties to remove the vehicle with the least amount of damage to the person beneath. When feeling helpless, we may think it would be better to just pick up the car, but we cannot see the situation in totality. I do not know for sure, but now that I look back at the moment I watched my cat dying, praying to God for her healing, had God spoken to me, the lack of foundation and support around me might have crushed the hope of God regardless. And my Father, all of time existing for Him in an instant, allowed for that lie because He knew that one day I would be driving in Montana, and He would have an intimate moment with me that would bring redemption and spark the restoration of our relationship.

For those who think that you have to be a born-again believer in Christ, or a pastor or priest to hear from God, I can testify that is not true. While getting in a quiet environment may help us hear Him, God can speak to you despite what your perception of Him is, despite your circumstances, despite your beliefs and surroundings, simply put, despite you. If He couldn't, none of us would be saved in the first place.

He initiated our relationship in the beginning. He followed up by redeeming its brokenness through Jesus. And He restores our relationship daily through our relationship with the Holy Spirit.

Even when we have let tares be planted in our garden, He is not afraid. He assures us that when He tells the harvesters to pull up the thistles, they are to be bound and thrown in the fire. When His Truth is revealed, in His perfect timing for our lives, the harvesters bind the lies, and throw them in the fire, the pit of Hell, where they belong. The thistles aren't merely laid to the side, allowing them a chance to germinate again; they simply burn up. Even better than that, take note that the wheat, the truth, is not bound, but is gathered to be stored in His barn. We are that barn. We are referred to as God's temple, a container for the Holy Spirit to live in. A container for His Truth.

He is in us and so is His absolute Truth. We just have to be willing to dig down and find it.

Take me to the shouting grounds
A prodigal lost was found,
I should be dead right now
But I am alive
I just want to see your face
You're calling me from my grave
Take me to the shouting grounds
It's gonna get loud!
- "Shouting Grounds" David Crowder

Steven Cohen

19
How to Believe and Live Truth

What LIES Beneath

Every Independence Day in the Dallas/Fort Worth area, a local radio station throws a huge celebration called *Celebrate Freedom*. Although I have only gone a few times, I've always had a blast. Starting mid-morning, the entire day is filled with concerts and performances by some of the world's best artists. Those artists are also Christian, which makes this day full of God-honoring fun in a worship-filled atmosphere. The Holy Spirit's presence feels like a cool spring fog, minus the fog. He is thick, covering the grounds, penetrating every area.

While we are there to celebrate the freedom we have here in America and honor those who serve us so bravely, selflessly, and heroically in our armed forces, it is also an excuse to get together and celebrate the freedom we have in Christ. It is something that we can and should celebrate. We were not made to live downcast and beat up. Sometimes that may happen, but it is not where we were designed to stay. We are designed to live in the shouting grounds, yelling at the top of our lungs how great our Father is. Much like that field in the beginning of July, we get to shout how remarkable our Creator is, how living free is so freeing. As Crowder states, "It's gonna get loud!"

As we know in this country, just because we are free doesn't mean that freedom isn't going to be challenged or attacked. And knowing we are going to be attacked should not prevent us from living in truth or celebrating *our* freedom.

One of my pastors hit the nail on the head when she said, "Being free doesn't mean you aren't attacked; it just means you identify the attacks more freely, more easily."[71] By identifying attacks faster, we have the opportunity to defend them much sooner. That defense involves asking God about the situation. He is our Defender and Protector and we need to trust, or have faith, in Him. He is the "Perfecter of our Faith,"[i] and that faith is perfected through hearing His Word. We already know it is an attack, so

---
i   Hebrews 12:2

hearing His Truth and letting Him protect our minds are the most important steps to living in Truth.

> *Faith comes from hearing and hearing through the word of Christ,*[ii]

or as *The Message* phrases it,

> *Before you trust, you have to listen. But unless Christ's word is preached, [unless the Truth is told] there is nothing to listen to.*

In order to believe something, we have to first hear it. In order to hear something, you must first open your ears and listen.

But what about fiction, creative stories, main stream music, and drama? If we are to only tell what is true, then these methods of entertainment and communication should not and cannot be used to spread truth. In a recent small group meeting, I brought this topic up and one reply to this was, "So if I create a bedtime story or an example to help my kids learn something, you're telling me I'm a liar?" And I looked straight in their eyes and said, "Yes."

Now, this is a group that has given each other permission to talk into each other's lives, challenging ways of thinking and living. Do not try this at your local super market, unless of course God leads you to, but even then, you should listen for His way of delivering that line.

I really enjoyed the reply I received. It was a huge face full of "you're crazy" looking right at me. This idea was challenging the group just as it challenges me. It's not a good versus evil thing; it's not a right versus wrong thing. It sounds extreme, but it's a Christ thing.

> *Unless Christ's word is preached, [unless the Truth is told] there is nothing to listen to.*[iii]

---
ii   Romans 10:17 ESV
iii   Romans 10:17 The Message (Emphasis Mine)

> *Hear O Israel, the Lord our God, the Lord is one. Love Adonai your God with all your heart and with all your soul and with all your strength. These words, which I am commanding you today, are to be on your heart. You are to teach them diligently to your children, and speak of them when you sit in your house, when you walk by the way, when you lie down and when you rise up. Bind them as a sign on your hand, they are to be as frontlets between your eyes, and write them on the doorposts of your house and on your gates.[iv]*

These two scriptures are crucial to deepening our relationship with God. The first we already discussed: unless something is of God or points to God, it's not worth listening to. The second verse tells us how often and where we are to talk about Him, to seek Him. The short of it: always and everywhere. We, in every moment of our existence, are to connect our being, our essence, our worship to the God who created, saved, and redeemed us. We are to share God's words and show His Love to our children every moment we have with them. Every moment we spend teaching them something else is a moment we take away an opportunity for them to establish a deeper relationship with their Father.

So, why did God give us such creative minds if we are not to use them? Jesus Himself used fiction, right? He used parables, fictional creative stories, to portray truths to people, right? Or did He? We know Jesus used parables, but what if they were not fictional, but instead reality-based? What if the stories He told simply had identities and time periods changed to protect the innocent?

We are taught that Jesus used fictional parables, but who started the theory that they were fictional? I ask because, if Jesus can simply make up false stories (aka: fiction), then can't He tell lies?

---
iv   Deuteronomy 6:4-9 TLV

And if He can tell lies, then what else *did* He lie about? Maybe being the Son of God, or that He is the only way to the Father? What if He made up that He is *"the way and the Truth and the Life?"*[v] What if He lied about liars going to hell?[vi] Those questions and accusations sound a lot like an accusation satan used against Jesus just after the Father proclaimed Jesus to be His Son. They also sound like the genuine questions that keep people doubting in the authenticity of Christ, and the accusations many atheists use on a regular basis to argue against the Godship of Jesus.

So, was Jesus lying? Outside of Jesus' story about the prodigal son, we haven't heard of a historical son who actually ran away to eventually eat with the pigs, but what if there was? What if these paradoxical parables were true? What if they are reality which had simply not come to fruition yet? Are they any less true? The story begins, "There once was," which says that at some point in time this event occurred, which implies it has already passed. But if you stand outside of time and can see everything all at once, as God does, then all of existence could be referred to as, *"There once was."*

Although I cannot prove it with fact, that does not mean it is not true. There is the possibility, a likelihood, a most definite probability that Jesus was simply telling a true story, just one unfamiliar to people at the time. This reality, freshly revealed to them boggled minds, yet resonated with their spirits, leaving them perplexed, desiring more. Much like when God revealed my orphan spirit, I didn't get it at first, but then He brought me to the parable of the wheat and the tares and revealed how both were growing simultaneously in me. The tares were simply creatively masked lies, woven into who I was. But He knew that if He stripped away the tares when I was not ready, then it would damage the wheat. I believe Jesus uses these illustrations to show us how invasive lies

---
v John 14:6
vi Revelation 21:8

can be, but just because they are illustrations doesn't mean they are lies.

The same day that God revealed these principles about fiction, a message from our pastor (that I wasn't planning on being able to attend) confirmed them. A meeting with my mentor was cut short because it was "mysteriously" not saved in his calendar. While we did get to talk briefly, he had get back to the business that had replaced our time slot. While it was a little disappointing at first, I knew God was up to something. Since my meeting took place at church, I popped in to catch the end of the message.

As I sat down, my pastor made a point about the parable of the rich man and Lazarus, that "there was a Lazarus, there was a rich man, Abraham was real, and there is a real hell."[72] God made sure, just a few short moments after He would challenge my brain about whether parables were fiction, to confirm through the pastor of a thirty-thousand-plus church who delivered the same message. All to confirm what He told me to tell you.

Just as He knew that my appointment was going to be cut short because the entry in my mentor's calendar would not save, He knew what our pastor was teaching on. He knew what stories to pull from reality and insert into that realm of time, and He knows that you need to hear this. The expanse of God's Truth and reality is not limited by our ability to comprehend. But, with Him, His Truth can expand our ability to comprehend reality.

Our understanding, or lack thereof, does not invalidate truth. The parables Jesus spoke were a way to point people to the Father. Examining what lies beneath works for discovering truth as well. Remember, we need to dig down until we find Jesus. If you tell made-up bedtime stories, does that mean you are going to hell? To my knowledge, no. I have referenced *The Shack* many times in this book and, while *The Shack* is technically fiction, it does speak the truth, pointing people to the Father. Is everything in *The*

Shack accurate? No, but that's not because God's Truth doesn't exist. It's because, although He is perfect, we are not. We do not have omniscience to pull our stories from. We have limited minds and limited understanding of our experiences, and sometimes we fill in the gaps. But as long as we are relying on God and making an effort to point others towards Him and His Truth, I believe He honors it. This, I believe, is how a brand-new believer can tell others about God, even though their theology may not be spot on. We all fall short of His Truth because we are not perfect, we are not Jesus, but we can always strive towards Him.

If you are struggling with this concept of reality in the stories Jesus told, seek Him, ask Him. I am not saying if you disagree with me that you are wrong. Hang in there and seek His Truth. Ask Him to reveal what you need in order to get closer to Him.

We need to be aware of what we are listening to, what we are accepting in our lives. Are cartoons or bedtime stories good or bad? Are movies good or evil? That really isn't the point. Instead, let's ask: What are they based on and who do they point you to? What are we concentrating on when we rise, as we drive to and from work, as we ready ourselves for sleep? In my case, while in Montana, my ears were open to everything in the world. While it was good that they were open to anything flowing in, so that I could hear God when He spoke, I was also opening myself up for an astonishing amount of evil to flow in. In Zach Neese's teaching, *Entertaining Demons Unaware*, he asks the question.

> **What's the spirit being entertained [or welcomed into] here? Are you being entertained by the Spirit of Christ, or is there something darker that is being beautified...?**[73]

I am not saying that the only thing we can do is listen to hymns, read Scripture, and watch cheesy movies that try to act out the Bible word-for-word. Even those hymns and Bible-based movies will be infused by some level of brokenness through an actor, director, writer, or artist.

We see things in this world that do not align with His Word, but as Neese points out, the question we should ask is: "Is this worth listening to? What is it doing inside me? ...[and when we watch or listen to these things] what spirit is being welcomed into our house?" Is this loving God with all that I am, or am I laying here on the couch filling myself with something not of Him?

If faith comes by hearing and there is nothing worth listening to other than Christ's Word, then we must be alert and choose intentionally what we are going to listen to. We must be purposeful to get the filter out before we listen. We need to make the decision to seek the kingdom, and unless it is Christ's Word, the Truth, that returns, there is nothing to listen to. Identifying the spirit as it knocks on the door is a great way to keep from letting it in. God loves to be that barrier. As we let His Word redefine our beliefs, redefine who we say He is, it redefines who we are. These don't have to be long prayers; by saying something as profound and simple as confirming that some other spirit is trying to make its way in, and that He is our Protector and Redeemer, we choose to refuse entry to any other spirit. Confirmation that what has been said is a lie, that death is death, is Truth. Revealing the light to the darkness makes the dark area dark no longer; it has light.

Just as our prayers need not be long and drawn out, God's response doesn't need to be either. Like a child who wants to argue with his parents because he has not been given a satisfactory reason why he must stop playing or go to bed, we too are often unwilling to accept a short answer from God. We want a dissertation from God explaining who is attacking, what the attack is about, what it is going to feel like, where it stems from, when it all started, when it is going to get the most intense, or even why it is happening. But all we need to know is that He says it is not Him, which means it is a lie. That is all we need in order to deny or reject what is being said to us. If it's a lie, it's a lie and if it's truth, it's truth. All of the other who, what, where, when, and why stuff is simply the knowledge of good and evil. Does it really matter? To paraphrase *The Message*, if it's not Christ's Truth, there is nothing to listen to.[vii]

Short, simple communication with God is sometimes the most impactful, helpful, and fruitful.

"God is that a lie?"
"Yes"
"Okay, thanks. I love You and trust You.
I am not going to believe it."
or
"No."
"Okay. Thank You for confirming what I heard. I may not understand it all right now, but I trust that You will continue to reveal Your truth to me.

These are complete conversations. It won't look like that all of the time, but it often can. Hearing His Truth is how faith develops and strengthens. Coming into agreement with His Truth is how we believe it. As we believe His Truth more and experience Him more, we become freer, increasingly like the person He had in mind when He created us. That then allows us to live in His reality.

Although our freedom is under relentless attack, we do not need to live defeated lives. Often when we are being attacked we are right on the cusp of something great in our relationship with our Father. Worshiping Him, pouring adoration and gratitude on Him, should not be lost in that attack. As the attacks get greater, much like the Crowder lyrics found at the beginning of this chapter, the celebration of our freedom should become stronger and louder. Made in the image of such a creative Creator, it's only natural for us to be creative. Our celebrations should reflect the unique beauty He made within us. Sometimes we just need to go to the shouting grounds and pour out our love on Him.

---

vii Romans 10:17

Think about this.
Wrap your minds around it.
This is serious business, ...
Take it to heart.
Remember your history,
your long and rich history.
I am God, the only God you've had
or ever will have—
incomparable, irreplaceable—
From the very beginning
telling you what the ending will be,
all along letting you in
on what is going to happen,
assuring you, 'I'm in this for the long
haul, I'll do exactly
what I set out to do,'....
I've said it,
and I'll most certainly do it.
I've planned it,
so it's as good as done.
- Isaiah 46: 8-11 (The Message)

Steven Cohen

20
The Nature of Truth

Truth has no birthdate. It, like God, has always been. If God is Truth, then, like Love, it would have existed prior to Day One within our concept of time. Remember, Truth is *reality*, not fact. God can see the beginning from the end and the end from the beginning.[i] Consider Revelation 22:13:

> *I am the Alpha and the Omega, the first and the last, the beginning and the end.*

God dwells outside of the realm of time. So has it been with truth; it is not time dependent.

In the beginning, God spoke existence into existence. The key *truth* here is that God spoke Truth. He speaks reality. He created them both, and that reality is the key to life. *He* is the key, the origin, not just of life as we know it, but of Life in its totality. Many times that brings up the question: if He created life and He is alive, then how did He create Himself? This is a valid, logical question, like the chicken and the egg; with our limited minds, or until God reveals it to us, we will never be able to *figure* it out. This is where the liar has plagued so many people with thoughts like, if God is hiding that from you, then what else is He hiding? Or, why won't He just tell you? Does He not trust you? Love you?

It may just be that He is protecting us. Is it possible that we are not ready for reality? Were we created to know truth in its entirety? Or were we created to walk with Him, talk with Him, and continually be in relationship with Him? Giving us everything we want and sending us on our merry way doesn't cultivate relationship.

If our minds are blown by some of the simplest things here on this planet, how much more intense would total revelation be? Read the book of Revelation, the last book in the Bible. How many people read through it on the first time and get it, truly get it? Sometimes our minds simply can't fathom how mind-blowing the

---
[i] Isaiah 46:10

The Nature of Truth

answer is. Could it be that we would spontaneously explode in awe of the truth behind the truth? This mystery very well could be the component of heaven that those who say they would be bored worshiping God all the time are missing. I think getting to see the behind-the-scenes action will be part of that worship. Every time we see how something works, or He answers another question, we will simply be in such great awe that we will praise Him as He deserves, as He's deserved since the beginning.

I like to imagine what it would have been like as He spoke existence into existence. Questions come to mind: Did it all form at the first sound, or did it unfold as the words rolled off His tongue? Does He even have or need a tongue? Does the kingdom of heaven's physics play by the same rules as Earth's? If not, sound will likely not function as it does here, so what did the sounds of creation sound like? Did He hear them? While I want to know, I must also acknowledge that our understanding, our science, our laws and theories, and how everything works may just be blown away like dust once unveiled truth is revealed.

What if God is simply waiting to share the totality of beauty and awe with His children when we are all sitting in heaven with Him. This is where faith and truth collide. Although we may not understand and have not experienced His ultimate reality, we have a choice whether or not to believe it. And if we cannot, or we choose not to believe that He is the beginning and the end of all existence, then reality is impossible to grasp. Without truth, there is death and bondage. With truth, comes life and freedom.

Some religions are afraid to release their followers to be who they were created to be. Countless stories follow people who have joined sects, religions, and cults who, with their families, are being held hostage. The leaders, through manipulation, secrecy, and fear keep followers under their influence, under *their* influence. Behind the guise of religion and spirituality, people have Truth hidden from them. Many times, those hiding from the Truth are also unaware of reality because they themselves are deceived. They believe that the rules and regulations, and our obedience of them, are how we establish and stay in relationship with God. But rules and regulations are simply bondage, even the ones we think we have received from God.

Much like the statement God made in the Garden about the Tree of the Knowledge of Good and Evil, the "rules" or "laws" were also warnings full of compassion. Yes, if broken they bring consequences, but like a Father warning His children of impending danger, those rules were put in place to help guide us to Him, not protect us from His wrath. We are not designed to be in bondage. He created us for freedom, to rule over this domain. Our hearts desire freedom. We seek the sky and long for the beauty of the stars. We hike to mountaintops, gazing on the horizon and its beauty. We feel the desire and freedom to roam, even in our captive spaces. Peter says in 1 Peter 2:16,

> **Live as people who are free, not using your freedom as a cover-up for evil, but living as servants of God.**

If God came to set the captive free and we are to live free, why do we bind each other with rules and regulations? God recognizes structure here on earth and even yielded to the demands of the Israelites to give them a king.[ii] But that does not mean that was the way He desired it. At that time, God was speaking through the prophet Samuel to bring His Word to His people. But, as God said,

> *[My people] have rejected Me from being king over them... According to all the deeds that they have done, from the day I brought them up out of Egypt even to this day, forsaking Me and serving other gods... Now then, obey their voice; only you shall solemnly warn*

---

ii 1 Samuel 8:6-22

The Nature of Truth

them and show them the ways of the king who shall reign over them.[iii]

God was supposed to be their King. He is supposed to be our King. The nature of truth is that it restores the kingship to the King. It returns the honor, power, and glory to the One who deserves it and frees those who are in the kingdom of the King. Truth originates with Him, resides in Him, and is given freely by Him to His children.

So Jesus was saying to those Jews who had believed Him, "If you continue in My word, then you are truly disciples of Mine; and you will know the truth, and the truth will make you free."[iv]

When we have a relationship with Jesus, when we continue to stay in His Word, we will be set free. This word, *word*, has been twisted in a manner that makes it seem as though Jesus wanted us to read our Bibles all day long, or that there was a minimum requirement as to how much we have to read or memorize in order for us to be His disciples and be free. We must remember that Jesus is called *the Word* and we are to continue to seek Him, walking with Him in the cool of the morning. The original Greek for this instance of the word, *Word*, is *logō* meaning a statement, a speech, or a word (embodying an idea).[74] While the Bible is invaluable, our relationship with the Author of it is so much more important. People can buy a Bible, read a Bible, even quote the Bible and never be in relationship with Christ. Jesus wants us to seek Him, to be counseled by His Holy Spirit so that He can teach us, be with us, love on us in the cool of the morning. His Truth, the only truth, will reveal His nature, so that we can know Him, be set free, and experience His true Love.

---

iii 1 Samuel 8:6-8
iv John 8: 31-32 NASB

> Darkness cannot drive out darkness; only light can do that. Hate cannot drive out hate; only love can do that.
>
> – Martin Luther King Jr.

Steven Cohen

21
The Fruit of Truth

What LIES Beneath

The phrase *truth in love* is often laced with pride, hatred, and jealousy, and comes from a place of judgment and self-righteousness. Because we are not the source of truth, nor are we righteous on our own, we make horrible judges. We often base our thoughts on the thoughts of those before us, the thoughts of those who have based their thoughts on those before them. Our judgments are regularly based on the judgment that was placed on us. Our opinions are our perceptions of truth.

But, as Martin Luther King said, "Darkness cannot drive out darkness; only light can do that." Our bias cannot fix another's bias, nor can our brokenness fix someone else's brokenness. Only love can do that. In recent years we have seen the continual erosion of love. Our emotions rule us. We become slaves to our thoughts and perceptions and, through that slavery, we allow perceived, relative truth, to replace absolute truth. While relative truth is the only truth we can personally know, once we become stagnant in it we become complacent in our own darkness. We cannot help others nor can we drive out our own darkness. This is why self-help books don't work. We, living in the darkness, are trying to enlighten those around us with our own attempts to create light. But being mere reflectors we cannot create light; we need the light to reflect through us.

That light is the Way, the Truth, and the Life that Jesus spoke of: Himself. The Pharisees knew the principle that we are to be reflectors. The Law said that there must be two men to testify in order for something to be deemed true. They told Jesus He could not testify about Himself. In the same principle that darkness cannot drive out darkness, individuals cannot bring the truth about themselves. People see themselves from an altered perspective, but Jesus countered their argument, "Even if I testify about Myself, My testimony is valid. For I know where I came from and where I am going." He continued, "I am one witness for myself, and the Father who sent Me bears witness for Me."[i] Although He was and is Truth, He still fulfilled the law that required two witnesses. Just as the

---
[i] John 8:14 &18

Source of light can provide light to drive out darkness, the Truth can tell the truth about itself.

So, what is the fruit of all of this? Love. The fruit of truth is Love. When we hear the truth about someone, we are able to have compassion and our perspective changes, especially when we combine that with hearing the truth about ourselves. Love sets us free to be patient, kind, and content, preventing envy, pride, conceitedness, tastelessness, and selfishness. Love does not get riled up, nor does it manipulate others, keep records of wrongs, or celebrate the mistreatment of others. Love "rejoices in truth; it bears all things, it believes all things, it hopes all things, it endures all things. Love never fails."[ii]

This does not mean that Love is gullible; quite the opposite. Love rejoices in truth. That truth, that love, allows us to love others despite what is done to us. It encourages and enables us to love someone, bearing all they have done to us, to believe that no matter what, they are a child of God and are lovable; to hope in restoration, redemption, and for true relationship, enduring all hardships. Love never fails, it rejoices in truth.

Love sets us free. We are not bound by our judgment, hate, biases, or lenses. Instead we are free from the toxins that pollute our minds, preventing us from seeing who He has created us to be.

If the Son sets you free, you will be free indeed.[iii]

So what is the fruit of truth? What it really boils down to is love and freedom, two things only God can truly provide. As truth is revealed, the Father's love pours over us and we are set free. The lies and bondage we have found ourselves in are broken off, revealing who He created us to be, loved as He has always wanted.

[ii] 1 Corinthians 13:4-8a TLV
[iii] John 8:36

"Nothing is more rare in any man," says Emerson, "than an act of his own." It is quite true. Most people are other people. Their thoughts are some one else's opinions, their lives a mimicry, their passions a quotation.
- Oscar Wilde, De Profundis

Steven Cohen

22
The Role of Truth

In an age where quotes like the one opening this chapter are readily available and social media provides a platform to voice our opinions, it is easy to get caught up liking and sharing what others say, ending up not being ourselves, but other people.

Growing up, it was different. We didn't have social media or the readily available mass of data at our fingertips. But I still witnessed, as I imagine you also did, situations where people took on someone else's identity. We see a person we think we like and we try to emulate them. My children do this, many times to their detriment, mimicking me, proclaiming, "I want to be like daddy when I grow up." Not that daddy is a bad person to be; it just isn't them. This isn't a nature versus nurture debate. It's a creation thing. Authentic identity is what Psalm 139:13-14 talks about:

> For you formed my inward parts;
> you knitted me together in my mother's womb.
> I praise you, for I am fearfully and
> wonderfully made. (ESV)

The TLV version says it this way,

> For you have created my conscience.
> You knit me together in my mother's womb.
> I praise You, for I am awesomely, wonderfully made.

The role of truth is to feed authentic identity. God created us. We are awesomely and wonderfully made. We are created, not evolved, and we are created in His image. Not as mini-me's or minions, but as remarkable creations of God, tasked with the calling to reflect His nature. Plain and simple. If we cannot grasp that our foundation is Him and that we are amazing creations grounded on Him, then we will continue to struggle with who we are.

Many times, we get in our own way. A dear friend of our family one day told me that I did not realize my full potential. When he said that, my wife and I looked at each other, silently agreeing to disagree with him. We know that God has created us for much more than what we were being utilized for at that time. We both had been given visions of God's plan for us, and where we were was not it. So, we knew our potential, because God had shown it to us. But what my friend said turned out to be more accurate than I wanted to admit. After talking with God about it one day, He pointed out that we had not realized and allowed our potential to come to fruition because we were not relying on Him. We gave Him credit, but we weren't really pressing into Him as our foundation.

> *It was a blow so appalling that I did not know what to do, so I flung myself on my knees, and bowed my head, and wept, and said, "The body of a child is as the body of the Lord: I am not worthy of either." That moment seemed to save me. I saw then that the only thing for me was to accept everything. Since then - curious as it will no doubt sound - I have been happier. It was of course my soul in its ultimate essence that I had reached. In many ways I had been its enemy, but I found it waiting for me as a friend. When one comes in contact with the soul it makes one simple as a child, as Christ said one should be.*

This realization by Oscar Wilde apparently came at a time after he went through a significant identity crisis. It didn't come until he gave up everything to rely on God for each and every thing. Wilde reached his "ultimate essence," when he gave up being who he thought he should be and submitted to his Creator. Often, we make things too complicated; we rely on our own understanding about how the world operates, casually throwing around platitudes like, "You can do anything you put your mind to." But we don't see how this excludes God and puts you in His place. God is the Creator of our minds, He is the creator of our souls and, as Wilde says, when we come in contact with our soul, it makes us as a simple as a child, just as Christ said we should be. As we have already seen, Wilde continues:

> *It is tragic how few people ever 'possess their souls' before they die. 'Nothing is more rare in any man,' says Emerson, 'than an act of his own.' It is quite true. Most people are other people. Their thoughts are some one else's opinions, their lives a mimicry, their passions a quotation.*
>
> - De Profundis – Oscar Wilde[75]

How are we other people? As we earlier discussed, one way we "become" other people is through this thing called social media, where we are so easily swayed and agreeable to others' thoughts, which are often simply quotations of someone else. Additionally, we become other people when we are not living as we were created to be. We will never be unrecognizable to God because He sees us and knows us. But the lies we have believed can keep us from living as the people He wants us to be.

In Psalm 139, David reveals how wonderful it is to have a God who knows us so intimately, even before we came to be. We are to be children, we are to love and trust Him with "faith like a child." When we do, we get out of our own way and can be the individuals He created us to be. But, in order to do that, we need to seek who He says we are.

This is different from what Paul was saying when he said he was, "all things to all people." The core of who Paul was did not change when he was around others. Instead, he found ways to relate to them, to have empathy for them. Again empathy, not sympathy. You do not see Paul, or Jesus for that matter, taking on the burdens of others in a manner that caused them to forget who they were. Yes, Jesus wept when Lazarus died. His friend was dead and His other friends were hurting. He felt their sorrow. He felt their pain. Jesus Himself felt that loss, but He did not let it overwhelm

Him. He did not let it create doubt in who He was. Lazarus' death gave Jesus an opportunity to show who He was. Even in the hardest of times, especially in the hardest of times, we have a Creator who knows us so intimately that He knows the importance of reminding us who and whose we are. Often, the hard times are tools He is using to burn away impurities and expose our true identity.

My wife's book, *Refining Identity*, speaks exactly to this point. Using the illustration of God as our Refiner, she walks through Scripture, hand-in-hand with readers, to encounter the Refiner and His process to reveal our true identity. From the violent, dirty extraction of the hidden gold from deep within the earth's crust, to the hot crucible used to melt away the impurities that have become a part of us, He rejoices in some of our hardest times, not because He likes to see us suffer, but instead because He enjoys seeing us come closer to who He created us to be. As we are broken free from bondage and junk that has attached and woven itself into our lives, we are revealed. I can only imagine His smile as He sees more of the people He created us to be, exposed from beneath the piles of lies.

As our truth, or what God says is true about us, is revealed to us, we can begin to see what we are to build our understanding and our lives upon. Many times, our foundations are buried deep beneath layers, like a long, lost city. Just as time and circumstance cover over magnificent ruins, so do years of beliefs cover us. Sometimes this process feels difficult or uncomfortable, as we may have to dig cavernous holes in our soul. But it is through those layers of adversity that we can begin to see what is truly us and what lie's beneath. I would like to tell you exactly who that is, but that conversation is between you and your Creator.

What LIES Beneath

Steven Cohen

SECTION 5
Applying Truth

Truth is like sunscreen; it should be applied and reapplied often and should even be used on cloudy days. REI, a resource for outdoor enthusiasts, offers these sunscreen guidelines:

- Apply liberally 15 minutes before exposure.
- Reapply a) after 40 or 80 minutes of swimming or sweating, b) immediately after towel drying, and c) at least every two hours.[76]

I remember the day the local REI opened on I-85 in Atlanta. It was the first time I could climb a rock wall inside a store. (Anytime I see an REI today, I feel nostalgic, wanting to go inside just to see if they have a wall to climb too.) I guess their marketing strategy really worked on me. When I think of adventure and outdoors, that's where my mind goes.

The sunscreen guidelines above are intended to help REI clients prevent the harmful effects of UV rays. The goal is not to rid the world of the cause of sunburn, as that is not feasible for them. The same is true for our spiritual lives; it is not possible to rid ourselves entirely of the devil or his demons, nor is it our responsibility. Throughout Scripture, we are told that God will take care of His people and their circumstances, specifically in the book of Revelation. However, it is possible for us to have protection against the enemy's harmful effects.

Even cloudy days require protection. These principles of protection are important every day, even, and perhaps especially, on the days you think you don't need them. As we continue to become less susceptible to bondage through our reliance upon truth, our enemy is going to take every chance he can to get us back in a rut.

Often, in the Bible, God refers to our relationship with Him as a marriage covenant. He calls us His bride. What kind of marriage would exist if the husband and wife put in their schedule a planned, purposeful, and dedicated time to talk, but then they didn't talk to each other for the rest of the day or week? What if, during that appointment, the husband and wife simply spewed all their struggles, all their hurts, all of their desires out on their spouse, but they did not take the time to listen to their mate? Maybe, on occasion, at the dining room table or at a restaurant they repeated a habitual line of communication, "Sweetheart, you're so good, thank you for this food," and then chowed down. For the first few times, the thought may be nice, but once it has lost its genuineness, once it became just a patterned line of communication it would lose its meaning, its heart. Is that truly a relationship?

Much of what lies beneath requires day-to-day, hour-by-hour, minute-by-minute application. While setting aside purposeful, dedicated time for prayer is beneficial, it is not the only time we should be talking to God and building our relationship with Him.

The application of truth has been woven all throughout this book. The following chapters are a summation of that application and are designed to be a quick reference guide when needed.

You will never cease to be the most amazed person on earth at what God has done for you on the inside.
- Oswald Chambers, My Utmost For His Highest

Steven Cohen

23
Our Testimony Is Powerful

What LIES Beneath

We have explored how satan attacks who we are, who God designed us and desires us to be. It may seem that we should strive to be perfect or to desire to be flawless. And, while perfection will be our reality once we step fully through the veil into the eternal presence of God, it is impossible to achieve until that point. We are vexed by this knowledge of good and evil we have. While we can reduce the lies we believe, there is no power within us to overcome our lies if we do not share the testimony of what God has done in our lives.

So, what is a testimony? First let me ask, what is the difference between a pattern and a formula? Go ahead and think about that for a moment. Don't continue reading until you do. No, seriously, stop reading, dog-ear the page, close the book, and think about it.

God asked me that question one morning during a quiet time as I contemplated the design of a tattoo. (Ironic, isn't it? According to many people, tattoos are sinful and God cannot be near you if you are sinning, right? What if God is bigger than the limitations we put on Him? Simply put, He is.) To backtrack a bit, when I was in my teens, I got a tattoo of a scorpion on my right shoulder. I had believed for so long that my personality, my emotions, and my future were already designed and destined by the stars. After becoming a Christian, I learned and discovered that, while I am created and designed in a specific fashion, it is not by the stars. As God later revealed, that is a great example of worshiping the created instead of the Creator. Our Creator created the stars. He showed me how worshiping the stars is no different than worshiping a golden calf; either way, I make something out to be greater than He is.

As I contemplated the difference between a pattern and a formula, I came up blank. Some guesses came to mind, but I was drawing at straws hoping to avoid looking stupid in front of God. How embarrassing would that be to admit to God that I had no idea? Without condemnation or telling me that I was stupid for failing to comprehend what He was getting at, He simply told me, "*The difference is who gets the credit.*" I was stumped. I didn't understand what He meant by *who gets the credit.* So, He asked me about my belief in astrology and how that worked. I replied that people had looked, over thousands of years, for ways to identify characteristics and traits of people, born at certain times and dates, in relation to the stars. He showed me that what people had discovered were patterns, patterns that He created, much like the pattern of the seasons, time, and governing of light during the day and night. But astrology took those patterns, created formulas, and took credit for the patterns. That's like reverse engineering a cake, making a recipe, and then giving credit for the recipe to the cake. By doing so, it strips the Creator of the credit due, placing that credit on the pattern, making it self-sufficient. Doesn't that sound a lot like Genesis 3, where satan tells two of God's most intricate creations that they do not need God, because, basically, they could be *like* God? The point of a formula is to allow for duplication of the same results based on something we *do*, instead of identifying a pattern in what God *has done* or *is doing*.

    A testimony is a pattern. We will not see it unless we are looking for it, but He has a unique pattern in each and every one of us. I have been involved in small groups since just a few months after my salvation. At a recent, promotional weekend event, called a small group block party, at our church, God told me to move from the back of the church where I stood to the front door. The front entry was saturated with greeters and small group leaders, so I couldn't understand His reason for wanting me there. Then I saw a man and his wife, on a mission to get to service; God told me to go disturb them. So, I did. The man didn't look too happy that I stopped him; he seemed a little off-put that someone was keeping him from his destination. However, he was respectful and tolerant of my conversation, and, by the end, he seemed to have relaxed a bit and was even willing to receive my invitation to group the next morning. I wasn't sure if I would ever see him again, but I enjoyed the conversation and it was interesting to see what God was up to.

To add some context, earlier that week I had come to the end of my rope with an earwig infestation at our house. Not only were they in our yard, they also continually came inside, and I was tired of it. (You may ask how earwigs have anything to do with our testimony, which would make you much better at looking for patterns than me.) I was simply frustrated that the exterminators were not doing their job. With at least two earwigs in our hallway every morning, the treatments we had been paying for obviously weren't working. I contacted another company we had previously used and I recognized the voice on the other end. I remembered him as a student of mine from many years back when I had been a self-defense instructor. I knew he owned the company, but he rarely, if ever, answered the phones. He said they could do a few extra treatments that my current pest control company was not doing, which sounded like a plan, but, first, I had to figure out a way to cancel my current contract; so we left it at that.

Back to the morning after our block party: the gentleman I had spoken to at church came into the restaurant where my group met. A strange feeling came over me as I recognized him from somewhere. (You might be thinking that I recognized him because I had just seen him the night before, but this recognition was different than that. I sensed God telling me that I knew him from somewhere else, though I hadn't realized it the night before. Our small group met and, as conversation progressed, he said something that triggered my memory. I realized then that he was my old student. The night before at church, he had told me he felt God calling him back after he had walked away from Him, and then this morning it all came together. We discussed how God had orchestrated connections, patterns, "signs," that would confirm answers to his prayers from the previous weeks. Seeing the pattern of how God had orchestrated my call earlier in the week, then sending me to the front of the church as this man walked in, and how God was revealing Himself through this pattern of events filled my former student with hope and restored his faith in God, his Father, whom he had walked away from some time ago.

Patterns tell our story, much like a patchwork quilt. When we are in the midst of experiencing our journey, it is difficult to see the beauty or benefit of each moment. Some moments are easier than others. I couldn't imagine how an earwig infestation would bring glory to God, nor did I even wonder about it at the time. But now that part of my testimony can bring hope, faith, and love to others as well. When we step back and ask for God's viewpoint, we get to see how He is, and always has been, with us. As those patterns are revealed to us, it also builds *our* hope and faith and is an encouragement to look for Him more and more.

If we try to tell someone else how to live, modeled after how we have lived our life, then we are making our pattern a formula. We are taking God out of the place of power He deserves and making circumstances and decisions our god. That has no power for those we talk to and no power for ourselves. When we share what God has done and we show others how we have been able to see the pattern in our lives, it helps build hope and faith, not because it is something we have done, but because it encourages them to build a deeper relationship with their Creator, their Savior, their Redeemer, and the love He has for us.

> Truth will sound like hate to those who hate the truth.
>
> — Unknown

Steven Cohen

24
Confronting the Lies of Others

Confrontation doesn't always look like it does on TV or like it may have in your home growing up. Confrontation can seem very non-confrontational. Some of the best military, police, and negotiation tactics include de-escalation. And, make no mistake, while de-escalation is made to seem as though it is not, it is a very specific and calculated form of confrontation.

The first thing we need to consider when we confront someone is our motive. Confrontation is biblical. Matthew 18 gives a perfect illustration about how we are to confront a brother who sins against us. But what if they are sinning against themselves? What if they simply believe a lie that prevents them from growing in their relationship with Christ, or worse, keeps them from reconciling with their Savior. The answer is still very similar. With Love. As we've discussed, Loving others, is different than just showing people love or doing good for others. When we Love others, as God Loves us, it allows us to give bits of God to those around us. If we do not bring Love, bring God, then we are not Loving them. This means that the confrontation is all about us and we have no power to change them.

The most important approach to begin with is prayer. We need to listen for what our Father says about our brothers and sisters. If we are not sure that we are hearing clearly from Him about someone else, then we should not approach them as if we are. That's prideful, controlling, and manipulative, none of which are fruits of the Spirit. Paul desires most that we have the gift of prophecy for a reason. I believe it is because we must hear from God in order to deliver an authentic word from God.

Empathy is also very important when approaching someone about a lie they may have believed. Empathy is the experience of understanding another person's condition from their perspective.[77] If we can take a moment and place ourselves in their shoes, it can go a long way when sharing our testimony with them. If we cannot understand where they are at, simply asking for them to share can open up a channel of communication and understanding that was missing and preventing healing from taking place. Many times, simply bringing the death hiding inside to the light helps bring healing and freedom. Remember to continually ask God what He says about the situation and be sensitive to allow only His input, not yours. Keep in mind that, unless you are a licensed counselor and this person has approached you for assistance, you should not present yourself in the role of a counselor.

Remember, there is a difference between sympathy and empathy. As we discovered earlier in this book when we considered the issue of deception, sympathy opens us up to take on burdens which were never ours to begin with. Sympathy is a feeling of pity or sorrow for someone else's misfortune.[78] As we witness someone experience trauma, tragedy, burden, or offense, it can be easy to pick up those emotions and carry them, but they are not ours to bear. Each one of us has our own struggles that we are to submit to the Lord. If we are confronting someone out of sympathy or our own emotional duress, there is likely an issue that we need to address in our own life first.

Jesus does not mince words on this topic:

> **You hypocrite, first take the log out of your own eye, and then you will see clearly to take the speck out of your brother's eye.**[i]

This is a strong statement meant to ensure that we seek God first. If we do not, then we are likely not seeing things clearly in the first place and we might try fixing something that isn't as broken as we think it is. We must seek God regarding our issues and to gain His vision on how to approach others. Make sure the only benefit we strive to attain from the confrontation is God's approval. If you are trying to impress yourself or someone else then the motive is tainted.

---

i   Matthew 7:5

Remember, our testimony has power. Often, simply sharing our story can break off shackles, having been exactly what someone needed to hear in order to be free. With that being said, keep in mind that it's easy to talk about ourselves more than others want to hear. Letting them speak not only allows for an open lane of communication and understanding, but it also allows for trust to form. Sharing a testimony is good, but the moment we turn that pattern into a formula, we remove God from the moment.

> The truth is everybody is going to hurt you: you just have to find the ones worth suffering for.
>
> - Bob Marley

Steven Cohen

25
Loving Others Despite Their Lies

Bob Marley's quote has inspired many people to find the people in our lives who are worth suffering for. Oh, to grasp this statement through God's eyes.

Imagine the Trinity is sitting down for breakfast one morning, perhaps on day four or five of creation week, as they discuss how they are going to bring about the next phase of creation. One person, perhaps the Holy Spirit, says to another, maybe Jesus, "*Every one of them* is going to hurt us. You'll just have to find the ones worth suffering for." Jesus replies, "*Every one of them* is going to hurt us and every single one is worth it. It's not suffering when you love them as we do."

The Bible tells us to love others. When asked, Christ said the greatest commandment was to love God with all your heart, and the second greatest which was equal, so second in order, though not by magnitude or importance, is to love others. So, it is just as important that we love those around us as it is that we love God. He did not say to love only the ones who are lovable.

It is also written that if we do not love our brothers and sisters, people whom we can see, then we cannot love God, whom we cannot see.[i] Wow. That is hard to swallow. If we do not love others, if we cannot love others, then what we believe to be love for God, our Father, isn't love at all. Hmm. Why is that so? I suppose a more important question would be, what is love? Is it an emotion, a feeling, a gesture, an action? No. Scripture says God is Love. Not that love is God; we are not to worship love. But the essence of love is God, love is made up of God. When we love God, we are actually presenting a portion of Himself to Him. When we love others, we give or impart part of God to them. That is one reason why it feels so good for both parties.

This makes statements like, "Love your neighbors," and, "Love your enemies," more understandable. He wants us to share Him with everyone we encounter: friends, family, neighbors,

---
i 1 John 4:20 edits mine.

enemies, and strangers. But what if they have offended us? What if they have wronged us in some way? What if they are the bane of our existence? What if we cannot stand them? Then we do not truly see them for whom God created them to be.

What about the ruler of a totalitarian government or the leader of a gang? What about the originator of a prostitution ring or a mass murderer? Remember that God loved you well before you knew Him, and, as such, He loves all of those people as well. They are His children, just like you. If you cannot get over what they have done, then it is a good indication that you need Him to help show you who He sees them to be. What if the thing that bothers you the most is simply an agitator, used by God to break you free something?

What if part of your testimony is exactly what that person needs in order for them to be able to see how God sees them. You are not going to save them, you are not going to fix all that they have done wrong, all the things that you hate most about them, but by showing them God and how He sees them, He can. Even though He doesn't need us to be a part of His restoration and reconnection to His kiddos, it is so awesome that He allows to be anyway.

Nick Vujicic, an international evangelist who was born without arms or legs shared a story about an international mission trip where he had gone to minister and speak. Standing at the altar with his in-country host, Nick noticed a woman in her nineties approach. Her frail body stood hunched over. She had been unable to walk upright for years. Even at her late age, this woman accepted Christ and received miraculous healing. She walked out of the church upright for the first time in many years. Elated and astounded, Nick's host asked if he knew who she was. To Nick's surprise, he learned that she was the originator of the sex slave trade in that country. Thousands of women had been bought and sold into slavery as a result of this woman's actions.

Although we may be appalled by the actions or the words that someone speaks, we should let the Holy Spirit reveal to us their value in the Father's eyes. Let Him tell us how much suffering they are worth. Let Him show us how they got so broken, not so that we can feel sorry for them, but so that we can understand the lies they have believed and we can share with them how much God cherishes them regardless. Our place is not to judge others to be good or bad, worthy or not. We are only to consider how we can share the love God has rained on us and what part of God they need to know in order to set them free.

Loving Others Despite Their Lies

Guard your heart diligently, for from it flow the springs of life.
- Proverbs 4:23

Steven Cohen

26
Guarding Against New Lies

As the G.I. Joe cartoon used to end its public service announcement, *"Knowing is half the battle."* Without knowing we are in a battle it's hard, if not impossible, to defend ourselves. Now that we know how lies are used against us and how our enemy wants to destroy us through them, we must be aware that the attacks will not stop. As I mentioned earlier, the attacks will likely even get worse or they will at least be noticed much more commonly. It is essential that we stay on guard, seeking the kingdom in all we do, in all we allow ourselves to believe, in every thought that enters our mind. We must remain diligent. We must trust our Father as our Protector.

      One very common Christianese statement is, "Take your thoughts captive," but what does that mean? Like finding your identity in Christ, it sounds great, but so many people struggle to understand. And beyond understanding what it means, how do we do it practically?

      Regardless of your opinion of law officials, for this example, remove all preconceptions or judgments about them and imagine the ideal law officer. Not the one who lets us get away with everything and doesn't uphold his oath to serve and protect. Many of us have been living with that law officer at the helm for much of our lives, and it hasn't helped one bit.

      This law officer has an in-depth understanding of the spirit of the law. That spirit of the law is infused into the officer's desire to ensure your safety and it drives the officer's passion to serve you, to know you intimately, to honor you, to counsel you, and to love you. This is your personal, spiritual, and emotional security guard.

      As a thought enters or is created in our mind, it passes by the guard shack where that ideal officer stands on duty. The cool part about this guard shack is that it has no fence attached. There is no wall with a weak point or a blind spot to it. Rather, this guard shack encompasses your entirety, extending beyond your boundaries, warning of impending attacks. The guard isn't reliant on sensors that could fail or cameras that could be hacked or disabled; he fills the shack, there is no way to slip by him.

This guard isn't there to filter through all the thoughts for us, to allow only good, to shelter us, or to prevent us from choosing evil. He works with us to allow or disallow thoughts from entering. It is ultimately our choice as to what passes through. Any thought that we know doesn't align with God's character can be stopped at our command. The guard can deflect or protect against a thought's entry in our mind simply by aligning with the warning God gives. Anything suspect of violating God's will for us should be arrested, detained for further investigation. It is critical that we do not just leave these thoughts unprocessed because they can pile up and become overwhelming.

A detention center exists in our mind when we let a thought in. If we do not tend to it quickly, it will age and mature and develop, affecting other thoughts. If we are not paying attention to it, there is also the possibility of its escape from detention, where it can simply run rampant, affecting us in ways we never imagined. It is important to examine the thought quickly, comparing it with truth. Anything other than what aligns with God's Truth must be submitted to the Judge to be convicted and thrown into the pit of Hell.[79]

You may be wondering where this guard is and why you have never heard from him or seen him. He has, in reality, been there since before you were created and desires to introduce Himself. Our guard is the Holy Spirit, His tremendous depth and understanding of the Law, of God's Word, is innate to Him, because *He*, God, is *Him*, the Spirit.

The best security guards intimately know who they protect so that they can understand their activities, their personality, their capabilities, and how they might react to various situations. That relationship builds trust and friendship. While there is nothing we can do to make the Holy Spirit stronger or better at His job, there are things that we can do, disciplines and practices that we can implement to strengthen our relationship with Him. The most important part is to introduce yourself to Him, invite Him into you, and let Him take residence inside you.

How that looks is simple, like you would invite anyone into your home. Open the door, greet them with a smile and say, "Come on in." You might say, "But I already did that with Jesus; I already have a relationship with Him." So did the disciples. So did many people in the Bible who were born again, yet they were also baptized with the Holy Spirit even after being born again, after being baptized in the name of Jesus.

If you have never done so before, take a moment now. It is as simple as saying something like this:

> Holy Spirit, I want to know You like never before. I want You to be a part of me in ways I have never imagined possible. I want to do life with You, to feel Your love and acceptance. I want Your protection, wisdom, guidance, counseling, and most of all friendship. Welcome Home.

Once you have established a relationship with the Holy Spirit, there are many ways to strengthen that relationship with Him. Many of these ways sound religious or like a list of rules, but they are relationship-building tools. They are known as disciplines. Not like the punishment or penalties you received as a consequence for wrong actions, but instead simply something you do on a regular basis. Not because you must, but instead because you get to. Two of my favorite disciplines are:

- Quality time with God – Whether that involves taking a drive while worshiping Him and His creation or isolating yourself in a closet in the back of your house, the key to this is not how quiet you can be or how grandiose your prayers are. The key to your quality time with God is that it's quality time with God. This is up to you and God. If you are in prayer and He shows you something that makes you want to dance, then dance. If you feel like shouting, then shout. Being still as some scriptures mention may or may not be the way you relate to Him. Be as still as you can while moving, or move as much as you can while being still. The key to being still is that your heart and mind are not all over the place in panic or worry, but you are instead present with God, concentrating on Him.

- Worship – This isn't just music. This is an activity and posture of the heart. Pouring love and adoration on God. Giving Him credit where credit is due and not blaming Him for what you think is bad. As we have discussed, lamentation is a God-thing which helps bring you back to Him. I believe lamenting is a way of worshiping Him, because He is the only one who can help you get through your challenges.

These two are by no means a comprehensive list on the disciplines. At the end of the book I've included resources which further expand on spiritual disciplines and how they can greatly influence your heart towards and relationship with God.

I do want to address and guard against the lie of the enemy that these disciplines themselves save us. They do not; there is nothing we can do to save ourselves. These disciplines are simply tools to help foster a more intimate relationship. Like dating your spouse, hanging out with friends, writing a pen pal, the more we do with them, the more transparent we are, the more genuine the effort, the closer we are, and the better we know each other. The better we know someone, the easier it is to let them guard, serve, minister, and love on us.

WRAPPING UP

So, what lies beneath? The answer, a lot. And what lie's beneath? I hope fewer than when you started.

What's next? Please know that there are no expectations on you now that you have finished this book. You do not have to be perfect, nor do you have to be completely free. Like my own freedom journey, you likely may need to go through this message again and again and again. I have lost track of how many messages I have heard, freedom-based books I have read, classes I have personally attended, and sessions and small groups I have facilitated. I stopped counting after about fifty events because it became less and less important about how many check marks I had next to my name and more and more about what bondage was being broken off. Every time I have the opportunity to be a part of anything I feel that will bring me closer to God's design and desire, I jump on it, knowing that it is not the event that is going to reveal God's Truth, it is God who will do that, in whatever dosage I am ready for at that time.

The key to take away from *What Lies Beneath: From Lies to Love* is simply that there is always something beneath. We are never perfect and neither are our neighbors, friends, family, co-workers, other drivers, people at the checkout line, customer service reps, or bosses. But we are called to love on them, not require love from them. We are to love people as we would like to be loved. In order to do that, we need to know what real love is and what it is not. There is only one place to learn that.

> **This is how we've come to understand and experience love: Christ sacrificed his life for us. This is why we ought to live sacrificially for our fellow believers, and not just be out for ourselves.**

The apostle John continues with an acutely convicting statement:

> *If you see some brother or sister in need and have the means to do something about it but turn a cold shoulder and do nothing, what happens to God's love? It disappears. And you made it disappear.*[i]

Does that mean you have control of God and His love? No, but it does mean that your choice to reflect His glory or not can make it diminish to those who desperately need it around you.

> *... let's not just talk about love; let's practice **real love** This is the only way we'll know we're **living truly**, living in God's reality... For **God is greater** than our worried hearts and knows more about us than we do ourselves.*[ii]

    A question to consider as we wrap up *What Lies Beneath*: What is keeping you from being who you were created to be? And do you want whatever that is to be what your life, faith, hope, and dreams are built on? Or, would you be willing to step out in faith and let the Holy Spirit guide you, love on you, and show you how amazing He is and how marvelously you have been created?

    What lies beneath will go many layers deep and may never seem to end, but God will meet you where He needs you to be, where He wants to heal you, where He wants to set you free, where He can take you from Lies to Love.

---

[i] 1 John 3:16-17 MSG
[ii] 1 John 3:18 & 20 MSG "Emphasis Mine"

Steven Cohen

RESOURCES

The God I Never Knew by Robert Morris

After You Believe: Why Christian Character Matters by N. T. Wright

The Spirit of the Disciplines by Dallas Willard

Hearing God: Developing a Conversational Relationship with God by Dallas Willard

Frequency: Tune In. Hear God. by Robert Morris

Celebration of Discipline by Richard J. Foster

Satan Unmasked: The Truth Behind the Lie by Dr. James Richards

How to Stop the Pain by Dr. James Richards

MEET STEVEN COHEN

When people first encounter me, they notice a passion in my eyes. Countless times I have heard how my eyes pierce with intensity, almost intimidating. That intensity many people perceive is simply my desire for everyone I have the honor of meeting to see and feel the ardent passion that God has for them.

Whether through teaching, writing, leading a team, facilitating group discussions, or being a husband and father, I try to approach life with that same intensity, calling God's design and desire out of others. But it wasn't always that way.

As an atheist for most of my life, I debated the existence of the very God I love today with that same passion and intensity. I searched for a solution to the unceasing, unquenchable desire for something greater than me. I explored multiple religions, belief systems, and cultures, only to be temporarily satisfied. Ultimately, I was left lacking true hope or understanding of who I was. I know now that God continued to pursue me, saving me from myself time and time again.

In 2002, I experienced complete love and the true fulfillment of my longing for more. It wasn't found in things or through my efforts to reach an enlightened state. This deep satisfaction was achieved only when I surrendered myself, my desires, my will, and my pride to the world's Savior, Jesus Christ.

Shortly after that moment, God revealed that He desired for me to share with the world that, although we may feel alone, unfulfilled, lacking, depressed, or abandoned, we are never too lost to be found.

This is the heart of Now Found Ministries: that you would know and be known by your Creator, Savior, and Counselor, and that you would experience His undying love for you.

ENDNOTES:

1. Hamp, Bob Alpha Summit, Gateway Church, Southlake, March, 2012. Lecture
2. History.com Staff, "History.com," A+E Networks, 2009, https://www.history.com/topics/world-trade-center.
3. The New York State Museum Staff, "NYSM.NYSED.gov," University of the State of New York, March 18, 2015, http://www.nysm.nysed.gov/wtc/about/facts.html.
4. "WolframAlpha.com," Wolfram, March 18, 2017, http://www.wolframalpha.com/input/?i=average+human+height.
5. King, Hobart M. Ph.D. RPG, "Expansive Soil and Expansive Clay: The Hidden Force behind basement and foundation problems," Geology.com, 2017-03-18, http://geology.com/articles/expansive-soil.shtml.
6. Willard, Dallas, "Truth and Reality Do Not Adapt to Us," Renovare, May 8, 2017, https://renovare.org/articles/truth-and-reality-do-not-adapt-to-us.

Chapter 1

1. Liptak, Adam, "Justice Sharply Divided in Gay Rights Case," New York Times Company, December 5, 2017, https://www.nytimes.com/2017/12/05/us/politics/supreme-court-same-sex-marriage-cake.html.
2. "Fact Definition," Google, 2018, https://www.google.com/search?q=fact+definition&aqs=chrome..69i57j0l5.3827j0j4&sourceid=chrome&ie=UTF-8.
3. "Bill Nye Debates Ken Ham – HD," Answers in Genesis, 1:10-1:12, 2014, https://www.youtube.com/watch?v=z6kgvhG3AkI.

Chapter 2

4. Phillips, W, "Lessons from the Fall: An Overview of Genesis 3," Answers in Genesis, May 31, 2009, https://answersingenesis.org/sin/original-sin/lessons-from-the-fall/.

Chapter 3:

5. *Matthew Henry's Concise Commentary* "John 1 Matthew Henry's Commentary," BibleHub.com, March 18, 2017, http://biblehub.com/commentaries/mhc/john/1.htm.

Chapter 4:

6. O'Keefe, James H. MD, Bhatti, Salman K. MD, Bajwa, Ata MD., DiNicolantonio, James J. PharmD, Lavie, Carl J. MD, "Alcohol and Cardiovascular Health: The Dose Makes the Poison...or the Remedy," Mayo Clinic Proceedings, Mayo Clinic, March 2014, https://www.mayoclinicproceedings.org/article/S0025-6196(13)01002-1/fulltext.
7. Gerszberg, Caren Osten, "If You Think a Glass of Wine Will Help You Sleep, Read This," Huffington Post, May 22, 2012, http://www.huffingtonpost.com/caren-osten-gerszberg/wine-and-health_b_1372082.html.
8. "Inhibitions Definition," Google 2018, https://www.google.com/search?q=inhibitions+definition&rtz=1C1CHBF_enUS756US756&oq=inhibitions&aqs=chrome&ie=UTF-8.
9. Hodanbosi, Carol and Johnathan G. Fairman, "The First and Second Laws of Motion," National Aeronautics and Space Administration, August 1996, https://www.grc.nasa.gov/www/k-12/WindTunnel/Activities/first2nd_lawsf_motion.html.
10. "-ion | Define -ion at Dictionary.com" Dictionary.com, September 1, 2018, https://www.dictionary.com/browse/-ion.
11. "Deception – Dictionary Definition," Vocabulary.com April 16, 2017 https://www.vocabulary.com/dictionary/deception.
12. Herold, Thomas, "Do You Know the Multiple Layers of the Root Word Ception?," Evolving Wealth Foundation, January 30, 2016 https://www.evolvingwealth.org/

multiple-layers-root-word-ception/.
13. "Strong's Greek 3806," BibleHub.com, September 01, 2018, https://biblehub.com/greek/3806.htm.
14. Metcalf, Linda, "Marriage and Family Therapy: A Practice Oriented Approach," Springer Publishing Company: New York, New York, 2011, p 72.
15. "Galatians 6 Commentary," BibleStudyTools.com, Salem Media Group, April 21, 2017, http://www.biblestudytools.com/commentaries/jamieson-fausset-brown/galatians/galatians-6.html.
16. Taylor, Shelly E. and Jonathon D. Brown, "Positive Illusions and Well-Being Revisited: Separating Fact From Fiction," Psychological Bulletin American Psychological Association, July 1994, Vol. 116, No. 1, p 21-27.
17. Brehm, Jack W and Arthur R. Cohen, "Explorations in Cognitive Dissonance," Hoboken, NJ, US; John Wiley & Sons Inc., APA PsycNET, 2016, http://psycnet.apa.org/books/11622/.
18. Alon, Anna, "Cognitive Dissonance Theory – IS Theory," TheorizeIt.org, November 12, 2014, https://is.theorizeit.org/wiki/Cognitive_dissonance_theory.
19. Curley, Allison, "The Truth About Lies: The Science of Deception," BrainFacts.org, BrainFacts/SfN, March 20, 2013, http://www.brainfacts.org/in-society/in-society/articles/2013/the-truth-about-lies-the-science-of-deception/.

Chapter 5:
20. Morris, Robert, "My Career Calling," GatewayPeople.com, Gateway Church, *Why Am I Here* Series, 2015, http://gatewaypeople.com/ministries/life/events/why-am-i-here-a-gateway-series/session/2015/08/15/my-career-calling.
21. Morris, Josh, "Freedom Basics 104," GatewayPeople.com, Gateway Church, *Freedom Basics* Series, 27:54 – 28:40, http://gatewaypeople.com/ministries/freedom/events/freedom-basics/session/2015/08/11/freedom-basics-104.
22. "Haughty Definition," Google March 18, 2017, https://www.google.com/webhp?sourceid=chrome-instant&ion=1&espv=2&ie=UTF-8#q=haughty.
23. Morris, Robert, "The Brother's Battle," GatewayPeople.com, Gateway Church, Lost and Found Sermon Series, https://gatewaypeople.com/ministries/life/events/lost-found-a-gateway-series/session/2015/10/24/the-brothers-battle.
24. Young, William P., *The Shack: Where Tragedy Confronts Eternity*, Paperback, Windblown Media, 2007, Newbury Park, CA, p. 91.
25. Lucado, Max, *You Are Special*, Crossway, Wemmicks Series, 2007 p. 31
26. Jenn F., "Big Toe No No: Five Common causes of Flexor Tendonitis (and How to Get Rid of It)," HealingFeet.com, Dr. Geldwert, November 2, 2012, https://healingfeet.com/foot-care/big-toe-no-no-five-causes-of-flexor-tendonitis-and-how-to-get-rid-of-it.
27. Farrell, Heather, "The Real Meaning of the Term 'Help Meet'," WomenintheScriptures.com, November 9, 2010, http://www.womeninthescriptures.com/2010/11/real-meaning-of-term-help-meet.html.
28. "Is Mary's Lineage in one of the Gospels?," Bible.org, January 1, 2001, https://bible.org/question/mary%E2%80%99s-lineage-one-gospels.
29. Ekman, Paul, "Emotions Revealed: Recognizing Faces and Feelings to Improve Communication and Emotional Life," Times Books, 2003, p. 32.
30. "Time Definition," Google, March 18, 2017, https://www.google.com/search?num=20&safe=active&q=time+definition&oq=time&gs_l=serp.1.0.0i71k1l8.0.0.0.44604.0.0.0.0.0.0.0.0.0..0.0....0...1c..64.serp..0.0.0._QJ8spFfX4o.
31. "Mortal | Define Mortal at Dictionary.com," Dictionary.com, Random House Unabridged, Random House Inc., March 18, 2017, http://dictionary.reference.com/browse/mortal.
32. "Did One Third of the Angels Fall With Lucifer?," GotQuestions.org, Got Questions Ministries, June 22, 2017, https://www.gotquestions.org/one-third-angels.html.
33. Deffinbaugh, Bob, "Satan's Part in God's Perfect Plan," Bible.org, March 17, 2004, https://bible.org/seriespage/3-satan-s-part-god-s-perfect-plan

34 3. Satan's Part in God's Perfect Plan.
Chapter 10 Lie 1:
35 "Death | Definition of Death by Merriam-Webster," Merriam-Webster.com, Merriam-Webster, March 18, 2017, http://www.merriam-webster.com/dictionary/death.
36 *Dorland's Illustrated Medical Dictionary, 31st Edition*, republished on the website of Merck & Co, defined death as (accessed May 11, 2007) http://euthanasia.procon.org/view.answers.php?questionID=000197.
Chapter 10 Lie 2:
37 *The Devil's Advocate*
38 Josh Morris "The Kingdom," http://gatewaypeople.com/ministries/young-adults/events/off-topic-2015/session/2015/12/08/the-kingdom, 9:01 minutes.
39 "Strong's Greek Lexicon: 4053," Biblehub.com, February 18, 2018, http://biblehub.com/greek/4053.htm.
40 "GreekLexicon.org: Dictionary Entry for Strong's Number 4053," GreekLexicon.org, February 18, 2018, http://greeklexicon.org/lexicon/strongs/4053/.
Chapter 10 Lie 4:
41 *The Devil's Advocate*
42 "Obesity and Overweight," World Health Organization, February 16, 2018, http://www.who.int/mediacentre/factsheets/fs311/en/.
43 Rumsfeld, Donald, "NATO Speech: Press Conference US SoD – NATO HQ, Brussells – 6 June, 2002," NATO, March 2, 2018, https://www.nato.int/docu/speech/2002/s020606g.htm.
Chapter 10 Lie 5:
44 *Moscow on the Hudson*, DVD, directed by Paul Mazursky, Columbia Pictures, 1984.
Chapter 10 Lie 6:
45 KB, "Anomaly," Album *Weight and Glory*, Reach Records, 2012.
46 "Judgment | Define Judgment at Dictionary.com," Dictionary.com, August 20, 2017, Definition 4, http://www.dictionary.com/browse/judgment?s=t.
47 "Strong's Greek Lexicon: 840," Biblehub.com, August 25, 2017, http://biblehub.com/greek/840.htm.
48 "Austere | Define Austere at Dictionary.com," Dictionary.com, August 25, 2017, http://www.dictionary.com/browse/austere?s=t.
49 David Crowder Band, "How He Loves," Written by: John Mark McMillan, Church Music, Sixsteps, 2009.
Chapter 10 Lie 7:
50 *Star Wars: Episode V -The Empire Strikes Back*, DVD, directed by Irvin Kershner, Lucasfilm, 1980.
Chapter 10 Lie 8:
51 Richards, James R., *Grace: The Power to Change*, paperback, Whitaker House, 1993, p. 13.
52 Casting Crowns, "What the World Needs," *Altar and the Door*, Beach Street/Reunion, 2007.
Chapter 10 Lie 10:
53 "White Lie | Define White Lie at Dictionary.com," Dictionary.com, March 18, 2017, http://www.dictionary.com/browse/white-lie.
54 The Devil's Advocate
Chapter 10 Lie 13:
55 Kreeft, Peter, "Peter Kreeft quote: No culture in history has ever embraced moral relativism and...," AZQuotes.com, July 17, 2017, http://www.azquotes.com/quote/791714.
56 "Relate | Define Relate at Dictionary.com," Dictionary.com, July 18, 2017, http://www.dictionary.com/browse/relate.
57 "Relate | Definition of Relate in English by Oxford Dictionaries," English Oxford Living Dictionaries, Oxford University Press, July 18, 2017, https://en.oxforddictionaries.com/definition/relate.

58 "Relate | Define Relate at Dictionary.com," Dictionary.com, July 18, 2017, http://www.dictionary.com/browse/relate.
Chapter 10 Lie 14:
59 Close, Kelly, "The Government Lost Money on Every Penny It Made in 2016," Time.com, Time Inc., Dec 27, 2016, Aug 24, 2017, http://time.com/money/4618271/penny-cost-make-worth/.
60 "Paul's Letters to the Romans: Part 1 of 2," The Bible Project, July 27, 2018, https://thebibleproject.com/videos/romans-1-4/.
61 Richards, James Dr., *Satan Unmasked*, Milestones International Publishers, 2004, p. 46.
62 *Satan Unmasked*, p. 46 [modification mine].
Chapter 15:
63 Cohen, Courtney, *Refining Identity*, Now Found Publishing, LLC, 2013, pg. 124-125.
64 *You are Special*, p. 29.
Chapter 17:
65 *Satan Unmasked* p. 50.
66 "Freedom | Gateway Church," GatewayPeople.com, Gateway Church, 2017, http://gatewaypeople.com/ministries/freedom.
67 "2 Timothy 4:2 Lexicon," BibleHub.com September 08, 2017, http://biblehub.com/lexicon/2_timothy/4-2.htm.
68 "Strong's Greek 1909," BibleHub.com September 08, 2017, http://biblehub.com/greek/1909.htm.
69 "Strong's Greek 5091," BibleHub.com, September 08, 2017, http://biblehub.com/greek/5091.htm.
70 *The Shack*, p. 227.
Chapter 19:
71 Jones, Kelly, "Freedom Leaders Meeting," Gateway Church, June 2017.
72 Morris, Robert, "The Priority of People," GatewayPeople.com, Gateway Church, September 23, 2017, https://gatewaypeople.com/ministries/life/events/individual-messages-2017/session/2017/09/23/the-priority-of-people.
73 Neese, Zach and Joni Lamb, "Entertaining Demons – Zach Neese (J1015)," Daystar, September 8, 2017, http://www.daystar.com/ondemand/video/?video=2491413864001.
Chapter 20:
74 "John 8:31 Lexicon," Biblehub.com September 11, 2017, http://biblehub.com/lexicon/john/8-31.htm.
75 De Profundis.
Section 5 Intro:
76 Chien, Andy MD PhD and David Kulow, "How to Choose and Use Sunscreen," REI.com, REI Coop, March 17, 2017, https://www.rei.com/learn/expert-advice/sunscreen-how-to-use.html.
Chapter 24:
77 "All About Empathy," *Psychology Today*, Sussex Publishers LLC, August 28, 2017, https://www.psychologytoday.com/basics/empathy.
78 "Sympathy Definition," Google.com, August 28, 2017, https://www.google.com/search?safe=active&rlz=1C1CHBF_enUS756US756&q=Dictionary#dobs=sympathy.
Chapter 26:
79 Jimmy Evans, *Tipping Point Series*, 2015, Gateway Church, https://gatewaypeople.com/ministries/life/events/tipping-point-a-gateway-series-with-pastor-jimmy-evans.
Chapter 8:
1 Truth and Reality Do Not Adapt to Us
Chapter 9:
1 Evans, Jimmy, *When Life Hurts*, Baker Books, 2013, p. 22.
Chapter 14:
1 *The Shack*, p. 189.
Chapter 16:
1 *The Shack* p. 191.

AVAILABLE
on Kindle, Google Play, Nook, and iBooks.

ALSO AVAILABLE
in print and eBook from

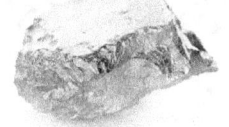

COMING SOON
from
NOW FOUND
PUBLISHING

NOW AVAILABLE
from

Both print and eBook versions available at Amazon, Google Store, and most major bookstores and eReaders.

LIVE, CREATE & SHARE YOUR STORY

Your story is powerful. Do you have a message you long to share with others, but aren't sure how to begin? Do you want to see lives changed, but writing isn't your strong suit? Do you long to see your heart's message in print, but are overwhelmed with the idea of becoming published? If so, we would be honored to serve and assist you.

At Now Found Publishing, we walk alongside authors through every step of the writing and publishing process. We provide services including proofreading, all levels of editing, coaching, cover design, and formatting while maintaining the heart of your message and your individual voice. Contact us at authors@nowfoundpublishing.com to live, create, and share your story.

For information on Now Found Publishing and our inspirational and life-changing resources, visit NowFoundPublishing.com.

www.ingramcontent.com/pod-product-compliance
Lightning Source LLC
Chambersburg PA
CBHW052052110526
44591CB00013B/2178